THE EVOLUTION OF ELECTRONIC MUSIC

The Evolution
of Electronic Music

David Ernst

SCHIRMER BOOKS
A Division of Macmillan Publishing Co., Inc.
NEW YORK

Collier Macmillan Publishers
LONDON

SCHIRMER BOOKS
A Division of Macmillan Publishing Co., Inc.
866 Third Avenue, New York, N.Y. 10022

Collier Macmillan Canada, Ltd.

Library of Congress Catalog Card Number: 76–41624

Printed in the United States of America

printing number

1 2 3 4 5 6 7 8 9 10

Library of Congress Cataloging in Publication Data

Ernst, David.
    The evolution of electronic music.

    Bibliography: p.
    Includes index.
    1. Electronic music--History and criticism.
I. Title.
ML1092.E76   789.9   76-41624
ISBN 0-02-870880-6

To Marisa and Eugenia

TABLE OF CONTENTS

LIST OF EXAMPLES

PREFACE

Electronic music has been in existence for more than a quarter of a century. Its large and diverse repertory poses considerable obstacles for those interested in studying composition. This book has been developed as an aid for teachers and students in an attempt to correlate historical developments with structural procedures within the electronic medium.

In order to facilitate an understanding of the works presented, only commercially recorded compositions are included. I can nevertheless present a comprehensive overview of our subject, because examples of all forms of electronic music have been recorded.

Because so many recordings of electronic compositions have been made, and since a good number of these are now out-of-print, it has been impossible to include every recorded electronic composition within our text. Although every effort has been made to obtain out-of-print recordings, a few pieces have been omitted; this should not be considered a negative reflection of these works. In order to be as thorough as possible, I have included recordings released during the first quarter of 1976. In addition, since new compositions are continuously being recorded and released, I project revised editions of this text. Despite these problems, I will discuss well over ninety percent of all electronic compositions that are available as recordings.

The basic problem with an historical survey of electronic music is how to categorize its diverse compositional styles. Without some method of stylistic division, however, we cannot hope to understand either its evolution or its compositional aesthetics. I have therefore developed three general classifications: solo tape, performer with tape, and live electronics. I have divided these categories according to the nature of sonorous elements and the type of transformations employed. The consequences of this procedure are twofold: concentration upon small groups of pieces is possible, and, therefore, structural relations between them become apparent. The resulting continuity should enable the reader to grasp the overall nature of this topic.

Particular emphasis has been placed upon areas that have been largely neglected until now: the use of electronics in jazz and rock music, the appearance of voice in electronic works, and the compositional aesthetics of early musique concrète and electronic composers. In addition, Part IV is devoted to some practical considerations of compositional techniques. I have included both electronic processes and formal structural designs, and illustrated the application of these procedures and concepts within live performance.

I have developed the materials in this text over the past two years for my courses and lectures on electronic music. I possess both compositional and performance experience in this field, and I hope that the discussions and explanations that follow are clear and readily accessible to a general audience.

I want to thank a former student, Grant Harders, for typing this manuscript, and for his assisting in the research and procurement of records. Thanks are also due to: Professor Lejaren Hiller, who helped me to obtain an out-of-print recording of his music; the graduate faculty of Rutgers University, especially Professors Henry Kaufmann, Martin Picker and Alfred Mann, whose extensive knowledge of music theory is reflected in the Introduction; and Ken Stuart, editor of this text, for his valuable guidance and suggestions. A special debt of gratitude is owed to Professor Robert Moevs, also of Rutgers, whose encouragement and critical evaluation have made this book possible.

D. Ernst
York College, City University of New York

INTRODUCTION

LIKE OTHER ARTISTIC DEVELOPMENTS, electronic music has resulted from a number of transformations within different areas of a single tradition. Music theory, composition and instrument design stem from mathematical and physical laws, beginning with ancient Greece, and they can be traced throughout the history of Western music.

The study of music in Greek antiquity was grounded in mathematics, as we can see in the inclusion of music in the quadrivium along with geometry, astronomy, and mathematics. Music theory was also closely related to performance practice, for a variety of tuning systems were derived from mathematical formulas. Both the subdivision of the octave and the derivation of consonant intervals were mathematically determined. Pythagoras formulated these concepts, which were based upon the characteristics of a single vibrating string. He discovered the existence of a fundamental relationship between the length of a vibrating string and arithmetic ratios. If a string is divided into two equal parts, the resulting pitch is one octave higher than the original pitch; the ratio is thus 2:1. The intervals of the fifth (2:3) and the fourth (3:4) were derived from divisions of a string into three and four equal parts.

It was the interval of the fourth, or the diatesseron, that generated the Greek system of scales contained within the Greater and Lesser Perfect Systems. The diatesseron was also subdivided in three different ways to produce the diatonic, chromatic and enharmonic intervals. The last of these was particularly important in instrument design in the sixteenth, late nineteenth and twentieth centuries, for the enharmonic type included the interval of the quarter-tone.

The significance of the quarter-tone is twofold. In Western music the octave has traditionally been divided into twelve more or less equal parts, but the quarter-tone produces twice as many divisions, so that the distance between successive pitches is smaller. The use of the quarter-tone scale was common among the ancient Greeks, but gradually disappeared as Western music evolved, although African and Asian cultures have maintained this subtle distinction between pitches to the present day. It was not until the middle of the sixteenth century that the Italian composer and theorist, Don Nicola Vincentino, attempted to revive the ancient Greek musical tradition. His achievements were so vehemently attacked by his contemporaries, however, that Vincentino's use of these concepts remains an isolated example in the history of Western music to the Renaissance.

Very little is known about ancient Greek music and its theory because most of it was based upon an aural rather than a written tradition. The extant writings of Pythagoras, Euclid, Aristotle, Aristoxenos, Ptolemy and Plato which contain discussions on music were introduced to Medieval Western civilization by the Roman philosopher and mathematician Boethius (ca. 480–524) and his contemporary Cassiodorus (ca. 485–560). Mathematical concepts involving proportions were perhaps ancient Greece's most important contribution to music, for they dominated the evolution of music theory until the seventeenth century. During this period proportional relationships were applied to pitch (consonance and dissonance), duration (rhythm), and tuning systems. Both the symmetry and logic inherent in mathematical procedures provided the basic framework for Western music.

The definition of a "musical" sound has been progressively extended to include all sounds. The Pythagorean concept of harmony of the spheres ascribes pitches within the Greater and Lesser Perfect Systems to individual planets. The sun is identified with the central note (mese) of these systems, and the revolution of each planet was thought to emit a particular scale of pitches. These ideas, in conjunction with mathematics, helped to relate the derivation of pitch to the cosmic structure. These theories are explained in treatises by Boethius and other medieval theorists.

In *De institutione musica*, Boethius divided music into three general categories: *musica mundana* (the harmony or rhythm of the universe), *musica humana* (the harmony or proportions of the body), and *musica instrumentalis* (vocal and instrumental music).

The first category is analogous to the Greek harmony of the spheres, and propounds the modern concept of sound waves. Both the Pythagoreans and Boethius realized that movement produces sound, for it was believed that the motion of the planets yielded specific pitches. Furthermore, both believed that the extreme velocity of the planets' movements produced frequencies so high as to be imperceptible to human ears.

Boethius's division of instrumental music into percussion, string, and wind sonorities, was adopted by his contemporary, Cassiodorus, and by Isidore of Seville (570–636), both of whom also categorized music according to harmonic, rhythmic, and metric principles. The writings of these theorists provided the basis for early medieval musical thought, as exemplified in the mid-ninth century treatise *Musica disciplina* by Aurelian de Réome, in which entire chapters are derived from the aforementioned writers. The late ninth century work, *Musica enchiriadis*, reaffirms the Aristotelian relationship between music and mathematics, while the work of the tenth century theorist, Regino of Prüm, refers to the "science of music," based upon arithmetic rules.

Like Boethius and the ancient Greek writers, Regino believed that sound travelled in the form of waves, but he divided music into two parts: natural and artificial. Artificial or instrumental music is analogous to the *musica instrumentalis* of Boethius. Natural music consists of the movement of the heavens, or the harmony of the spheres, in addition to vocal sounds that include animal noises. The concept of the combination of *musica mundana* and *humana* to form natural music not only departs from Boethian procedures, but the inclusion of animal sounds also exceeds the limits set by Boethius of *musica humana*. Regino's definition of natural music can include the Sirens mentioned in Homer's *Odyssey*, as well as the yells of the three-headed dog Cerberus and the shreiks of the Harpies which appear in "Purgatory" (VI, 13–14, 28–32; XIII, 10–15, 22) of Dante's *Divine Comedy*. The harmony of the spheres which underlies Dante's thought is directly referred to several times, beginning with Canto XXVI of "Paradise." Francis Bacon's later *The New Atlantis* (1627) contains "sound houses," where all sounds exist.

Once the definition of music was firmly established, later theorists like Guido of Arezzo, Franco of Cologne, Anonymous IV, and Johannes de Grocheo could concentrate on compositional procedures and notational problems. During this period, from the eleventh through the thirteenth centuries, proportions were applied to pitch, tuning systems, and the determination of consonant and dissonant intervals. By the early fourteenth century, however, the works of Marchetto da Padua and Philippe de Vitry display increased rhythmic complexity which is derived from duple subdivisions of durational values, in addition to the more common triple divisions. This era, referred to as the "Ars Nova," was followed by an extensive reliance upon proportional relations for the derivation of rhythmic structures.

An important treatise from this period, *Proportionale musices* (ca. 1475) by Johannes Tinctoris, provides principles of proportions for composers and performers. Proportions of equality and inequality are applied to duration, and are accompanied by definitions and notational procedures. The rhythmic relations within such a composition assume a complexity equal to some of the piano works of Henry Cowell and such later serialists as Stockhausen and Boulez. Some of the more complex proportions found in the *Proportionale* are 5:4 (sesquiquarta), 6:5 (sesquiquinta), 9:8 (sesquioctava), 5:3 (superbipartiens tertias), 7:4 (supertripartiens quartas), 7:3 (duple sesquiteritia) and 13:5 (duple supertripartiens quintas). The *Practica musicae* (1497) of Franchinus Gafurius contains similar theories, but the elements that had been used by Tinctoris were generally restricted to academic exercises. The "Missa Prolationum" of Johannes Ockeghem and the "Choralis Constantinus" of Heinrich Issac, both Flemish composers, provide examples of compositional use of proportions during the Renaissance.

Vincentino's theoretical concepts, derived from the three Greek genera, led him to design and construct a multi-keyboard instrument, the "Archicembalo" (1555). This instrument was capable of dividing the octave into thirty-one steps, and displayed a sense of pitch awareness that had long been absent in Western music. The "Archicembalo" was improved upon by Colonna's "La Sambuca lincea" (1618), and foreshadowed the emergence of a similar class of new micro-tonal instruments that began to appear in the eighteenth century. These instruments are an important aspect of the concepts which eventually led to the emergence of electronic music, for they helped to both broaden and refine composers' attitudes toward pitch. Many keyboard instruments from the sixteenth through the nineteenth century possessed extra keys which provided enharmonic equivalents, e.g., E^b–$D\#$, A^b–$G\#$.

Harmony of the World (1618), by the German scientist Johannes

Kepler, was one of the most comprehensive treatises to appear since ancient Greek writings. It contains five separate books on geometry, music, astrology, astronomy, and epistemology. The rationalization of consonance was derived from geometry, and marked a departure from previous mathematical processes. Using the sun as a reference point, Kepler determined harmonic consonances by comparing the slowest and fastest motions of individual planets to the stationary position of the sun. Early Pythagorean theory had identified the sun with the central note, "mese," of its scale system; both methods associate music theory with ideas outside the discipline.

The mathematical theories of Greek antiquity remained operative until the first quarter of the seventeenth century, when the science of acoustics began to supersede them. A long line of French theorists, beginning with Marin Mersenne, developed revolutionary theories following Descartes's scientific method of 1618 based upon empiric procedures. Many physical properties of sound became known and understood as a result of extensive experimentation with a single vibrating string, or monochord, which had been the vehicle for this type of research since Pythagoras's time. The seventeenth century theorists began to incorporate acoustical laws, rather than purely mathematical ones, in their theories. The difference between the old practice and the new is primarily the gradual discovery of the overtone series, which was formulated in its entirety by the French scientist Joseph Sauveur in 1701.

During the last third of the seventeenth century more French theorists began to publish treatises involving acoustics. Among the most important are those of Jacques Rouhault and Claude Perrault, whose discoveries assume particular significance when we consider electronic compositional techniques. Rouhault was concerned with aural perception and its relationship to the brain, manifest by the resonant capacity of the ear. Perrault determined that timbre depends upon the presence of upper partials, in addition to subsidiary noises associated with percussive, blown and bowed sounds. Because the amplitude of these elements is considerably less than that of the fundamental tone, we only perceive timbral changes.

The importance of Sauveur's work cannot be overestimated, for he not only formulated new acoustical theories, but he also refined preexisting concepts of earlier French theorists. Sauveur clarified Mersenne's measurement of consonance and dissonance by basing his calculations upon beats that result from simultaneously sounding two pitches that are not in tune. He also defined the limits of human aural pitch perception as being between 16 and 32,718 cycles per second. Although the upper limit is actually approximately double that number, the lower is correct; this is an amazing accomplishment for the first quarter of the eighteenth century.

Sauveur also experimented with micro-tonal tunings and related tuning systems, which was an activity that had increasingly occupied composers, theorists, and instrument builders since the sixteenth century. This led Sauveur to do further work in the realm of aural perception. He concluded that the ear could perceive 301 equal divisions in an octave, or 50 divisions within a whole-tone. It seems rather unlikely that we possess such a refined sense of hearing, but Sauveur did design an instrument, the "Echometer," that could measure the micro-intervals within an octave. Unquestionably, however, Sauveur's most important discovery, which appeared in his *Système Général des Intervalles des Sons, et son application à tous les Systèmes et à tous les Instruments de Musique* (1701), was that of the overtone series.

The overtone series is a physical phenomenon that is expressed as a fundamental pitch (frequency) that is always accompanied by an infinite series of higher pitches (partials) of decreasing amplitude. Since the frequency relationships between successive partials and their fundamental exist in the ratios of $2:1$, $3:1$, $4:1$ etc., it should be apparent why the abstract application of proportions gave way to empirical methods during the Age of Reason. The discovery of the overtone series not only supported previous mathematically based rationalizations of music theory, but also provided a foundation for the subsequent attempts to control the timbral characteristics of sound, which were begun at the end of the nineteenth century by the German physicist Hermann von Helmholtz.

For practically two centuries, the impact of Sauveur's work was restricted to purely theoretical topics within the discipline of music. The French theorist and composer Jean Phillipe Rameau (1683–1764) employed Sauveur's discoveries in his treatises on music theory, but it was not until Helmholtz's work appeared that these new concepts actually influenced musical composition and the design of new instruments.

The first of Rameau's nine works, *Traité de l'Harmonie Réduite à ses Principes naturels* (1722), applied the concepts of the overtone series only to the first six partials of a vibrating string. In his second volume, *Nouveau Système de musique théorique* (1726), Rameau concluded that resonant bodies produce the same overtones as vibrating strings. He followed this with a discussion of sympathetic vibration in *Génération harmonique* (1737). Rameau eventually accepted up to the forty-fifth partial to justify vertical sonorities in his eighth book, *Code de musique pratique* (1760).

From the Middle Ages through the eighteenth century, the formulation of theoretical concepts and their employment within musical compositions were emphasized. The only instruments designed during this time were Vincentino's "Archicembalo" and similar ones by his contemporaries Zarlino and Salinas. Throughout the eighteenth and first part of the nineteenth centuries there were many attempts in the area of new instrument design, the most important of which was Benjamin Franklin's Glass Harmonica, which appeared in 1763. Both Mozart and Beethoven wrote compositions for it. The glass harmonica contained a series of revolving glass discs which could be set in motion by a foot pedal; they were kept wet by passing through a trough of water. The discs were of increasing thickness, so that when the performer touched one of their edges a specific pitch was produced.

From the beginning of the eighteenth century the design and construction of new instruments flourished. One of the prime areas of concentration was the division of the octave into more than the traditional twelve semi-tones. These instruments took Vincentino's octave divisions so far that it is questionable whether those inventors could actually have heard the minute pitch differentiations which their instruments produced. Sauveur, for instance, included twenty-five tuning systems in his *Table générale des systèmes tempérés de musique* (1701). Some of his octave divisions are 17, 43, 53, 67, 74, 98, 105, 112, and 117. Other eighteenth century theorists who divided the octave into more than 50 parts include Henfling (1710), Mattheson (1722–25), Jackson (1726), and Romieu (1758).

Nineteenth century experiments in England, France and Germany carried on this tradition. The most significant were by Liston (1812), Delezenne (1826–27), Poole (1850), Oplet (1852), Drobisch (1855), Helmholtz (1863), Bosanquet (1874–75), Koenig (1876) and Tonaka (1890). The most radical instrument these men developed is Koenig's "Tonametric," which could divide four octaves into 670 equal parts, or approximately 167 steps per octave.

The first experiments in electronic music would never have occurred without previous technological advances in the area of sound reproduction and storage. Alexander Bell succeeded in transmitting the voice by means of electricity in 1876, the same year that Koenig's "Tonametric" appeared. By the next year Emile Berliner had perfected both a telephone receiver and a disc record. Thomas Edison's phonograph in 1878 was the next significant technological advance to take place. Although this phonograph eventually proved to be inadequate for the sophisticated sound manipulations associated with electronic music, it was employed extensively by a few French, German, and American composers from the 1920's through the next two decades.

During the final years of the nineteenth century three events occurred to provide composers with both the theoretical and practical resources which would ultimately permit them to structure sounds in a new way. First, in 1863 Helmholtz published his book *Sensations of Tone,* a pioneering work in the field of acoustics that delineated new compositional techniques for composers of future generations. Helmholtz was the first to systematically explain timbre to be a result of a fundamental tone and its harmonic content, a concept grounded in the works of Joseph Sauveur from almost two centuries before.

Second, one of the first instruments whose design was based on the theory of the overtone series appeared more than thirty years after Helmholtz's book. Thaddeus Cahill's "Sounding Staves" (1897) was involved with timbre control, which was regulated by varying the number of upper partials, or the harmonic content of a fundamental tone. The quality or timbre of a tone was altered by the addition or elimination of upper partials. The aural effect was analogous to a change of instruments in traditional music as, for example, switching from flute to clarinet, but differed in the possibilities afforded by the "Sounding Staves," which exceeded the number of conventional orchestral instruments. Cahill was therefore able to produce sounds whose quality did not necessarily resemble that of familiar instruments.

Third, in the following year, the Danish scientist Vlademar Poulsen presented his "Telegraphone," the first magnetic recording machine, which was sometimes referred to as the wire recorder. From a compositional point of view, Poulsen's invention had far greater potential than its predecessor, the phonograph, but its limitation lay in the difficulty of working with the wire upon which the recording was made. This problem was solved in 1935 by the invention of the magnetic tape recorder.

The achievements of Helmholtz, Cahill, and Poulsen ushered in twentieth century music. Although some musicians maintained an interest in pure theory, the emphasis had shifted to the construction of new instruments and to musical composition. Early in 1906 Cahill introduced his "Dynamophone," which was capable of generating sounds by means of a series of electronically driven dynamos (electrical generators). Both his "Sounding Staves" and Helmholtz's acoustical theories influenced many early twentieth century composers, whose work manifested an acute awareness of timbral relationships. Arnold Schoenberg's use of *Klangfarben-melodie* (tone-color-melody) in his "Fünf Orchesterstücke" (1909), in which he distributed successive pitches of a melody among various instruments, is a clear indication of Schoenberg's concern with instrumental color. In his footnote to the third piece of this set, "Summer Morning by a Lake," Schoenberg specified that "only the difference in color becomes noticeable." Timbre was also given a prominent role in the piano music of the American composer Henry Cowell. In 1911 Cowell employed tone clusters, which are simultaneously sounding groups of adjacent pitches. His subsequent compositions utilized a variety of sounds produced in the interior of the piano including the strings themselves.

Some of the most significant upheavals in musical thought have originated in Italy, as we have seen in Vincentino's "Achicembalo," his theories, and his compositions. The Italian Futurist movement, founded by the playwright and poet Filippo Marinetti in 1909, included these three areas of concentration. Marinetti's *Foundation and Manifesto of Futurism* (1909) initiated a series of events that would exert profound influence upon subsequent musique concrète composers, John Cage, and the recent compositions of Karlheinz Stockhausen.

Futurism includes painting, sculpture, poetry, drama, opera, dance, music, and cinema, and its followers generally engaged in more than one of these disciplines. Public readings of Futurist manifestos and poetry in 1910 led in the next few years to productions of short, one-act plays that often employed nonsense speech or dramatic visual effects. The glorification of machines, of speed and strength, and perhaps also the Futurists' advocacy of the destruction of historical monuments, created a turbulent atmosphere that was later exploited by Mussolini and the Fascists (1922).

Some primary correspondences between Futurism and Fascism are the advocacy of war and opposition to the monarchy. Concerning the former, Marinetti said: "War is the culminating and perfecting synthesis of progress." The Futurists demanded war against Austria, and incited Italian university students against their pro-German professors. Both Marinetti and Mussolini were arrested in Rome at a pro-war demonstration in 1915, and many of the Futurists enlisted in the army at the outbreak of the First World War.

One reason that the Futurists opposed the monarchy in Italy was because of its close association with the Catholic Church, a symbol of a meaningless past that obstructed according to the Futurists, political, economic, and social reforms. Mussolini initially desired a "tendentially republican Fascism"; however, the subsequent dictatorship established by Mussolini is an obvious digression from this ideal, and bears no political relation to Futurism.

The growth of the Futurist movement was hindered by political and economic unrest in Western Europe after the First World War. Therefore, the effects of Futurism upon music, for instance, were not significant until the middle of the century.

The major vehicles for the dissemination of Futurist ideology are the manifestoes and the performance pieces. Manifestoes that involve music were written by Francesco Pratella, Luigi Russolo, and Filippo Marinetti. The spirit of Pratella's *The Technical Manifesto of Futurist Music* (1911) is summarized in his statement: "Young musicians, once and for all, will stop being vile imitators of the past that no longer has a reason for existing and imitators of the venal flatterers of the public's base taste." Pratella advocated the use of microtones, which he referred to as "enharmonic" pitches. He emphasized the need for experimentation with a "found object," that is, an "everyday" sound, as a new sonorous source. Finally, Pratella referred to repetitive rhythm as "the disgraceful umbrella of all the impotents who teach in the conservatories."

Although Pratella was a musician, not all the manifestoes on music were written by musicians. Luigi Russolo, for instance, was a painter, but his *Futurist Manifesto* (1913) is concerned with musical topics. Russolo not only criticized the stifling of harmony that he believed had been precipitated by the theories of the ancient Greeks; he also pointed out that noise was actually a product of the machine age. Russolo considered the growing complexity of polyphony, harmony and timbre in nineteenth and twentieth century music to be the forerunners of "musical noise." He advocated breaking away from the small group of conventional musical instruments that had hitherto restricted musical sound, in favor of the more interesting, and unlimited, noise sounds now available. Russolo's cryptic description of the concert hall, "a hospital for anemic sounds," is evidence of the urgency of his ideas, for he strongly believed that musical sounds must be expanded to include noises.

Russolo applied his theories to his inventions, the "Intonarumori," (1913) and the "Psofarmoni" (1926). The former are mechanical "noise" instruments that produce hisses, grunts, pops, etc., while the latter are keyboard instruments that imitate animal and nature sounds. The sonorities produced by the "Psofarmoni" not only encompass the medieval concept of "natural" music, but the reappearance of this idea in Futurism suggests that the Western definition of music was no longer adequate.

Russolo's next manifesto was *Enharmonic Notation for the Futurist "Intonarumori"* (1914), in which he devised the "line-note," a horizontal line to signify duration. This system is now employed by many contemporary composers, including Stockhausen, Kagel, and Penderecki. The Futurist movement has not received the attention that it deserves; yet many of its ideas and techniques, like the concept of "noise" as music, the "Intonarumoni," and new notational systems are used by many contemporary musicians to whom Russolo and Pratella are unknown. It is astonishing to hear Pierre Schaeffer, the originator of musique concrète, say that he was unaware of Futurist experiments with noise.

Further references to music appear in some of Marinetti's manifestoes. *The Variety Theatre* (1913) suggested that Wagner's "Parsifal" be reduced to forty minutes; this version was later performed in London. Marinetti also recommended that a Beethoven symphony be played backwards, beginning with the last note. The homemade instruments employed in a composition by Francesco Cangiullo in 1914 are described by Marinetti in the *Dynamic and Synoptic Declamation* (1914). Fortunato Depero called for "composed noises" including the sounds of machines and engines, in *Notes on the Theatre* (ca. 1916). The last manifesto of this movement, the *Futurist Radiophonic Theatre* (1933) by Marinetti and Pino Masnata, is an extension of the "Intonarumori." The authors discuss amplification of inaudible sounds (an idea John Cage later adopted and referred to as "small sounds"); they also mention amplification of "vibrations from living beings" (see the later "brain wave" music of Evangelisti, Lucier *et al*.).

Although the Futurists published these theoretical justifications of their ideas, their greatest efforts lay in demonstrating these concepts in live performance. Futurism was more than a purely academic movement, for it strove to combine all art forms in practice. In 1910, the initial Futurist efforts involved only poetry and the theater, but Pratella's opera "La Sina d'Vargöun" (1909), which was based on a text written in free verse, indicates that these new concepts were shared by other artistic disciplines as well. Pratella's "Musica Futurista per Orchestra" (1912) uses conventional instruments, whereas his "Saggio di Orchestra mista" (1914) combines a mixed ("mista") orchestra composed of instruments, "Intonarumori," and vocal shouts. Pratella used Russolo's notational method for the "Intonarumori".

The "Intonarumori" received their premier, under Russolo's direction, at the "Art of Noises" concert in Milan in 1913. Russolo had composed six "Noise Networks" for a noise orchestra that consisted of buzzers, bursters, thunderer, whistlers, rustlers, gurglers, shatterer, shriller, and snorter. Marinetti later used these instruments for sound effects in his play, "Il Tamburo di Fuoco" (1922).

"Feu d'Artifice" (1917), by Giacomo Balla, is based upon Stravinsky's 1908 orchestral composition of the same title, and was staged by Balla for Diaghilev. Lights were shined on an enlarged reconstruction of a painting by Balla, so that continually changing shapes emerged. In 1928, Enrico Prampolini combined the "Intonarumori" with lighting effects in "Santa Velocità," a theater piece without actors. These works predate Varèse's "Poème Electronique" by more than thirty years.

Shortly after the introduction of Russolo's "Intonarumori," Francesco Cangiullo derived sound effects from "Tofa," a homemade wind instrument made from a large seashell; "Scetavaisse," a saw from which rattles and pieces of tin were suspended; "Pitipu," a box covered with skin; and "Triccabballacche," a variant of the lyre, in which thin strips of wood were attached to wooden blocks, and substituted for conventional strings. These instruments, described by Marinetti in the *Dynamic and Synoptic Declamation*, were combined with vocal effects in Cangiullo's "Piedigrotta" (1914).

Inspired by Russolo's noise concepts, Fedele Azari experimented with the sonorous possibilities of airplane engines in "Aerial Theatre" (1918), for which Russolo designed a special hood and exhaust to increase resonance and modify timbre. Azari's subsequent manifesto, *Futurist Aerial Theatre* (1919), describes the "flying Intonarumori" in which each airplane was painted by a Futurist painter.

Sometimes familiar "musical" sonorities like percussion and voice, satisfied the needs of Futurist theatrical performances. Marinetti, for instance. used the bass drum to represent bombs in "Simultaneità di Guerra Volutta" (1921). Gun shots, screams, cries, and laughter appear in "Sintesi delle Sintesi" by Guglielmo Jannelli and Luciano Nicastro; and Balla's "Macchina Tipografica" (1914) uses the voice in a non-human context. In this piece, the sounds of a printing press are represented by phonetic and syllabic fragments: "lalala," "sta . . . sta . . . ," "riórió," "scsc . . . spsspsscsc . . . ," "ftft," and so on. The performers physically imitate the mechanical operation of gears and levers. The treatment of the voice in these compositions extends its function beyond traditional literary, musical, and syntactic ones, and foreshadows its use by Luciano Berio.

Most Futurist works appeared between 1910 and the mid-1920's, and various artistic media were gradually fused to yield highly integrated works. Speech, for example, was reduced to vocal sounds, and resulted in an affinity with "musical noise." All forms of movement were defined in terms of rhythm, so that movement too was associated with music. Since sound and/or movement characterize all media of expression, it was easiest to combine various art forms when these elements were reduced to their purest and simplest states. This reduction, however, resulted in increased abstraction, so that a universal interpretation of the meaning of sonorous or visual events became impossible. The phoneme "s," for instance, does not possess any intrinsic semantic value; it is a "pure" sound that may assume "musical" connotations.

Music is particularly suited to illustrate this concept because it is, by nature, the most abstract art form: it does not need to transcend visual images and their associations. While literary and visual artists attempted to approach "pure" sound and rhythm, their experiments helped to extend the boundaries of music. Although Russolo spoke of "musical noises," he was primarily concerned with non-vocal elements; but the literary and theatrical works of Marinetti, Balla, Jannelli, and Nicastro actually included vocal sonorities in a musical context. These experiments, along with those performed at the Bauhaus, contributed significantly to subsequent developments in the sphere of musique concrete.

The final Futurist works, a set of five short pieces for radio by Marinetti, appeared over a period of seven years, from 1930 to

1937. These examples of the Radiophonic Theatre foreshadow the "Imaginary Landscapes" (1939) of John Cage and the musique concrète repertory of Pierre Schaeffer and his associates. Marinetti mixed discrete sounds with silence, thus elaborating on the concept of the "found object" that had appeared in the manifestoes of Pratella and Russolo. Although Webern employed silence in his instrumental music (1908), Marinetti extended those periods of silence to as long as three minutes in some instances, which was much beyond those employed by Webern. "Battaglia di Ritmi" exemplifies this procedure. The silences in "I Silenzi Parlano fra di Loro" range from eight to forty seconds in length, while sound sources consist of isolated appearances by flute, trumpet, piano, motor, a baby's cry, and "Amazed oooooo's from an eleven-year-old little girl." An authentic musique concrète atmosphere pervades "Un Paesaggio Udito," in which the sound of "lapping" water repeatedly alternates with short segments of crackling fire, until the whistle of a blackbird concludes the piece. In "Drama di Distanze," Marinetti included sounds from a boxing match. Some of Cage's tape collages, as well as Stockhausen's "Telemusik" and "Hymnen" are reminiscent of this piece.

More sophisticated electronic instruments began to appear during the first quarter of the twentieth century with the formulation of new electronic theories. In 1915, Lee De Forest invented the oscillator, a device that produces electronically generated tones. The oscillator is not only one of the principal sound sources in electronic music, but is also the heart of the modern synthesizer. The "Theremin", an extension of the oscillator, was devised in 1923 by the Russian scientist Leon Theremin. Although it consists of an oscillator to generate electronic tones, the Theremin eliminates the standard pitch and amplitude control dials found on an oscillator. These functions are controlled by the relative distance of the performer's hand from an antenna that extends vertically from the Theremin. An upward movement of the hand produces higher pitches, and an increase of amplitude results from moving the hand closer to the antenna. Three years later Theremin conceived the "Electric Harmonium," which was capable of producing pitch deviations beyond what humans could perceive: 1/100 of a tone, or 1200 divisions per octave. Such fine gradations of pitch can be obtained only with electronic sound generating equipment. The compositional value of these scientific experiments was only realized much later, most notably at the electronic music studio in Cologne during the early 1950's.

The phonograph was one of the first machines to receive widespread attention by composers. Shortly after Russolo's "Concert of Noises" (1913), the French composer Darius Milhaud, along with the German composers Paul Hindemith and Ernst Toch, began to use variable speed phonographs to alter the characteristics of preexisting sounds. Their enthusiasm for these new sonorous possibilities rapidly spread to the film medium, in which the technique of "drawn sound" was developed. Filmmakers derived sounds by registering fingerprints, facial profiles, lettering, and geometric figures directly on the film sound track. Sound was first combined with film in Germany in 1928 by Walther Ruttmann, and this work was continued at the Bauhaus by Paul Arma, Oskar Fischinger, Lászlo Moholy-Nagy, and Friedrich Trautwein. During the 1930's in France, sound tracks for motion pictures were manipulated by Maurice Jaubert, Arthur Hoéreé, and Arthur Honegger, who were the first French composers to employ this technique.

During the First World War, many French and German artists fled their homeland to neutral Switzerland, where Hugo Ball opened the Cabaret Voltaire in Zurich in 1916. The cabaret attracted the artists Tristan Tzara, Hans Arp, Marcel Janco, and Richard Huelsenbeck; they used the term Dada to identify their activities and published the first Dada Manifesto that same year.

Unlike Futurism, Dadaism is not an artistic movement. The spirit of Dada was summarized by André Breton: "Dada is a state of mind . . . Dada is artistic free-thinking . . . Dada gives itself to nothing . . ." Continual negation distinguishes Dada from other contemporary trends, but it does contain associations with the Futurists and the Bauhaus artists. Tzara, for instance, was in contact with Marinetti; Ball had worked with Kandinsky in Munich, prior to 1916, to establish an Expressionistic theatre; the aforementioned Cabaret Voltaire Exhibition of 1916 included Futurist works; and Klee and Kandinsky lectured in Zurich the following year, two years before the Bauhaus was established.

Huelsenbeck prepared the first German Dada manifesto in 1918, and Dada was introduced in France by Tzara the following year. Similar concepts also appear in New York during this period, revealed in works of Marcel Duchamp, Man Ray and Max Ernst. These developments are subsequently reflected in the music of

John Cage, particularly his adoption of collage and chance, or aleatoric, procedures.

Dadaist ideas concerning music parallel those of the Futurists. In his third manifesto, *Proclamation without Pretension*, Tzara proclaims: "MUSICIANS SMASH YOUR INSTRUMENTS." The last line of the poem, "Information Please" (1921), by Paul Eluard, expresses similar, though less violent, attitudes toward music: "I do not like music, all this piano music robs me of all I love." When the Dadaists used traditional music, it usually consisted of compositions by such composers as Satie, Stravinsky, Milhaud, Auric, and Schoenberg, or of popular tunes. Even though they employed "noise music," it was frequently related to poetry or the theatre.

The poetic transformations employed by the Dadaists can be grouped in three categories: "sound," "simultaneous," and "chance" poems. The first genre includes verse without words, as, for example, "gadji beri bimba" from "Flight from Time" by Hugo Ball, and "Ursonata" (1924) by Kurt Schwitters. Unlike the Futurists, both rely on sonorous characteristics rather than on semantics. Schwitters further distills poetry to a single letter in "W" (1924), which only phonemic distinctions of "w" are articulated during the performance.

Tzara adopted the Futurist idea of simultaneity in both poetry and theatre. This resulted in multi-lingual poetic recitations in attempts to transform the nature of poetry. "Simultaneous" poems presented at the Cabaret Voltaire were accompanied by whistles, drums, and bells.

Tzara invented "chance" poems, which first appeared in *Littérature* in 1919. A newspaper article is cut up into separate words. These are shaken in a bag, and then copied in the order in which they are removed from it. John Cage uses chance procedures in his tape collages; György Ligeti used this method as late as 1958 in his tape composition, "Articulation," in order to maintain a homogeneous distribution of diverse sonorous elements.

The Dadaist writers' interest in language began as early as 1916, when Hugo Ball declared: "We have developed the plasticity of the word to a point which can hardly be surpassed." It was not until the 1950's that the electronic composers Schaeffer, Henry, Berio, Cage, and Stockhausen applied analogous procedures to tape compositions, and extended the plasticity of the word.

Kurt Schwitters was among the first Dadaists to emulate the

Futurists' presentation of stage works in which all the elements are inseparable; and their use of "noise music." One of his theatre scores that displays these characteristics is *Merz* (1920): "Materials for the score are all tones and noises capable of being produced by violin, drum, trombone, sewing machine, grandfather clock, stream of water, etc." Schwitters goes on to say that "Materials for the text are all experiences that provoke the intelligence and emotions." His broad definition of textual elements is comparable to that of later musicians. Initially, musicians were not very concerned with these processes because tape recorders, which were the means to accomplish such transformations, were not yet available. Aside from the Intonarumori, only nominal experiments with phonographs were executed at this time.

The Bauhaus, founded in 1919 by the architect Walter Gropius, was comparable in many respects to Futurism and Dadaism. It included architecture, painting, photography, film, typography, commercial art, and reflected-light composition, in addition to workshops in stone sculpture, woodcarving, cabinetmaking, metal, pottery, stained glass, wall-painting, weaving, bookbinding, printing, interior design, and the stage. Since the Bauhaus was primarily concerned with visual arts, there was less concern with linguistic transformations. The sole exception is the theatre, in which some syntactic and semantic modifications, in addition to musical and noise sounds can be found.

The first stage workshops at the Bauhaus, in 1921, were directed by Lothar Schreyer, but dissatisfaction with Schreyer led to his replacement by Oskar Schlemmer two years later. Schlemmer's "Gesture Dance" (1927) incorporates piano, gong, timpani, and a fanfare played on a phonograph, but aside from the fanfare, no precise directions are given to the musicians. Three actors, dressed in yellow, red, and blue respectively, coordinate their actions, or movements, with the musical sounds, so that the score includes a description of a theatrical event.[1]

The concept of form, which stems from architectural principles, is an underlying factor in all Bauhaus creations. Schlemmer's "The Two Solemn Tragedians" (1924), for example, bases

[1] Prior to the "Gesture Dance," Schlemmer, Lászlo Moholy-Nagy, and Farkas Molnár contributed a series of articles to a book on the Bauhaus theatre, the fourth in a projected series that included approximately fifty titles. *The Theatre of the Bauhaus* (1924) is one of the fourteen books published. Gropius and Moholy-Nagy were coeditors of the "Bauhaus Books" series, which terminated in 1930.

amplitude relations upon proportions, and employs megaphones to amplify voices according to the relative size of the stationary figures. Moholy-Nagy, in "Theatre, Circus, Variety" (1924), makes amplified voices correspond to visual magnification by mirrors. He predicted the appearance of electro-mechanical acoustical equipment, "speaking or singing clamps," and new amplification systems, in addition to the placement of loudspeakers either under seats or beneath of floor.

In "Man And Art Figure" (1924), Schlemmer explores further possibilities of sonorous transformation: "Mechanical reproduction by means of various kinds of technological equipment is now capable of replacing the sound of the musical instrument and the human voice or of detaching it from its source, and can enlarge it beyond its dimensional and temporal limitations." Unfortunately, the author does not specify the "technological equipment" that he refers to, but he probably meant the Theremin, or devices that produce sound from oscillators. Since the megaphone is used in some of the theatre pieces of this period, its inclusion within this category is also reasonable. The Intonarumori were a unique family of instruments, and it is doubtful that they were either popular or well known outside of Italy. The modern tape recorder was not available until 1935. In all probability, he was describing phonograph speed transformations; a less likely possibility (due to its cumbersome manipulation of sonorous elements) is Poulsen's wire recorder.

Spatial relations between sound and movement are mentioned by Molnár in his "U-Theatre" (1924). Four stages, one of which is reserved for sound sources, are distributed within a large performance area. Like Schlemmer, Molnár refers to "Mechanical music apparatus, combinations of modern sound-effects instruments, radio." Again, there is no indication concerning the nature of this equipment.

Moholy-Nagy's the "Mechanized Eccentric" (1924) offers a clearer description of musical resources. Megaphones replace sounding boxes of conventional instruments, while sound effects, noise makers, and sirens are also required. Although instrumentation is not specified in the score, lights, films, odors, motion, color, and form are graphically indicated.

Musical concepts of form also influenced Bauhaus creations, most notably in the reflected-light compositions of Ludwig Hirschfeld-Mack in 1925. The initial experiments in this medium had been executed three years earlier by Joseph Hartwig and Kurt Schwerdtfeger, and were followed by public performances in Berlin and Vienna in 1924. Music, or sound, is used to reinforce the visual perception of time sequences by means of simple rhythmic patterns. According to Hirschfeld-Mack: ". . . we endeavor to create a fugue-like color composition that is strictly organized and each time derived from some particular theme of color and form." Unlike the "Mechanized Eccentric," the music for the reflected-light compositions is precisely notated in the score, along with color and light combinations.

The basis for much of this work is "The Creation of Living Form through Color, Form and Sound" (1923) by the Bauhaus artist Gertrude Grunow. She attempted to determine fundamental relations between sound and color by searching for a lawful order, the state of equilibrium: "Every living force, and thus every color, corresponds to a lawful order, to a sound." Since equilibrium is related to the ear, Grunow concludes that sound affects one's state of equilibrium, and since colors are ordered to correspond to the chromatic musical scale, color may produce similar effects through its association with music.

Amidst these revolutionary, albeit sometimes scientifically invalid, experiments with sonorous transformation, the invention of new instruments continued. In France, Maurice Martenot introduced various methods for controlling timbre in 1928, and the following year Laurens Hammond did so in America. Both the "Ondes Martenot" and the "Hammond Organ" utilized principles similar to Cahill's for timbral modifications. Composers Paul Boisselet, François Bayle, and Edgard Varèse, among others, have written pieces for the "Ondes Martenot," and both instruments are still useful to composers.

A precursor to the modern synthesizer and computer also appeared during this time. In 1929, two Frenchmen, A. Givelet and E. E. Coupleux, devised a machine that consisted of four oscillators controlled by punched paper rolls, thereby incorporating De Forest's oscillator with the principles of the player piano. An equally significant aspect of this prototypic synthesizer was the degree of automation involved. The punched paper rolls activated the oscillators in much the same manner that IBM cards are used to program a computer. It is therefore not surprising to find computers assuming an important role in the synthesis of electronic music beginning with the late 1950's.

Even though electronically generated sounds and sonorous transformations via the phonograph were available in 1930, composers were still intrigued by the possibility of deriving new timbres from conventional instruments. Henry Cowell had already liberated the piano from its traditional tone color by clusters and playing on the interior of the piano by 1911, but the piano alone could not satisfy musicians searching for new timbral resources. In "Ionisation" (1931), his composition for percussion ensemble, Edgard Varèse was the first to demonstrate the wide range of instrumental color available from percussion instruments.

During the first few decades of the twentieth century, articles on the "new" music increasingly appeared in periodicals in France, Italy, Germany, and the United States. Contributions were made by both composers and scientists, including the scientists Givelet and Robert Beyer and the composers Ferruccio Busoni, Edgard Varèse, and Henry Cowell. Scientific advances had become so numerous by this time that Joseph Schillinger compiled a survey of them in 1931, and in the following year the conductor Leopold Stokowski published a speech entitled "New Horizons in Music." Stokowski not only supported the new methods of controlling timbre, but he called upon scientists and musicians to work together to investigate the emotional responses attributed to music.

By the 1930's, virtually all the prerequisites for the realization of electronic music had been satisfied. Composers were beginning to think in terms of timbral relations; oscillators and instruments capable of controlling timbre had been perfected; and the means for sound storage and reproduction were available. Both the phonograph and the wire recorder, however, were inadequate for sound manipulation except for the most basic transformations. The appearance in 1935 of the "Magnetophone," the first magnetic tape recorder, completely changed this situation. It was now possible for composers to play sounds backwards, to vary speed during playback, to alternate between two or more sounds by splicing, and to superpose any sounds or entire segments of a composition by overdubbing. None of these techniques is possible without the aid of machines, which opened up both a new world of sound and a different compositional approach in order to deal with these sounds.

The visionary composer Edgard Varèse continued to probe new compositional procedures. He discussed the close relationship between science and art, sound masses, timbre control, and the use of graphic scores which could be realized by machines. His ideas were shared by the Mexican composer Carlos Chavez, who also advocated the synthesis of all art forms via film. Chavez even spoke of elaborate mixing panels, dubbing, and filtering for film sound tracks, and of the necessity for musicians to learn about sound engineering if they were to work with film.

Carlos Chavez talked about film in 1937, but the combination of sound with film had already begun in Germany and France almost a decade earlier. By 1939 these European experiments had influenced the Canadian filmmaker Norman McLaren, who was living in New York. He extended the technique of "drawn sound" to include the scratching of geometric patterns directly on film, so that these shapes frequently corresponded to visual imagery.

In Hollywood the following year, James and John Whitney developed a new approach for combining sound with film. Basing their work upon abstract films produced at the Bauhaus, the Whitney brothers used a series of manually activated pendulums whose movement controlled the amount of light passing through an aperture to which the pendulums were connected. An optical sound-track was guided past the opening so that changing light patterns were registered on the film. Since the rate of the pendulums' movement was intrinsically slow, the optical sound track had to be played back at a greater speed in order to avoid sub-audible sounds, the frequencies below 16 Hz. Because they had been forced to work at such slow speeds, the Whitneys were able to synchronize precisely the temporal relationship between sound and visual imagery. In addition, they became aware of a timbral change when they increased the playback speed. This technique was employed by Karlheinz Stockhausen twenty years later in his electronic composition, "Kontakte."

Among those interested in the work of Henry Cowell and Edgard Varèse was the American composer John Cage, whose "Imaginary Landscapes" utilized a wide array of sounds. "Imaginary Landscape No. 1" (1939) was intended as a radio broadcast similar to Marinetti's "Radiophonic Theatre." Its sound sources consisted of two RCA Victor test records played on a variable speed phonograph, a large Chinese cymbal, and the interior of a piano. A percussion quintet in combination with a coil of amplified wire constituted the sound materials for "Imaginary Landscape No. 2" (1942). His third "Imaginary Landscape" was completed in the same year, and retained the percussion instruments and amplified wire, but added tin cans, a buzzer, a muted gong, oscillators, frequency test records played on a variable speed phonograph, and a marimbula connected to a contact microphone. Cage's choice of sounds in this last composition is reminiscent of Russolo's (1913) "Noise Networks," while his use of a variable speed phonograph recalls work carried out during the 1920's by Milhaud, Toch, and Hindemith.

Following the appearance of the tape recorder in 1935, a number of primitive synthesizers, based upon the principles of a similar machine designed by Givelet and Coupleux in 1929, were invented. The most significant were built in America by Percy Grainger and Burnett Cross, and by J. M. Hanert between 1944 and 1945. Grainger and Cross collaborated and employed eight oscillators that could be accurately synchronized. Hanert's synthesizer operated on the principle of punched cards, which replaced paper rolls of the earlier French machine. From this time onward, it was chiefly the Americans who developed synthesizers for commercial use.

The compositions of the Parisian Paul Boisselet, beginning in 1944, clearly indicate the direction that many composers were taking. Boisselet frequently combined instrumental ensembles of various sizes with oscillators and the "Ondes Martenot," to produce music for radio, ballet, and the concert hall. Boisselet's compositions predate the current practice of combining musicians and electronic music in live performance.

This brief survey explains the development of electronic music. The evolution of this "new" music was not only logical, but it satisfied a basic need on the part of composers to deal with sounds themselves—with *all* sounds. It is not surprising to find ancient Greek concepts present in contemporary electronic works; for the Greeks' mathematical procedures, founded on proportions, illustrate a universal phenomenon: that human aural perception is based upon proportional relations of the overtone series. Just as important, the ancient Greek and medieval peoples' awareness of the existence of sound waves, indicates their understanding of the nature of sound, even though their knowledge was a product of deductive reasoning rather than scientific method.

These fundamental concepts, formulated more than two thousand years ago, were kept alive and developed in theoretical treatises throughout the intervening centuries, and remain the basis of acoustical thought today. Sauveur was the first to scientifically substantiate these ideas. Their relevance to the electronic medium reveals the "new" music to be a part of this tradition, for the application of these scientific principles to music eventually produced both electronic sound generators, or oscillators; and storage-transformation devices, or the phonograph and the tape recorder. By the twentieth century technology was so sophisticated that these theoretical concepts could be applied to practical situations. This permitted the development of a new medium, musique concrète.

CHRONOLOGICAL LIST OF PRE-1948 EVENTS RELATED TO ELECTRONIC MUSIC

Greek Antiquity
 Odyssey

Pythagoras:
Proportions, monochord,
quarter-tones

Plato:
Ethical and political aims of music

Aristotle:
Aesthetics, education, musical
practice

Aristoxenos:
Equal temperament

Ptolemy:
Just intonation
5th century

Boethius:
De institutione musica

Cassiodorus:
Institutiones musicae
7th century

Isidore of Seville:
Etymologiarum sive originum
9th century

Aurelian:
Musica disciplina

Musica enchiriadis
10th century

Regino of Prüm:
De harmonica institutione
11th century

Guido of Arezzo:
Micrologus
ca. 1260

Franco of Cologne:
Ars cantus mensurabilis
ca. 1270–80

Anonymous IV:

Homer:
De mensuris et discantu
ca. 1300

Johannes de Grocheo:
Theoria
1307

Dante:
Divine Comedy
1318

Marchetto da Padua:
Pomerium artis musicae mensurabilis
ca. 1320

Philippe de Vitry:
Ars Nova
ca. 1475

Tinctoris:
Proportionale musices
1497

Gafurius:
Practica musicae
1552

Vincentino:
Archicembalo
1558

Zarlino:
19 divisions per octave
1577

Salinas:
19 and 24 divisions per octave
1618

Descartes:
Scientific method

Colonna:
La sambuca lincea

Kepler:
Harmony of the World
1627

Bacon:
The New Atlantis
1636

Mersenne:
Harmonie universelle
1671

Rouhault:

Traité de Physique
1680   **Perrault:**
Du Bruit and *De la musique des Anciens*
1701   **Sauveur:**
Overtone series, tuning systems
1710   **Henfling:**
Specimen de novo suo systemate musico; 50 divisions per octave
1722–25   **Mattheson:**
Critica musica; 55 divisions per octave
1726   **Jackson:**
A Scheme Demonstrating the Perfection and Harmony of Sounds; 55 divisions per octave
1722–60   **Rameau:**
System of harmony based on overtone series
1758   **Romieu:**
Memoire théorique & pratique sur les systèmes de musique; 31, 43 and 55 divisions per octave
1763   **Franklin:**
Glass harmonica
1791   **Mozart:**
Music for glass harmonica
1812   **Liston:**
An Essay Upon Perfect Intonation; 59 divisions per octave
1814   **Beethoven:**
Music for glass harmonica
1826–27   **Delezenne:**
Mémoire sur les valeurs numériques des notes de la gamme; 41 divisions per octave
1850   **Poole:**
Enharmonic organ with 50 divisions per octave
1852   **Oplet:**
Allgemeine Theorie der Musik; 22 and 43 divisions per octave
1855   **Drobisch:**
Uber musikalische Tonbestimmung und Temperatur; 43 and 74 divisions per octave
1863   **Helmholtz:**

Sensations of Tone
1874–75   **Bosanquet:**
Generalized Keyboard with 53, 56 and 118 divisions per octave
1876   **Koenig:**
Tonametric with 670 divisions over 4 octaves
                                                         Bell:
Telephone
1877   **Berliner:**
Telephone receiver, disc record
1878   **Edison:**
Phonograph
1897   **Cahill:**
Sounding staves
1898   **Poulsen:**
Telegraphone
1906   **Cahill:**
Dynamophone
1909   **Schoenberg:**
"Fünf Orchesterstücke"
                                                   Marinetti:
Foundation and Manifesto of Futurism
1911   **Cowell:**
Tone clusters
                                                    Pratella:
The Technical Manifesto of Futurist Music
1912
Translation of Marinetti's manifesto in *Der Sturm*
                                                    Pratella:
"Musica Futurista per Orchestra"
1913   **Russolo:**
Intonarumori, *Futurist Manifesto*
                                                   Marinetti:
The Variety Theatre
1914   **Cangiullo:**
"Piedigrotta"
                                                        Balla:
"Macchina Tipografica"
                                                    Russolo:
Enharmonic Notation for the Futurist "Intonarumori"
                                                    Pratella:
"Saggio di Orchestra mista"

Duchamp:
"Ready-mades"
1915   De Forest:
Oscillator
ca. 1916   Depero:
Notes on the Theatre
1916   Tzara:
Cabaret Voltaire
1916–17   Man Ray:
"Object Paintings"
1917   Balla:
Staging of Stravinsky's "Feu
d'Artifice"
1918   Huelsenbeck:
First German Dada manifesto
1919   Azari:
Futurist Aerial Theatre Manifesto
Bauhaus at Weimar
Tzara introduces Dada in France;
"chance poems" in *Littérature*
1920's   Milhaud, Hindemith, Toch:
Phonograph speed changes
1920   Schwitters:
Merz
1921   Richter:
"Rythmus 21"
                                            Eggeling:
"Diagonal Symphony"
                                              Eluard:
"Information Please"
1922   Marinetti:
"Il Tamburo di Fuoco"
                       Hartwig, Schwerdtfeger:
Reflected-light experiments
1923   Theremin:
Theremin
                                             Grunow:
"The Creation of Living Form
Through Color, Form and Sound"
1924   Schlemmer:
"Man And Art Figure" and "Two
Solemn Tragedians"
First performance of reflected-light
compositions in Berlin and Vienna
                                        Moholy-Nagy:
"Theatre, Circus, Variety" and
"Mechanized Eccentric"

Molnár:
"U-Theater"
                                          Schwitters:
"Ursonata," "W"
1925   Hirshfeld-Mack:
"Reflected-Light Compositions"
1926   Russolo:
Psofarmoni
                                           Theremin:
Electric Harmonium with 1200
divisions per octave
1927   Schlemmer:
"Gesture Dance"
1928   Ruttman:
Drawn sound
                                          Prampolini:
"Santa Velocità"
                                           Martenot:
Ondes Martenot
1929   Hammond:
Electronic organ
                                Givelet, Coupleux:
Synthesizer
1930–37   Marinetti:
5 radiophonic works
1931   Bauhaus:
Drawn sound
                                              Varèse:
"Ionisation"
                                         Schillinger:
"Electricity, a musical liberator"
1932   Stokowski:
"New Horizons In Music"
Bauhaus at Berlin
1933   Marinetti, Masnata:
*Futurist Radiophonic Theatre
Manifesto*
1933–37   Jaubert, Hoérée, Honegger:
Film sound tracks
1935 Allgemeine Elektrizitäts
                                        Gesellshaft:
Magnetophone
                                           Duchamp:
"Rotoreliefs"
1937   Chavez:
Toward A New Music
1939   McLaren:

Drawn sound

Cage:
"Imaginary Landscape No. 1"

1940 **Whitney:**
Drawn sound

1942 **Cage:**

1942
"Imaginary Landscape Nos. 2 and 3"

1944 **Boisselet:**
Compositions with oscillators

Grainger, Cross:
Synthesizer

1945 **Hanert:**
Synthesizer

Part One

Music for Solo Tape

It is by ruler and compasses that the Greeks discovered geometry—musicians might do well to be inspired by their example.

Pierre Schaeffer, 1960

CHAPTER ONE

MUSIC FROM VOICE AND INSTRUMENTS

THE FIRST MUSIC composed exclusively for either magnetic tape or phonograph appeared in Paris in 1948. Pierre Schaeffer, at that time a broadcast engineer for the Radiodiffusion-Télévision Française (R.T.F.), presented a concert of his compositions involving sound effects records and "everyday" sounds. This new music, called "musique concrète," was "realized" by subjecting natural, prerecorded sounds to any number of recording techniques, like speed changes, playing the sounds backwards or tape reversal, and overdubbing.

The following year Schaeffer was joined by another young French composer, Pierre Henry, and together they established at the R.T.F. the world's first center for tape composition. These first musique concrète pieces will be discussed in subsequent chapters, but it should be noted that the basic sound sources for these works included any sound that was not electronically produced, like trains, wind, birds, footsteps, voice, piano, and so on. Our study of electronic music will begin with compositions realized from a single sound source, the human voice. If we first treat familiar sounds, it will be easier for us later to understand those works built upon sounds that are electronically generated by oscillators.

The first composition derived solely from the voice did not appear until 1952. This work, realized by Pierre Henry at the R.T.F., was entitled "Vocalise." It is approximately two and a half minutes long, and uses only a single syllable, "ah." This extreme limitation of basic sound material would have been unimaginable to a com-

poser who did not use either mechanical or electronic modifications, but it quickly made apparent the tape recorder's compositional value.

Musique concrète and electronic composers did not totally
abandon the use of a theme and its development. The developmental techniques employed in musique concrète primarily involve the aforementioned tape manipulations. Those most frequently employed by Henry in his "Vocalise" consisted of speed
changes or tape transposition (change of tape record and/or
playback speed), splicing, and overdubbing (superposition of
sounds).

"Vocalise" begins with a clearly recognizable statement of the
syllable "ah." As the result of tape transpositions that involve first
playing the tape at a higher speed, and then playing the tape at a
slower speed, the timbre of the sounds is transformed to resemble
chirping birds, and the roar of a lion. Henry was able to produce
rhythmic patterns by splicing together various pieces of tape, and
the process of overdubbing enabled him to vary the texture between one and many voices.

Henry's use of a single syllable allowed him to concentrate on
pure music, and eliminated any concern with language and meaning. The Italian composer Luciano Berio, however, employed a
text from James Joyce's *Ulysses* in his piece "Thema" (1958), which
he subtitled "Omaggio a Joyce." Although it would seem that Berio
was attempting to incorporate language and meaning into the sonic
structure of this composition, he removed the words from their
context and treated them as independent "sound systems."

Berio's decision to deal with Joyce's text in this manner was
prompted by the sonorous nature of the text itself, which makes
extensive use of such onomatopoetic words as "smack," "chips,"
"trilling," and "hiss," and of alliterative ones like "blew blue
bloom," "jingle jingle jaunted jingling," "clock clacked," and
"Liszt's rhapsodies."

"Thema" is just under eight minutes long. Example 1 traces the
appearance of the text throughout the piece. Like "Vocalise,"
"Thema" begins with a statement of the basic material—in this
instance an unaltered reading of the complete text—which lasts
approximately one minute and fifty three seconds. The remaining
six minutes consists of a variety of tape manipulations and filtering
(suppression of selected overtones that results in a change of color
or timbre) applied to the original text. Berio's desire to create new

0:00   1:54

(Recitation of complete text)⌐⌐ D'ever.   A sail, a sail, a sail.   A veil awave.

                                                         2:07

Throstle fluted.   The spiked winding cold, silent.   Hissss hissss ssss.

                                    2:14   2:23

I feel loose.   A sail lonely blooming.   Hissss hissss hissss   ⌐ sā sā sā ..
                                                                    ⌞ War

                    2:37

⌐ ....   bl bl bloo bloo bloo blooming blooming
⌞ spike spike d'ever spike fight

        2:44   2:57   3:02   3:41

blooming.   D'ever   ⌐war   Bronze, spiked thesss (unintelligible).   Tingle,
                       ⌞spike

        3:44   3:47   3:49   4:21

tingle, frost (unintelligible).   So lonlely, lonely (untelligible).   Hissss.

4:28   4:32   4:42   4:44   6:49   6:54

⌐ The waves.   Rhapsody   Say yes (unintelligible).   Soft words, alas.
⌞ sails

                            7:04

Listen.   Each and for other plash   ⌐ and silent roar.   Pearls.   When
                                        ⌞ hissss   hissss   so sad   hissss

                    7:20   7:22

she left word the roar.   Alas.   Listen.   Hissss (unintelligible).   War.

7:35   7:51

⌐ Hissss Soft hissss....
⌞ War

EXAMPLE 1. Luciano Berio, "Thema"

types of sounds from preexisting ones resulted in a composition
that is his impression of Joyce's passage.

Berio focused on the onomatopoetic and alliterative elements of
Joyce's work. Two minutes and thirty-seven seconds into the piece,
Berio removed the "bl" from "blooming" and spliced a number of
these "bl" segments together to produce a stuttering effect. He then
lengthened this segment to include "bloo," and then "bloom," until

finally the complete word "blooming" appears three times in succession. Such processes are very similar to those employed by Pierre Henry in "Vocalise," and reflects both composers' concern with aural effects of their music.

One of the predominating sounds in "Thema" is "s," which not only appears rather obviously in the word "hiss," but also in more subtle contexts, with vowels as in "sail" and "rose," and consonants, as in "steel," "spiked," and "stars." The "s" is also found adjacent to both vowels and consonants, as in the words "flushed," "husky," and "listen."

Example 2 illustrates the frequency of the "s" sound. An extreme instance occurs throughout the last minute of "Thema," when the word "hiss" is superimposed on other words. The final sequence of words—"hiss soft hiss hiss"—produces a cadential effect, with the "s" sound now more significant than the actual words.

In France, Michel Philippot's "Ambiance II," derived from Stephane Mallarmé's poem "Toast Funèbre," appeared in the same year as "Thema." Philippot was one of the first composers after Pierre Henry to use the facilities at the R.T.F. regularly.

In many respects, "Ambiance II" is similar in design to "Thema." A literary text is once again the basis for the composition. Both composers employed essentially the same tape techniques: tape transposition, tape reversal, and various imitations by means of splicing. These two pieces do differ, however, in their overall structural organization. Whereas Berio's work is divided into two distinct sections, statement and development, Philippot juxtaposes Mallarmé's poem, unaltered and in its entirety, with modifications of the poem that result from his tape manipulations.

The only modification applied to the poem itself is the addition of reverberation, which helps to separate the poem aurally from the accompanying modifications. "Toast Funèbre" may be easier for the untrained listener to follow than "Thema," because the intact poem is used throughout the entire composition. As we will see, composers can ofteen be distinguished by the structural plan of their work. This type of understanding will enable the listener to better appreciate a work of art.

So far, the compositions discussed here were realized either at the R.T.F. in Paris or at the Italian electronic studio in Milan. During the early 1950's, there were at least three other major

Phonetic Structure of "Thema"

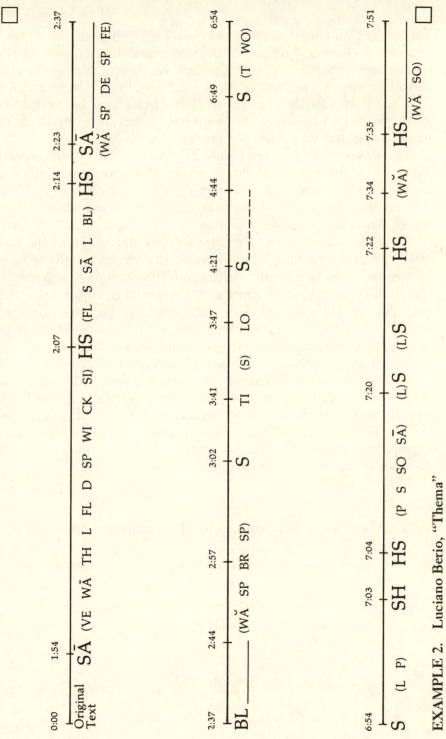

EXAMPLE 2. Luciano Berio, "Thema"

studios in Cologne, Toronto, and New York. They all encouraged composers the world over to utilize their facilities. The Columbia studio was founded by the composers Vladimir Ussachevsky and Otto Luening in 1952; in 1959 it merged with Princeton University as a result of a Rockefeller grant. It has been used by composers from more than twenty countries. One of the most important of these composers was Ilhan Mimaroglu, a native of Turkey.

In his composition "Le Tombeau d'Edgar Poe" (1964), based upon a Mallarmé poem of the same title, Mimaroglu established a highly sectional design as its structure. The poem is composed of four stanzas to which Mimaroglu added an introduction, three interludes and a postlude (Example 3).

As in the works previously discussed, the statements of the text itself are complete and unmodified. They occur simultaneously with a multitude of textual modifications that include tape transposition, filtering, and reverberation. It is clear in Example 3 that the introduction is particularly long in relation to the other sections, and it is one of the most complex segments in the piece. Mimaroglu's conscious sectional divisions become apparent when we note the gradually shortening durations of succeeding verses. There is very little durational difference between the four final segments, whereas the introduction, first and second verses, and interludes are characterized by rather large disparities of that kind. Therefore, as "Le Tombeau" approaches its conclusion, a state of structural equilibrium is reached. Well-proportioned sections characterize a number of other pieces by Mimaroglu as well.

EXAMPLE 3.   Ilhan Mimaroglu, "Le Tombeau d'Edgar Poe"

0:00		2:45		3:25	
	Introduction		1st Verse		1st Interlude
4:08		4:35		5:48	
	2nd Verse		2nd Interlude		3rd Verse
6:10		6:36		6:57	
	3rd Interlude		4th Verse		
6:57		7:08			
	Postlude				

During the 1960's, the young Japanese composer Toru Takemitsu realized a musique concrète work, "Vocalism Ai," that was reminiscent of Pierre Henry's "Vocalise". "Ai" is a Japanese word meaning "love." A man's and a woman's voices were utilized to record "ai," and the usual tape manipulations were then employed.

Takemitsu's compositional handling of this extremely sparse sound material primarily involved three aspects of speech. The first was the manner in which the word "ai" was pronounced: it was spoken, sung, whispered, screamed, and cried. The next was different pronunciations of "ai," which sound in English like "eye" and "ah-e." Finally, Takemitsu varied the articulation of the word by using such musical devices as staccato, legato, and portamento. Between these operations and tape transposition, reverberation, and overdubbing, the variety of shapes that "ai" could assume becomes staggering. Multiplying these possibilities by two (because there are two timbral sources, the voices of the man and woman) supplied Takemitsu with an almost unlimited repertory of closely related sounds. "Vocalism Ai" is a fine example of an economical choice of sound sources treated in such a manner that they are never monotonous or boring.

Steve Reich's composition "Come Out" (1966), derived from the phrase "come out to show them," is a similar instance. This piece is a by-product of a riot in Harlem in the summer of 1964, in which a black man, Daniel Hamm, was arrested for murder. When he arrived at the precinct house, he was beaten by the police; and in order to receive hospital treatment for his police-inflicted injuries, Hamm said, "I had to, like, open the bruise up and let the bruise blood come out to show them."

This statement appears unaltered three times in succession during the first twenty seconds of Reich's piece (Example 4), after which the final phrase "come out to show them" continuously repeats by means of tape loops for the remainder of the work, approximately twelve minutes. A tape loop is made by cutting a piece of recording tape to any length and splicing the loose ends together to form a loop. This loop is then placed on a tape recorder so that prerecorded sounds appear in a continuous series. Reich expertly executes relatively simple tape manipulations to produce very subtle aural effects throughout this section. This composition was realized on two channels, in stereo; therefore, it requires two loudspeakers for performance. Example 4 refers to the following description of the piece.

Mic →

A

"I had to, like, open the bruise up and let some of the bruise blood come out to show them."

Both channels in unison.

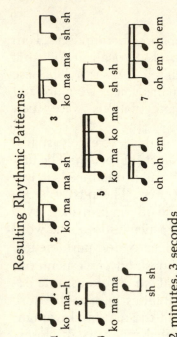

come out to show them

Begin to perceive pitch, rhythm and noise formants (sh).

Duration = 30 seconds

B

Channel 2 gradually moves ahead of channel 1.

Resulting Rhythmic Patterns:

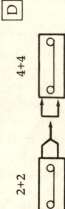
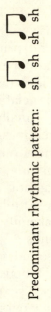

1 ko ma–h
2 ko ma ma
3 ko ma ma sh sh
4 ko ma ma sh sh
5 ko ma ko ma
6 oh oh em
7 oh em oh em

Duration = 2 minutes, 3 seconds

C

1+1   2+2

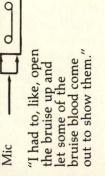

Vary phase relations within new 4-layer version to produce artificial reverberation

Resulting Rhythmic Patterns:

1 ko ma ko ma
2 sh sh sh
3 sh sh sh
4 sh sh sh sh
5 sh sh sh sh
6 sh sh sh sh

Duration = 20 seconds

Duration = 5 minutes, 31 seconds

D

2+2   4+4

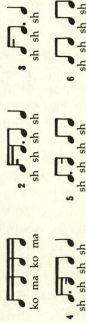

Only "sh" retains its character; all other syllables become indistinguishable.

Predominant rhythmic pattern:

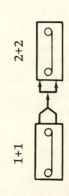

sh sh sh   sh sh sh sh

Duration = 2 minutes, 3 seconds

Duration = 4 minutes, 6 seconds

EXAMPLE 4. Steve Reich, "Come Out"

After the introductory statements, four main divisions occur as a result of an increasingly close juxtaposition of materials. The first of these A, may appear short in comparison to the remaining segments for it lasts only about thirty seconds. Both channels are in unison, so that the same material comes through both loudspeakers. Thirty seconds, however, is a relatively long time to hear nothing but a constant repetition of "come out to show them." This was Reich's intention, for by the end of this section the listener has become aware of three elements: pitch, rhythm, and noise formants. The pitches that gradually emerge are notated in Example 4 along with their appropriate rhythmic configuration. The noise formants, harmonically complex regions within the frequency spectrum, are produced by the "sh" of "show," and are reminiscent of a drum played with brushes.

Section B lasts approximately two minutes and three seconds, and is characterized by the gradual temporal separation of the two channels. Although both channels continue to possess the same material, channel two begins to move ahead of channel one. This technique is referred to as "phasing." Even though the time lag between the two channels is only a fraction of a second, many changes occur within the text. The hard "c" of "come" is broadened, and since the "e" is silent, the "m" is elongated. The "t" of "out" is not articulated, so that the words "come out" begin to sound like "kom ou." As the channels move increasingly out of phase, the "ou" of "out" becomes "ah." The various rhythmic patterns based on "kom ah" are notated in Example 4.

The other predominant sound is the "sh" of "show." First it is extended, and subsequently appears in patterns of two as "sh sh." The "ow" of "show" combines with the "em" of "them" (the "t" is not articulated) to yield the pattern "oh em".

The textures become twice as dense in Section C. By now, both channels of the previous section are out of phase, and are recorded on each channel of this new section. Both channels one and two contain the entire Section B. The interconnection of the tape recorders is depicted in Example 4. In order to create more complex patterns, both channels of Section C are recorded out of phase to result in some patterns which differ from those in Section B.

"Oh em" (numbers 6 and 7, Section B) occur in such close proximity that they now sound like a trill between C# and D# Furthermore, since the time lag is applied to essentially four channels, artificial reverberation is produced.

Finally, recording procedures idential to those employed in Section C are used throughout Section D to produce another twofold multiplication of density. The accompanying phasing between the two channels creates such a complex sound mass that all the words become totally indistinguishable. Only "sh," appearing in the form of equally spaced pulses, retains its character. Excessive reverberation resulting from the time lags also contributes to the incomprehensibility of the text and to the rather simple rhythmic patterns.

Structurally, "Come Out" resembles "Thema" in that both pieces start out with a completely comprehensible text which gradually loses any literary meaning, and where the words exist primarily as individual sounds. This happens to a greater extent in Steve Reich's piece because no meaning remains: a transformation from logical speech to "pure" sound has occurred. Perhaps John Cage was correct when he wrote in 1939 that "Tomorrow, with electronic music in our ears, we will hear freedom."

Extensive textual transformations characterize the work or Arrigo Lora-Totino who, assisted by Enore Zaffiri and Sandro de Alexandris, established the "studio di informazione estetica" in Turin in 1966. Lora-Totino's "English Phonemes 1970" was composed for the Fylkingen Festival in Stockholm and recorded at the Sveriges Radio. It is derived from three short texts written by the composer that contain mostly alliterative and onomatopoetic passages. The sonorous character of Lora-Totino's text resembles the one Berio used in "Thema."

There are three timbral shades in "English Phonemes" (the phoneme is the smallest unit of speech), the voices of a man, a woman, and the combination thereof. The original texts are read unaltered, and subjected to a series of syntactic and syllabic transformations, which consist of the words grouped according to their length, and verbal segmentation into three-letter aggregates which are combined to form meaningless words. A progressive loss of intelligibility is achieved by overdubbing, tape reversal, tape delay, and filtering.

Roland Kayn, a German composer who worked in Italy, realized "Cybernetics III" (1969) at the R.A.I. in Milan. Voices and animal sounds, subjected to extensive tape and electronic transformations, constitute a vocal continuum bounded by breath sounds and unintelligible speech. Selective filtering of the vocal spectrum, in addition to ring modulation, tape transposition and reversal, contribute to the dissolution of the semantic characteristics of speech, while phonemes and accents are further transformed by envelope contours superposed on them. Ring modulation is an electronic process whereby all the frequency components of two input signals are arithmetically added and subtracted to yield a harmonically complex sound; both input signals are attenuated at the output. The amplitude variation of a sound is referred to as an envelope; it is a graphic description of a sound with respect to time, hence the term "envelope contour." Since familiar sounds are often recognized by their characteristic envelopes, envelope modification produces many degrees of variation. Rich textures comprised of vocal imitation of oscillator tones, gongs, metal, wood, and short wave transmission, undergo smooth transitions, yet display great timbral variety.

One of the most recent tape compositions derived exclusively from the voice is "Bal Des Leurres" (Dance of the Decoys), realized by Ilhan Mimaroglu at the Columbia-Princeton Electronic Music Center. This short piece is the last of an eleven-movement work, "Music for Jean Dubuffet's Coucou Bazar" (1973), which was composed for Dubuffet's "Coucou Bazar". The text is a poem written by the painter. It is first recited, and then treated canonically by overdubbing and gives the impression of simultaneous conversations. This is the only manipulation employed, so that a partially intelligible text results.

Only a rather small number of tape compositions employing the voice alone have been commercially recorded. This seems peculiar, considering the number of such works that exist. However, quite a few pieces that involve the voice with other sounds have been recorded, and these will be treated in subsequent chapters.

The same problem arises in considering solo tape pieces derived from conventional musical instruments. Once again, Pierre Schaeffer conducted the initial experiments. His "Etude au Piano I" (1948) and "Etude au Piano II" (1948) were derived from a series of chords transformed by tape manipulations. The first étude, subtitled "Etude violette," is an imaginative transformation of piano sonorities. Schaeffer's splicing techniques include the dissection of recorded piano sounds into autonomous components that frequently bear no resemblance to the original sound. Rhythmic patterns are obtained from alternating between two diverse sonorities, usually of short duration. Appropriate lengths of tape are measured and spliced together. The superposition of these elements forms complex textures. Schaeffer's "Variations sur une flûte mexicaine" (1949) involved similar timbral alterations resulting from tape modifications.

Prior to the establishment of the Columbia-Princeton Electronic Music Center, Vladimir Ussachevsky and Otto Luening had begun to realize musique concrète pieces derived from piano and flute, the same instruments Pierre Schaeffer had employed a few years earlier. The first works to emerge from this period were a set of pieces, "Transposition," "Reverberation," "Composition," and "Experiment," realized by Ussachevsky during 1951–52. Piano was the sole source of sound for all these compositions.

As the title suggests, "Transposition" utilizes the technique of changing speeds to produce different pitches and durations from a single pitch, the low A on the piano. When the playback speed of the prerecorded pitch is increased, its frequency becomes higher while its duration is shortened. This strict limitation of sound materials forms a closely knit group of piano timbres.

The second piece extends the timbral spectrum by adding reverberation to "Transposition." "Composition" employs additional piano sounds. Special repeating devices with multiple playback heads, reverberation, and overdubbing constitute the primary modifications of the piano sounds in "Experiment." The repetitions are produced by passing the prerecorded tape across a series of tape playback heads, similar to the "Echoplex" that is now commercially available. Standard tape recorders possess only one playback head, therefore Ussachevsky's device may be considered an elaborate tape playback system.

One of the most important of Ussachevsky's early works is his "Sonic Contours" (1952). It is derived from the piano, and includes a short segment of reverberated voices at high speeds about two-thirds of the way through the piece. The piano is modified via tape transposition, tape reversal, reverberation, filtering, and overdubbing or mixing. Although the results of overdubbing and mixing are similar, the execution of these techniques differs. Due to the repeated recording of sounds, the former process entails a greater amount of time, and the fidelity of the initially recorded sounds is often inferior to that of the final addition. Since mixing is the simultaneous combination of sounds, there is no loss of fidelity. Furthermore, amplitude controls for individual sources permit discreet intensity changes during the recording process. Example 5 contains two instances of superimposed piano sonorities and illustrates Ussachevsky's continual emphasis upon a highly concentrated repertory of motives.

Otto Luening derived four tape compositions from flute in 1952. Artificial reverberation, an effect produced by means of adjacent multiple playback heads, or by overdubbing a sound with itself incorporating a short time delay, provides the majority of the flute alterations. "Fantasy in Space" is built upon a simple melody (see Example 6) which, with its accompanying juxtapositions, produces an impressionistic effect. Luening's other flute-derived tape compositions are "Invention in Twelve Tones," "Moonflight," and "Low Speed." This last employs tape transposition to obtain pitches beyond the normal range of the flute. One such example occurs at the end of the piece, where two pitches are superimposed (Example 7). The low B^b produced by slowing down the speed of the tape is beyond the range of the flute.

After listening to these compositions by Ussachevsky and Luening, we can see that both men were dealing with instrumental sounds in a similar fashion. It is therefore not surprising to find them collaborating on "Incantation" (1952). For the first time, they increased the number of sound sources to include flute, clarinet, voice, bell, and gong sounds, which undergo conventional tape manipulations. Ussachevsky's tendency to create larger sections from individual motives is achieved by tape transposition. "Incantation" continually subjects the woodwind instruments to changing speeds, a generating motive that appears regularly throughout the piece. The effect is easily distinguished because it is a glissando, and its frequent presence serves as a structural basis for the composition. "Incantation" will be discussed in more detail in the third chapter.

The French composer François Bayle, working at the R.T.F. in Paris, realized two pieces involving instrumental sounds. "Vapeur" (1962) incorporates bass clarinet, string bass, harp, and cymbals. At the beginning of this piece, the instrumental sounds are unaltered. During the course of "Vapeur," however, tape transformations gradually modify those initial sounds and extend the instrumental ranges and timbres.

Bayle made another attempt at producing new timbral combi-

ca. 4:27-4:45

ca. 5:47-5:53

EXAMPLE 5.   Vladimir Ussachevsky, "Sonic Contours"

ca. 1:15–1:50

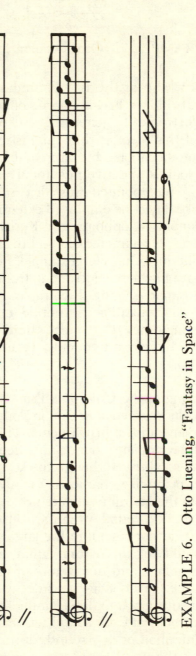

EXAMPLE 6. Otto Luening, "Fantasy in Space"

EXAMPLE 7.   Otto Luening, "Low Speed"

nations in 1963, also at the R.T.F. studio. "L'Oiseau-Chanteur" (The Songbird) utilizes French horn, oboe, and harpsichord, in addition to electronically generated and other concrète sources. The novelty of this piece is that the instrumental sounds do not undergo any modifications, but are combined with the electronic and concrète sounds to derive new tonal shades.

Ussachevsky incorporated this idea in "Of Wood and Brass" (1965) but unlike Bayle, he employed extensive modifications to the trombone, trumpet, xylophone, and Korean gong. Each of these instruments loses its characteristic timbre as a result of tape transposition and filtering. One such example, near the end of the composition, is partially derived from a trombone glissando. Even though the glissando is quite discernible, its source is not always obvious. The vast quantity of timbral changes among the instruments distinguishes this piece from Ussachevsky's earlier works, in which the piano frequently retained its character.

While working at the Columbia-Princeton Center in 1966–67, Ilhan Mimaroglu realized a set of préludes, three of which are derived from conventional instruments. The first one, number I, is based on the interior piano sounds obtained by playing the strings, cross-bars, and wood. Even though the keyboard is not played, the piece retains a piano-like character, mainly because the modifications applied to the instrument were not extensive.

"Prelude No. VI," employs guitar sounds, but contains some passages which do not resemble the guitar at all. This effect was obtained by modifying the natural guitar envelope by eliminating or altering the attack and decay times. The envelope essentially consists of attack, steady state and decay portions and with the overtones, is instrumental in determining the timbre of any sound. It is for this reason that each sound has its individual quality. The attack is the initiation of any sound, during which the amplitude reaches its peak; the attack-time for conventional instruments is less than one second. All sounds have an attack but they do not necessarily possess a steady state, where the amplitude remains relatively constant. The piano envelope, for instance, does not have a steady state, whereas a bowed violin tone may contain a steady state of considerable duration. The decay is characterized by either a gradual or an abrupt decrease in amplitude. With respect to the piano, a sustained tone exhibits a gradual decay, while a snare drum stroke possesses an instantaneous decay. If any or all of the envelope's constituent parts are changed, or if the overtone structure is altered, a different timbre will result. By modifying the guitar's envelope, Mimaroglu was therefore able to obtain a wide variety of new tonal colors.

In Mimaroglu's ninth prélude, a clarinet is modified to resemble a brass instrument. In addition, Mimaroglu applied vibrato, called frequency modulation, to the clarinet. This transformation is clearly audible at the beginning of the piece when the clarinet plays middle C. All three préludes contain frequent use of tape transposition and reversal, filtering, reverberation, and overdubbing.

These kinds of experiments were initiated in 1948 by Pierre Schaeffer at the R.T.F. when he divided a prerecorded bell sound into two parts. When the parts were played individually, the first was recognizable as that of a bell, while the second sounded more like an organ or wind instrument (Example 8). In 1957, Jacques Poullin and Alain de Chambure (also at the R.T.F.) continued the work Schaeffer had begun some years earlier. They removed the attack portion of a prerecorded guitar, and discovered that the guitar had lost its characteristic timbre and assumed that of a piano.

Schaeffer's "Etude aux objets" (1959, revised 1966–67) illustrates the compositional value of these new techniques. Schaeffer said of

EXAMPLE 8. Pierre Schaeffer, Experiment with prerecorded bell

direction of tape

———————————————————————▶

Bell Tape

2nd part	1st part
Organ/wind instrument sound	Bell sound

this work that he was primarily concerned with orchestral material, the idea of theme and variation, and a structure composed of separate movements. The five sections are: "Objets exposés" (exposed objects), "Objets liés" (related), "Objets multipliés (multiplied), "Objets étendus" (spread out) and "Objets assemblés (assembled) ou strette" (stretto). Instruments supply all of the source materials, while many tape manipulations, filterings and splicings provide sonorous transformations in the form of variations. Instrumental sonorities are clearly discernible in the opening section, and at times resemble *Klangfarbenmelodie*. Many glissandi derived from tape transposition characterize "Objets liés," whereas rapid timbral changes, reminiscent of the first movement, predominate in "Objets multipliés." "Exposés" and "multipliés" are differentiated by the treatment of timbral shifts as a function of rhythm in the latter section. "Objets étendus" contains more complex sonorities, but its relation to "exposés" is established by the appearance of easily discerned instrumental timbres. The final movement, as indicated by its title, employs extensive superposition of previous material, so that the structural plan embodies a logical culmination.

With his "Piano Music for Performer and Composer" (1966–7), Mimaroglu explored other means of deriving basic sound materials for a tape composition. Rather than treating the piano as a raw source of sound from which an entire piece would then be realized, Mimaroglu subdivided the compositional process into two stages. His first step was to record a pianist improvising, the improvisation being stimulated by aural and visual imagery supplied by the composer. Mimaroglu then realized a tape piece derived from the recorded piano improvisation. He considered this dual process to be similar to that of a film director who, after coaching the actors (in this case, the pianist) in their performance, proceeds to edit the film.

During the editing process Mimaroglu made use of standard tape techniques in presenting both modified and natural piano sounds. His refined control of timbre is in evidence near the work's conclusion; the unmodified piano is gradually subjected to filtering, which results in an extremely smooth transition in which the natural piano sonorities eventually disappear.

The final composition to be discussed is also derived from a combination of instrumental and electronically-generated sounds.

"Bozzetti" ("Sketches") was realized by the Polish composer Bohdan Mazurek in the Experimental Studio of the Polish Radio in Warsaw in 1967. It is divided into four parts or sketches. The primary instrumental sound is the harp, which frequently appears in transposed form: it is played back at higher speeds throughout the beginning of the piece. The harp sounds are then contrasted against electronically generated blocks of filtered noise. "Bozzetti's" conclusion is derived from the viola, and Mazurek again makes use of the tape transposition by which he obtained patterns of glissandi derived from a single chord.

A new concept of sound and its structural significance links all the compositions discussed in this chapter. Whether the sonorous material was vocal (with or without a text) or instrumental, the main objective of these works has been to extract new sounds from preexisting ones. In order to do so, composers have had to explore timbral relationships based upon tape manipulations. The relationship of timbre to structure will be particularly significant in the works discussed in the next chapter, as these pieces encompass a much wider range of sound sources than those we have explored thus far.

Discography

BAYLE, FRANCOIS
  L'Oiseau-Chanteur, Can.
  31025.

———

  Vapeur, BAM LD—072.
BERIO, LUCIANO
  Thema (Omaggio a Joyce),
  Turn. 34177.

HELLERMANN, WILLIAM
  Ariel, Turn. TV—34301.
HENRY, PIERRE
  Vocalise, DUC—9.
KAYN, ROLAND
  Cybernetics III, DGG
  2543 006.

LORA-TOTINO, ARRIGO
  English Phonemes 1970
  (excerpts), Source Record
  No. 5.
LUENING, OTTO
  Fantasy in Space, Folk.
  FX—6160 and
  Desto 6466.

———

  Invention in Twelve Tones,
  Desto 6466.

———

  Low Speed, Desto 6466.

———

  Moonflight, Desto 6466.

**LUENING, OTTO AND VLADIMIR
USSACHEVSKY**
Incantation, Desto 6466.

MAZUREK, BOHDAN
Bozzetti, Turn. 34301.

MIMAROGLU, ILHAN
Le Tombeau d'Edgar Poe,
Turn. 34004.

Music for Jean Dubuffet's
Coucou Bazar, Finn.
SR—9003.

Piano Music for Performer
and Composer, Turn.
34177.

Preludes I, VI, IX, Turn.
34177.

PHILIPPOT, MICHEL
Ambiance II, BAM
LD—071.

REICH, STEVE
Come Out, Odys.
32160160.

SCHAEFFER, PIERRE
Etude au piano II,
DUC—8.

Etude violette,
Philips 6521 021.

Objets étendus, Philips
6521 021.

Objets exposés, Philips
6521 021.

Objets liés, Philips 6521
021 and Can. 31025.

Objets multipliés, Philips
6521 021.

Objets rassemblés ou
strette, Philips 6521
021.

Variations sur une flûte
mexicaine, DUC—8.

TAKEMITSU, TORU
Vocalism Ai, RCA
VICS—1334.

USSACHEVSKY, VLADIMIR
Linear Contrasts,
Son—Nova 3.

*Of Wood and Brass, CRI
S—227.

Sonic Contours, Desto
6466.

**Transposition, Reverberation,
Experiment, Composition,
Folk. FX—6160.

* Incorrectly listed as "Piece for Tape Recorder."
** Incorrectly listed as "Underwater Waltz."

CHAPTER TWO

MUSIC FROM ELECTRONIC
AND CONCRÈTE SOUNDS

ALTHOUGH MOST OF THE WORKS discussed in the previous chapter fall into the category of musique concrète, they are not the earliest examples in this medium. The term musique concrète was employed by Pierre Schaeffer prior to 1950 to describe a new approach to the compositional process. Only three years after the atomic bomb had been dropped over Hiroshima, Schaeffer appropriately referred to this age as the "time of the atom and fusion." The concept of the atom, when applied to sounds, results in the disintegration of individual sounds. What remains from the sonorous macrocosms is the "found object," an individual sound susceptible to infinite modification. It is this concept of the isolated sound, or "found object," that predominates in Schaeffer's early musique concrète pieces.

The titles of Schaeffer's compositions from the period 1948 to 1949 actually describe the sound sources employed in each piece. Sound effect recordings of locomotives were the sources for the "Etude aux chemins de fer," while "Etude aux tourniquets" employed a xylophone, bells, toy whistling tops and variable-speed phonographs. Two of his works, "Etude au piano I" and "Etude au piano II," were derived from piano sounds, but the greatest number of sound sources is found in the "Etude aux casseroles," which was realized from pan covers (casseroles), canal boats, spoken and sung sounds, and a piano. The choice of such a variety of sounds clearly reflects Schaeffer's concept of an "ocean of sounds" which, together with the notion of the "found object," generated an entirely new compositional approach for dealing with sounds and their organization.

The techniques Schaeffer employed in his "noise études" have influenced many composers associated with the Paris studio. "Etude aux tourniquets," for instance, articulates simple rhythmic patterns by frequent timbral shifts and tape transposition, followed by the introduction of melodic elements. All materials are then combined to form a homogeneous texture. Tape loops using locomotive noises produce rhythmic patterns in "Etude aux chemins de fer," while train whistles supply contrasting melodic fragments. The sound of spinning saucepan covers, rhythmically extended by tape loops and transposition, is accompanied by voices and transposed piano sonorities in "Etude aux casseroles" (Etude pathétique). The basis of these études is the development of rhythmic elements. Stockhausen adopted similar processes a few years later in realizing his first electronic works. Incidentally, Stockhausen entitled these "Studie," the German equivalent of étude. Whereas Schaeffer manipulated tape loops which he subjected to transposition to produce rhythmic transformation, Stockhausen used them to generate timbre.

Of the many composers who made their way to Paris in order to work with Pierre Schaeffer, the first was Pierre Henry. The engineer and the composer subsequently collaborated in the realization of no less than eight works between 1950 and 1953. The "Symphonie pour un homme seul" (1950), which will be discussed in the following chapter, was the first composition to result from their association. Another work from the same year is "L'Oiseau Rai," in which the techniques of speed changes and tape reversal amply demonstrate the flexibility of the tape recorder.

Most of Pierre Henry's work, however, was not the result of collaboration with other composers. His ideas are particularly valuable because, unlike Schaeffer, Henry had been trained as a composer. His traditional musical background is reflected in many of his tape compositions. "Tam-Tam IV" (1951) has a rhythmic style similar to that of the 1950's jazz style; that is, it contains a well-defined rhythmic pulse. Wooden, metallic, and piano sounds predominate, with the piano being played both in the traditional manner and directly on the strings.

Perhaps one of Henry's most successful attempts to apply traditional compositional techniques to tape pieces is "Antiphonie" (1952), whose sonorous materials consist of voices, orchestral music, and metallic sounds. After he had subjected these elements to the usual tape manipulations, Henry distributed them among a series of rhythmic durations, employing the then popular technique of rhythmic serialization. Extremely rapid successions of sounds are produced, so that it is rather difficult to perceive individual pitches and timbres. This is another example of sonic fragmentation, involving the concept of the atom as a generative force.

Henry's preference for employing the piano, voice and percussion instruments in combination with noninstrumental sounds becomes even more apparent in "Astrologie" (1952), in which he includes wind, rain and storm segments. The whole gamut of tape manipulations—tape transposition, tape reversal, splicing, overdubbing—once again enhances the sonorous resources. This piece constitutes the first example of musique concrète used in a commercial French film. The music was also used by Maurice Béjart in choreographing his ballet "Arcane;" he subsequently choreographed many other tape compositions by Pierre Henry, in addition to Stockhausen's "Stimmung" (1968).

One of the characteristics of the early musique concrète pieces is their resemblance to conventional instrumental music, especially in the domains of pitch and rhythm. This was the result of composers focusing their attention primarily on the timbral results of their tape manipulations. The rhythmic construction of many of these tape compositions is reminiscent of Anton Webern's pointillistic treatment of sound and silence, which by the 1950s had become the vogue among the young generation of serialist composers like Pierre Boulez, Luciano Berio, and Karlheinz Stockhausen. An example of such rhythmic designs is Michel Philippot's "Etude I" (1952), in which silence is prominent. Continual changes of timbre are delineated by intermittent silences of varying durations, and the temporal relationship between sound and silence influences the degree of rhythmic complexity.

In contrast, in "Texte II" (1953), André Boucourechliev juxtaposed rhythmic activity against sustained sounds. Furthermore, he extended the idea of rhythmic contrast by preparing two separate tapes to be played on two tape recorders. The tapes were not synchronized, and could begin at different times. This created a multitude of sonorous possibilities. This procedure of arbitrarily combining musical elements is referred to as "indeterminate," since the will of the composer is not operative at some point during the compositional process, and the end result cannot be predetermined. This radical departure from the traditions of Western art resulted from opposition to the strict serial procedures of the aforementioned composers, and was developed by John Cage during the 1950s.

Like Henry and Philippot, Boucourechliev structured his "Texte II" upon musical procedures which were not uniquely tape compositional techniques, but he approached the problem of structural organization from the opposite direction. Both rhythmic relationships and all the sonorous elements appear in a somewhat indeterminate combination.

John Cage incorporated the technical procedures and editing techniques used in musique concrète in his tape collage "Williams Mix" (1952), but his compositional aesthetic was much different from Schaeffer's. Whereas Schaeffer dissected familiar sounds in order to derive new, related sounds, Cage juxtaposed segments of diverse categories of sounds: city, country, and wind-produced sounds, electronic and small sounds requiring amplification, and preexisting musical compositions. Rather than structuring this piece on a predetermined progression of timbral transformations, Cage employed chance operations and the *I-Ching Book of Changes* in order to determine the succession of sounds.

"Williams Mix" was realized at Louis and Bebe Barron's private studio in New York. Its haphazard succession of sonic events, the result of much splicing, produces a wide range of rhythmic and timbral complexities. In extreme instances the sounds are so fragmented as to be beyond recognition. Generally, however, the duration of each event is just long enough that its identity can be established. The listener feels bombarded by essentially unrelated sounds, and must decide for himself what the relationships between them are. A rather lengthy section consisting of applause, cheers, and jeers concludes this work and adds by chance a new dimension to the entire composition.

Pure electronic music was born in Germany in the early 1950s. It differs from musique concrète in that it employs electronic sound generators and modifiers rather than "natural" sounds in compositions. In 1948, the same year that witnessed the first musique concrète compositions of Pierre Schaeffer in Paris, Homer Dudley of Bell Telephone Laboratories introduced the "vocoder" to Werner Meyer-Eppler, a physicist and the director of the Institute of

Phonetics at Bonn University. The vocoder was a device capable both of analyzing sound and simulating speech. It provided the basis of Meyer-Eppler's lecture "Developmental Possibilities of Sound," which he presented the following year. Meyer-Eppler and Robert Beyer delivered additional lectures on electronic music in 1950 at Darmstadt. At that time, Beyer was working at the Northwest German Radio (WDR) in Cologne. In 1951 Meyer-Eppler succeeded in synthesizing sounds electronically by using the Melochord. Developed by the German engineer Harald Bode in 1949, the Melochord employed oscillators for the production of tones. By 1952 the Cologne studio was in operation at the WDR, and the following year Beyer collaborated with Herbert Eimert to produce the first purely electronic compositions; excerpts of some of these works are included in an album of recorded lectures, *Elektronische Musik*, by Eimert.

In the first of these lectures, "Akustische und Theoretische Grundbegriffe," Eimert lists pitch, timbre, tone mixing, and noise as the basic elements of electronic music. The process of mixing is reduced to two types. The first is simply an acoustical addition of tones, analogous to the way we hear an orchestra, which is that individual tones are heard in combination. The second involves a physical interaction among signals: the acoustical properties of tones affect individual sonorous characteristics to generate new timbres. Amplitude modulation, frequency modulation, and ring modulation are electronic processes that produce this kind of mixing; more will be said about these later in this chapter.

Next, Eimert explains that the electronically generated sine tone is a new musical element which cannot be produced by instruments or the voice. It is the simplest musical sound, in that it consists of a single frequency; no overtones are present. The timbral significance of the overtone series (later extensively explored by Stockhausen) is seen as both a means of composing and of fabricating new sounds. Atonality now is liberated from melodic and harmonic functions; each member of the overtone series may correspond to a pitch contained within a preconceived 12-tone row. Transformation (inversion, retrograde, and retrograde-inversion) and transposition applied to the overtone structures of a row yield diverse timbres which, in addition to their melodic and harmonic aspects, can be controlled by applying Schoenberg's 12-tone theory to them.

The record of "Zur Geschichte und zur Kompositionstechnik,"

a lecture presented by Eimert and Meyer-Eppler, includes the only commercially available recording of some early electronic compositions, including some by Eimert and Robert Beyer that were performed at the International Music Festival in Cologne. This recording includes two excerpts of unidentified pieces from this period, possibly Eimert's "Klangstudie I and II." Sine tones and pitches with a rich harmonic content constitute the sound sources, while modulation and filtering yield timbral and textural variants of them.

Eimert's piece "Struktur 8" (1953–4) reflects the influence of Webern in its use of the 12-tone row. Eimert employs only eight melodically associated pitches, which he subjects to modulation, filtering, and reverberation. Another composition of Eimert's that makes use of serial concepts is an electronic version of a 1924 string quartet. Originally canonic and 12-tone, the quartet was modified by tape transposition one octave lower, and by filtering; the electronic version was realized during 1955 and 1956.

Eimert and Meyer-Eppler together produced very intriguing sounds. Their exploration of vocal timbres was based upon principles of acoustics, phonetics, and information theory. Meyer-Eppler suggests the following techniques of vocal transformation: tape reversal and transposition, filtering, the extraction of voiced impulses, and the synchronized superposition of all of these. Tape manipulation of speech had already been carried out by the R.T.F. composers in Paris, but these additional techniques were more systematically investigated by their German counterparts.

Voiced impulses are the plosive elements of words. They possess a sharp attack, and their duration is only a fraction of a second. The following procedure may be employed to extract voiced impulses from speech. Record spoken material at a fast speed, preferably 15 inches per second (15 ips), so that the impulses consume a few inches of tape. (Slower recording speeds, as 7½ or 3¾ ips, yield extremely short pieces of tape per word, making impulse extraction almost impossible). After recording the basic sonorous material, listen to it at a slower playback speed (7½ or 3¾ ips) so that sudden amplitude peaks are easily detectable. Mark off these segments with a pencil, and remove them by splicing.

Degrees of filtering were set to correspond to vowel formants, and speech (voiced) impulses were often filtered or ring modulated. Each vowel is characterized by particular frequency and amplitude relations among the fundamental tone and the accompanying overtones; this distinction is referred to as a vowel formant. Synchronized superposition, the final technique described by Meyer-Eppler, consisted of recording the results of these procedures on individual channels. Each channel was synchronized; that is, each contained the same sequence of material. This synchronization was frequently accomplished with a slight time delay, so that a choral effect was produced. The execution of these processes, referred to as "Musik und Sprache," enabled composers to derive pitch, or music, from normal speech.

These techniques often appear in Eimert's later compositions. "Selektion I" (1959–60), for instance, is derived from four electronically generated and modified signals, and from noise found in any vocal sound mixed with sine tones. The vocal material consists of reading a text that describes the compositional processes and transformations applied to that text. The text is divided into four juxtaposed segments, each of which is assigned an individual channel in which timbral differentiation is maintained by isolating vowel sonorities. Channel one is composed of "a" ("Einsatzabstande," "Klange"); channel two is made up of "e" ("bestimmen," "metrische"); channel three uses "i" ("ist," "Häufigkeitsverteilung"); and channel four includes both "o" and "u" ("Spur"). The resultant textual disintegration mixed with sine tones produces an abstract rhythmic and melodic correspondence to the original text. When combined with these electronically generated elements, speech loses its meaning and becomes music.

Other pieces by Eimert that display similar processes are "Zu Ehren von Igor Stravinsky" (1960–62), in which intelligible speech is replaced by melodic orientation; and "Epitaph für Aikichi Kuboyama" (1960–62) in memory of a Japanese fisherman, which alternates between ring modulated and normal speech. Serialization and vocal transformation were fundamental principles of the early WDR studio, and they occupy a central position in the first electronic works of Karlheinz Stockhausen.

While these events were taking place in Germany, Stockhausen was at the R.T.F. in Paris, where he was occupied with the acoustical analysis of sounds. His work involved the study of timbre: Stockhausen was one of the first electronic composers to control timbre as a function of pitch and rhythm. Even in Pierre Henry's serial compositions, the constituent elements were not as structurally unified.

Stockhausen's timbral concepts were based on the electronic realization of the overtone series. This enabled Stockhausen to establish a continuum between a single pitch and white noise, where all frequencies appear at rapidly fluctuating amplitudes. The sine tone is the sole source in this process. At one extreme of the continuum was the pure sine wave, totally devoid of upper partials, or overtones. As overtones were systematically added in the form of sine waves the sound became increasingly complex. The noise portion of the continuum is comprised of what Stockhausen calls "note mixtures," a grouping of sine waves with harmonically unrelated partials; these do not adhere to the arithmetic ratios that constitute the overtone series. Example 9 is a graphic representation of Stockhausen's timbre continuum.

Stockhausen's "Studie II" (1954) provides an excellent demonstration of the application of his theories to timbre control. This piece, along with its immediate predecessor "Studie I" (1953), was realized at the Cologne studio of which Stockhausen is currently director.

A sine wave generator was the only sound source employed in "Studie II." In combining pure sine tones, Stockhausen constructed a series of closely related timbres by additive synthesis. Since timbral differentiation was his ultimate objective, Stockhausen treated pitch and amplitude variation, the envelope, as functions of timbre. His first step was to construct a pitch, or frequency, scale within the range of 100 to 17,200 cycles per second (cps), or Hertz (Hz). The intermediate pitches were determined by multiplying each successive frequency by the constant $\sqrt[25]{5}$ (approximately 1.07), which results in an 81-degree frequency scale. Stockhausen chose this constant because it yields minute pitch successions where individual tones can still be heard. A smaller constant would have produced frequencies so close together that

EXAMPLE 9.   Karlheinz Stockhausen, Timbre continuum

$\mathcal{N\!V}$ $\mathcal{N\!V}$

$\mathcal{N\!V}$ $\mathcal{N\!V}$

$\mathcal{N}$ $\mathcal{N}$ $\mathcal{N}$ $\mathcal{N}$ $\mathcal{N\!V}$

Note   2:1   3:1⟶Mixture⟶Noise

discreet pitch perception would be unlikely, whereas a larger constant would have destroyed Stockhausen's plan to create smooth timbral successions. Beginning with 100 Hz, the following series results: 100, 107 (100 × 1.07), 114 (107 × 1.07), 121 (114 × 1.07) . . . 17,200 Hz. An important feature of this series is that there are no octave doublings. All pitches exist as nonharmonic frequency ratios among one another; that is, they do not adhere to the arithmetic ratios that constitute the overtone series. They tend to produce noise bands when grouped into note mixtures.

Stockhausen subdivided this series into segments or note mixtures of five pitches. The first was 100, 107, 114, 121, and 129 Hz. The second note mixture was 107, 114, 121, 129, and 138 Hz. After constructing the first five note mixtures in this way, Stockhausen arrived at a second group of note mixtures, numbers six through ten, by skipping one pitch between each two successive pitches. Note mixture six was therefore 100, 114, 129, 147 and 167 Hz., and mixture seven was 114, 129, 147, 167 and 178 Hz.

Three additional groups of note mixtures were constructed in a similar fashion, numbers eleven through fifteen by skipping two frequencies between successive pitches, numbers sixteen through twenty by skipping three frequencies between successive pitches, and numbers twenty-one through twenty-five by skipping four frequencies between successive pitches. This entire process, encompassing twenty-five different note mixtures, was executed nine times beginning with 100, 138, 190, 263, 362, 500, 690, 952, and 1310 Hz. respectively, and resulted in a total of 193 note mixtures. Those that would have been exact repetitions of previous mixtures were deleted; they account for the 32 missing note mixtures. Example 10 illustrates the first twenty-five of these.

In order to treat this elaborate pitch scheme as a function of timbre, Stockhausen first recorded each of the five frequencies of a given note mixture. He then cut a short segment, approximately $5/100$ of a second, from each of these five frequencies. Next, he spliced these five segments together, beginning with the lowest frequency, and placed them on a blank tape loop. Since the five frequencies were recorded at the same amplitude, and since the ear is unable to perceive individual pitches that occur at the rate of twenty per second, the timbre becomes readily apparent to the listener. In order to emphasize the nonharmonic note mixtures that create complex timbres approaching noise, Stockhausen recorded the mixtures with microphones in an echo chamber. The

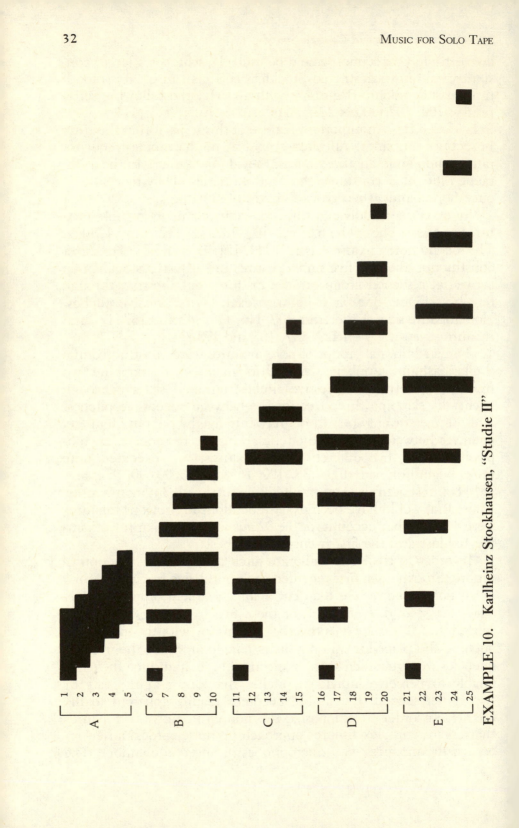

EXAMPLE 10.   Karlheinz Stockhausen, "Studie II"

additional reverberation time allowed for a homogeneous mixing of the nonharmonic pitches.

By studying Example 10 the structure of Stockhausen's timbre continuum becomes evident. Within each of the groups A–E, four frequencies are common between successive note mixtures so that if, for example, mixtures 1 through 5 were played in succession, the pitch would gradually rise and the timbre would become brighter. If, on the other hand, mixture 1 were immediately followed by mixture 5, the pitch and timbral transitions would be more abrupt.

Because the frequencies of group A are rather closely spaced, the transitions within this group will naturally be more smooth than those within group B, for the latter not only eliminates every other frequency, but it also encompasses a wider frequency range. Compare the range of mixture 1 (100–129 Hz.) with that of note mixture 6 (100–167 Hz.). Similarly, group B produces smoother transitions than group C, group C more gradual transitions than group D, and group E contains the most abrupt changes of pitch and timbre.

In addition to treating pitch as a function of timbre in the form of note mixtures, Stockhausen manually regulated the amplitude of each note mixture, thereby producing various types of envelopes. This procedure is analogous to Pierre Schaeffer's experiments six years earlier, when he separated the attack and decay portions of a prerecorded bell sound by splicing. Stockhausen's approach, however, is more sophisticated because he was able to construct whatever envelope he desired by manipulating the volume controls on a tape recorder, thus eliminating the often tedious work involved with tape editing. Example 11 illustrates some of the envelopes employed in "Studie II."

EXAMPLE 11. Karlheinz Stockhausen, "Studie II"

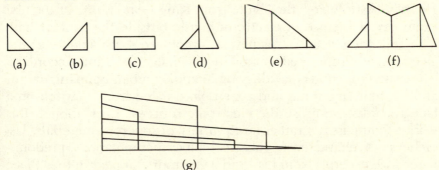

(a)   (b)   (c)   (d)   (e)   (f)

(g)

Envelopes (a), (b), and (c) constitute the three forms from which more elaborate envelopes may be derived. Envelope (d) is a combination of (b) and (a); (e) is the result of (a), (c), and (a); (f) is a combination of (b), (a), (b); and (a); and (g) is an example of the juxtaposition of five envelopes (a) of different durations.

The importance of "Studie II" should not be underestimated. First, it was one of the first purely electronic compositions; in addition, Karlheinz Stockhausen emerged as one of the most skilled composers within this medium. Stockhausen's concept of pitch, amplitude and timbre, as well as his reliance upon recording techniques, are probably the result of his analytical work in Paris. It was Stockhausen's ability to transfer these ideas from the field of musique concrète to electronic composition, however, that actually suggested new directions for composers to take.

Following the work of the Cologne composers, three kinds of tape pieces were composed: musique concrète, electronic music, and a combination of the two. Unfortunately, with the exception of "Studie II," no electronic works realized at the Cologne studio in 1954–5 have been commercially recorded. Examples from this period of musique concrète combined with electronic equipment are available, however. "Dripsody" (1955) by Hugh Le Caine was realized in Canada at the Elmus Lab, a division of the National Research Council of Ottawa. Its sound source is a single drop of water. Like the composers at the R.T.F., Le Caine employed a variable speed tape recorder to alter the sound's pitch so that it encompassed a range from 45 to 8000 Hz.

That same year, the Columbia University composers Luening and Ussachevsky joined forces to produce background music for Orson Welles's production of Shakespeare's "King Lear." Like Pierre Henry's "Astrologie," the "Suite from King Lear" is one of the first examples of the use of electronic music outside the concert hall. The following year, Ussachevsky employed both concrète and electronically generated sounds in his "Piece for Tape Recorder." The concrète sounds include gong, piano, cymbal, tympani, organ, and jet; four sine tones and a tremolo created from a switch on a tape recorder comprise the electronic sources. Even though this work encompasses a rather large variety of sonorous materials, Ussachevsky's characteristic classical tape manipulations predominate. Two excerpts from his "Sonic Contours" appear in the "Piece for Tape Recorder," from 1:37 to 1:53 and from 2:29 to 2:43. New timbres are sought by extracting the beginning, middle, and end of a prerecorded gong sound by splicing, a technique which reflects Schaeffer's influence. Additional timbral transformations result from tape transposition and reversal, filtering, and reverberation. Although electronically generated sounds appear, the piece is dominated by non-electronic materials.

This predisposition for concrète sounds, particularly musical instruments, characterizes Ussachevsky's tape compositions. His "Metamorphosis" (1957) is derived from prerecorded percussion sounds, in addition to sine tones and rapid modulations of pitch, which Ussachevsky refers to as "warble" tones. Even in his computer music Ussachevsky electronically synthesizes instrumental timbres, which is a common habit among electronic composers.

The compositions realized at the WDR studio in Germany during the mid-1950's made a lasting impression on other composers involved with tape composition, particularly those working at the famous R.T.F. studio, which had been known for its involvement with musique concrète techniques. Eventually, the Paris studio increased its facilities to include electronic sound generators and modification devices; consequently, many of the composers working there began to combine elements from both media.

Stockhausen's "Studie II" demonstrated many new ways of dealing with pitch, but this did not necessarily mean that composers always needed or wanted such a variety of approaches. Some works from this period exhibit a rather conservative attitude toward pitch, such as Henry Sauguet's "Aspect Sentimental", which was realized at the R.T.F. in 1957. Like Luening's flute pieces of 1952, simple melodic patterns are superimposed to form masses of sound. The beginning of Sauguet's piece evolves from an arpeggiated minor seventh chord (Example 12a), while the middle section is derived from breathing patterns and a simple rhythmic motive (Example 12b) that undergoes tape transposition and reversal. Beginning at about 4:48, a classical ABA structure is formed with the recapitulation of the opening section.

EXAMPLE 12. Henry Sauguet, "Aspect Sentimental"

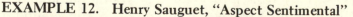

(a)   (b)

1958 was an important year in the history of electronic music in France, for Pierre Henry left the R.T.F. and founded his Studio Apsome, the first private studio in Europe. In addition, composer/engineer Pierre Schaeffer broke what had been a five year silence (with the exception of two collaborations in 1957 with Henry and Luc Ferrari for a film, and incidental music), with "Etude aux allures" (1958) and "Etude aux sons animés" (1958).

These new works display Schaeffer's changing attitudes toward the treatment of sounds. He deliberately chose sounds possessing a rich harmonic content for the "Etude aux allures," which is characterized by sustained sounds and silence. The piece moves slowly enough for the listener to be able to distinguish each sonic event; he can also make aural connections between the sounds, thus perceiving the composition's overall structure. Schaeffer feels that composers should concentrate on the building up of sounds rather than upon their dissolution, which for him is a new approach to the derivation of sonorous materials.

In order to understand this change in Pierre Schaeffer's fundamental concept of sound, the influence of Stockhausen and his colleagues at the WDR must be considered. The concept of disintegration, whereby the composer extracts portions of complex sounds, is by nature negative. On the other hand, electronically generated sounds provide the composer with the opportunity to construct whatever sounds he desires, with no limitations. The prophesies of Varèse, Cage, and other like-minded composers had finally come true.

In spite of the attractions of the newly founded Cologne studio, the R.T.F. continued to attract composers living outside of France. The Greek composer/architect Iannis Xenakis realized his "Diamorphoses" in 1957 (revised in 1968) at the Paris studio. The sound sources are concrète, and include jets, earthquake shocks, crashing railroad cars, and small bells, which are transformed by tape transposition and reversal, and filtering. Tape transposition of the bell sonorities produces glissandi which appear as a timbral contrast to the other "noisier" sounds. A sole concrète source, burning charcoal, provides the sonorous material for Xenakis's "Concret P-H" (1958) (also revised in 1968); tape transposition and filtering predominate. This work was transmitted by three hundred fifty loud speakers at the Philips Pavilion at the Brussels World Fair in 1958. The Philips Pavilion will be discussed in more detail when the music of Varèse is explored.

Xenakis's conceptualization of sound hinges upon architectural and mathematical principles by which sounds can be considered as masses evolving through varying degrees of density. Xenakis uses these concepts to build his overall structural forms. They also help to determine the timbre of the ensuing sounds, although the timbre often seems to be a by-product of the density relationships.

We have already observed the importance of rhythmic elements in some of the early pieces of Pierre Henry. Luc Ferrari was also working at the R.T.F.; he approached rhythm by relating it to speed. In his "Etude aux accidents" (1958), Ferrari subjected a metallic rhythmic pattern to a continual fluctuation of speed. Other percussive sounds, such as drums, appear later, but are treated more as embellishments than as principal events.

Ferrari's next work, "Etude aux sons tendus" (1958), is again centered around rhythmic organization, but this time the timbres are richer in texture, and yield more interesting sounds. His treatment of repetitive rhythmic patterns is also more refined here. Rather than constantly being present, these patterns appear and disappear, sometimes abruptly. Both studies utilize tape transpositions and reversal, splicing and overdubbing, but in the second study their use is more closely related to the structural organization of the piece as a whole.

In 1958, John Cage left New York to visit the Milan Studio di Fonologia Musicale of the Radio Audizioni Italiane (RAI). The RAI had been founded by Luciano Berio in 1955; he was joined at that time by Bruno Maderna. Since both Italian composers had spent some time at the Cologne studio prior to 1955, they constructed a similar studio in Milan.

Cage produced three works at the Milan Studio. Two of them—"Water Walk" (1959) and "Sounds of Venice" (1959)—were for television. The third is "Fontana Mix" (1958), a tape collage consisting of speaking, singing, instrumental music, electronically generated sounds, environmental sounds, barking dogs, and many other such sounds. Transposition and reversal frequently occur, but splicing is the most heavily used technique. Tapes of the sound sources were cut into a variety of lengths and painstakingly spliced together, often resulting in rapid successions of diverse sounds, complex rhythmic fragments, and quick timbral changes like those previously encountered in the "Williams Mix."

The Belgian composer Henri Pousseur, who had been closely associated with Stockhausen at the WDR, was also invited to work at the RAI studio. Here Pousseur produced his second electronic composition, "Scambi" (1957), which is not a complete composition, but rather separate sequences that could either be joined in succession or juxtaposed. Although Pousseur included detailed instructions for the realization of "Scambi," indeterminacy plays a prominent role in the piece. Pousseur and Berio each made two versions of this piece, only one of which has been commercially recorded.

Pousseur's intention was to unify asymmetrical sonorous elements into a coherent sound structure. He restricted the sound sources to a single element, "white" noise. White noise is electronically produced. It contains the entire spectrum of audible frequencies, and is characterized by continual, non-periodic changes of amplitude which result in a hissing sound. Narrower bands of "colored" noise can be produced by filtering. As the noise bands are filtered into separate and distinct parts, the most extreme limits of pitch can be clearly heard. The narrowest band of filtered noise is a pure sine tone. These filtering processes are commonly referred to as "subtractive synthesis;" they represent the antithesis of the additive process employed by Stockhausen a few years earlier. Pousseur treated noise bands as individual elements, so that their interaction produced moving masses of sound.

The Austrian-Hungarian composer György Ligeti spliced many electronically generated sounds in "Artikulation" (1958), which he realized at the Cologne studio. Structurally, this is one of the most complex electronic compositions to date, for Ligeti combined both an abstract idea and a definite musical structure. The abstract idea is an imaginary conversation that leads to a particular arrangement of the sonorous elements. Before he began working on this piece, Ligeti did a great deal of research in the field of phonetics to establish direct correlations between speech and "musical" sounds.

Ligeti began by choosing forty-two basic sounds, including sine tones, harmonic, subharmonic, and noise spectra—an array of frequencies within the harmonic, subharmonic, and noise ranges—impulses, and glissandi forms. The harmonic spectra were constructed above a fundamental pitch, dividing the octave into a given number of equal parts, whereas the subharmonic spectra were formed below a fundamental pitch, also providing for an equal division of the octave. Example 13 represents a harmonic

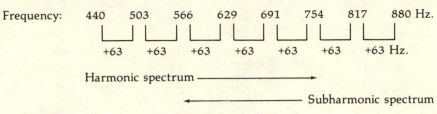

Frequency: 440 503 566 629 691 754 817 880 Hz.

+63 +63 +63 +63 +63 +63 +63 Hz.

Harmonic spectrum ——————→

←—————— Subharmonic spectrum

EXAMPLE 13. György Ligeti, "Artikulation"

spectrum. If the frequencies are read in reverse order, a subharmonic spectrum is illustrated.

The forty-two sounds were then grouped into ten "texts," or categories based on general sonorous characteristics. The texts were spliced together and subjected to conventional tape manipulations (tape transposition, reversal, splicing, and overdubbing) to form "words." Additional tape transformations, and electronic modifications such as reverberation, ring modulation, and envelope shaping were applied to the words, which resulted in "languages." These were spliced together to form "sentences," which underwent further tape and electronic modifications to produce "Artikulation." Example 14 contains a summary of these procedures.

This work not only exhibits a close resemblance to Stockhausen's employment of additive synthesis, particularly in Ligeti's derivation of the harmonic and subharmonic spectra; but it further indicates electronic composers' increasing awareness of the structural possibilities of language. These linguistic considerations were noted in the previous chapter as well, particularly in the works of Henry, Berio, Philippot, and Mimaroglu.

On the other hand, Ligeti's procedure of ring modulating two previously existing segments to produce a new but related sound—in this case, "sentences" ring modulated to form "Artikulation"—actually predates Stockhausen's concept of intermodulation. This technique will be examined in more detail later in this chapter when Stockhausen's "Telemusik" is discussed, but first it must be understood.

A ring modulator is an electronic processing device that accepts two input signals at once, and suppresses the original frequencies while adding and subtracting them. The result is usually a harmonically complex sound that ranges in quality from tremolo and bell-like sounds to dense sonorous masses bordering on noise. For

SOUNDS ——→ TEXTS ——→ WORDS ——→ LANGUAGES ——→ SENTENCES ——→ "ARTIKULATION"
sine tones;   ten categories   tape and electronic   tape and electronic   splicing together of   tape and electronic
harmonic and   derived from   modifications of   modifications of   LANGUAGES.   modifications of
subharmonic   SOUNDS.   TEXTS.   WORDS.   SENTENCES.
spectra; noise
spectra; impulses;
glissando forms.

EXAMPLE 14. György Ligeti, "Artikulation"

40

example, given input frequencies X and Y, the ring modulated output would consist of the frequencies X + Y, and X − Y. The increased number of frequencies, especially nonharmonic partials, accounts for the prevalence of dense textures and harmonic complexity.

Throughout the 1950's, the number of electronic music studios in Europe steadily increased. Most were sponsored by national radio stations. In the Netherlands, it was at the Nederlandsche Radio Unie (NRU) at Hilversum that Henk Badings began preparing his tape pieces for radio in 1952. The NRU, however, did not possess the facilities equal to those at the Cologne or Milan studios; it remained essentially a radio broadcasting studio with a limited availability of electronic generators and modifiers. It was not until 1957 that a permanent, fully equipped electronic studio, a subdivision of the research laboratories of Philips Gloeilamperafabrieken at Eindhoven, was established in the Netherlands. Once again, Henk Badings was responsible for most of the works realized at this studio.

Badings has not restricted himself to the electronic medium. Many of his compositions display sectionalized, neo-classical formal organization. "Evolutions" (1958) is a ballet choreographed by Yvonne Georgi. Its six movements—Overture, Air, Ragtime, Intermezzo, Waltz, and Finale—are reminiscent of the Baroque suite. The Intermezzo contains an example of timbral transformation that varies the waveform of the opening pitch.

Badings' "Genese" (1958), is divided into three movements: introduction, slow, and finale. Five oscillators comprise the sound sources. Although these compositions are purely electronic, their neo-classic orientation spearates them from the works of such composers as Stockhausen and Ligeti, who tend to establish structures that result directly from the sonorous materials rather than to fit the sounds into preexisting forms.

At the Philips studio at Eindhaven, Edgard Varèse realized his "Poème Electronique" (1958), which had been commissioned for performance at the Philips Pavilion at the 1958 Brussels World Fair. The pavilion was designed by Iannis Xenakis and the French architect Le Corbusier. It was the site of a multi-media event at which Le Corbusier used lighting effects and slide projections in conjunction with Varèse's tape.

"Poème" was composed of electronic and concrète sounds that were modified by tape manipulations and such electronic devices as filters and reverberation units. The sounds were recorded on a three channel tape, of which two were reserved for reverberation and stereo effects. The pavilion contained three hundred fifty loudspeakers, some of which were concealed behind the walls and above the ceiling. The taped sounds were distributed by telephone relays among various combinations of loudspeakers. These "sound paths" were determined by a fifteen channel control tape, each track of which contained twelve spearate signals. Therefore, 180 (15 × 12) control signals were available to regulate the sound routes, lighting effects and a variety of light sources which consisted of film projectors and projection lanterns, spotlights, ultra violet lamps, bulbs, and fluorescent lamps of various colors. The diagram in Example 15 depicts the elaborate interconnections of the equipment necessary for "Poème."

By the end of the 1950s, most European countries had at least one electronic music studio; it was often affiliated with a radio station. This accounts for the substantial number of tape pieces composed for radio at the studios in Paris and Hilversum. Surprisingly, only one such tape was realized at the Cologne studio, and four at the studio in Milan. The distinction between musique concrète and

EXAMPLE 15.   Edgard Varèse, "Poème Electronique"

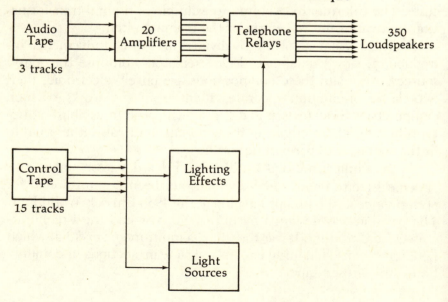

electronic music began to disappear at this time, and the individual studios lost their reputations for specializing in one or the other.

In Paris, the close of the 1950s marked increasing attempts to divide large works into a number of short sections, which were often based on technical manipulations that led to the creation of specific timbres for individual sections of a work. "Ambiance I" (1959) by Michel Philippot centers around periodic timbral shifts that result in a 17th century rondeaulike structure, while Luc Ferrari's "Tête et queue du dragon" (1959–60) is in three continuous sections, the last of which contains transformations of previously stated material.

Even though both the Paris and Cologne composers were deeply involved with timbre, there is a real distinction between the works produced at these two studios, which involves the choice of basic sonorous material. The Cologne composers were likely to restrict themselves to the use of pure sine tones which by definition do not contain any upper partials. The timbre of the source material was always the same because it was devoid of any harmonic content. While it is true that when sine tones are treated in an additive manner, they give rise to an infinite number of timbres, nonetheless, such a scientific approach often results in sonorities that sound like they have been artificially produced. Many electronic composers began to use these solely sine generated frequencies with extreme caution because of this. The use of the sawtooth wave, with its rich harmonic content, eventually helped to solve this problem. A sawtooth wave contains all harmonic partials whose amplitude is the reciprocal of the partial number. Given a fundamental frequency of 60 Hz., the third partial would be 180 (60 × 3) Hz.; this partial's amplitude would be one-third that of the fundamental.

The R.T.F. composers' approach to timbre control was still rooted in concrète sources at this time, so that they did not have the problem of generating timbres electronically. Besides, the particular sounds they employed already possessed a specific timbre. These composers had the flexibility of either removing some frequencies from the harmonic content of a sound by filtering, or subtractive synthesis; or of combining those sounds by overdubbing or mixing in order to derive more complex timbral relationships.

Composers' continual exposure to both methods of composition allowed them to decide for themselves which procedures to follow; often, they combined both techniques. This approach was fostered at the RAI studio in Milan from its inception.

Stockhausen's technique of generating timbres by means of note mixtures and tape loops in his "Studie II" was further developed in "Kontakte" (1959–60). Two versions of this work exist: the first is for solo tape, and the second includes piano and percussion instruments, and will be discussed in Chapter 5. In 1961, Stockhausen transformed the second version into a theatre piece, "Originale." The new version also contains an excerpt from the composer's orchestral piece, "Carré" (1959–60). Stockhausen's predilection for juxtaposing segments of preexisting works becomes a dominant characteristic in his later compositions.

The apparatus needed for the realization of "Kontakte" is more elaborate than that of "Studie II." It consists of an impulse generator, sine and square wave generators, filters, a tunable indicator amplifier, a ring modulator, a reverberation unit, tape recorders, and a rotation loudspeaker. The impulses' durations, adjustable within the range of 900 to .1 milliseconds, encompass such short durations that they are almost impossible to obtain by splicing, which was the method employed in the "Studie". The frequencies obtainable from the impulse generator range from 16 to .06 Hz., frequencies so low that they are perceived as separate impulses rather than as a continuous pitch.

The tunable indicator amplifier acts as a filter with adjustable decay rates, and it may be switched manually to operate within three overlapping frequency ranges: 45–400 Hz., 300–2200 Hz., and 1800–14000 Hz. The rotation loudspeaker was built at the WDR for the production of sound-rotation. A loudspeaker was mounted on a round table top whose shaft was attached to ball bearings, so that the loudspeaker could be rotated manually; a tape of prerecorded sounds was played through the loudspeaker. Four microphones were placed a short distance from the loudspeaker, and their height was adjusted parallel to the center of the loudspeaker cone. Each microphone was equipped with two amplitude controls; the first of each was connected to one channel of a four track tape recorder, and the second served as a modulation signal to the prerecorded tape. In performance, the four track tape is played over four loudspeakers located in separate corners. As the table is rotated the prerecorded sounds are rerecorded on each of four separate channels; but since the microphones are adjacent to one another, the ensuing sounds appear to be moving among the four loudspeakers during performance. Common designations such as "left," "quick," and "slow down" indicate the rate at which the table is turned.

Various timbres were produced by recording a series of impulses which were then played back at a faster speed by using a variable speed tape recorder. Because of the faster playback speed, some of the frequencies of the impulses were extended into the audible pitch range. By varying the duration and frequency of the impulse generator, additional timbral changes were produced.

This procedure of constructing timbres from chains of impulses was gradually implemented through the use of such modification devices and techniques as filtering, reverberation, and feedback loops. Example 16 illustrates some of the equipment interconnections that Stockhausen employed in the derivation of his basic sound sources.

The increasing complexity of the modifications applied to the impulses is immediately apparent from Example 16. After the original idea (a), amplification, filtering, and a feedback loop were added to produce new timbres (b). A feedback loop consists of connecting the output of a tape recorder to its input. The aural effects are regulated by volume controls, or potentiometers, and range from a slight tape delay to a massive, howling sound.

By reversing the positions of the filter and tape recorder, the configuration (c) is obtained, while (d) is the result of eliminating the feedback loop and incorporating three filters with individual frequency responses. Figure (e) is simply the combination of the three-way filtering with a feedback loop.

The most complex timbral structure is represented in figures (f_1)–(f_4). Filtering is the sole modification of the first stage (f_1), which is subjected to reverberation (f_2). This is sent through a feedback loop (f_3), and finally is retransformed by additional reverberation and filtering (f_4).

Stockhausen again developed a timbre continuum by a very gradual increase of modifications to the impulse successions. In "Studie II," a similar continuum was established by the pitch distributions of the note mixtures, whereas "Kontakte" achieved these gradations through electronic modifications and tape transpositions. "Studie II" and "Kontakte," however, reveal a rigorous structural scheme based upon timbral relationships.

"Kontakte" ushered in the electronic music of the 1960s. In New York, Richard Maxfield realized "Night Music" (1960) in his private studio. It was derived from supersonic frequencies and subaudio

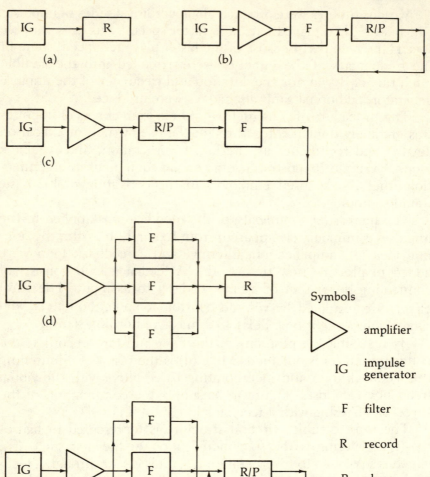

EXAMPLE 16.   Karlheinz Stockhausen, "Kontakte"

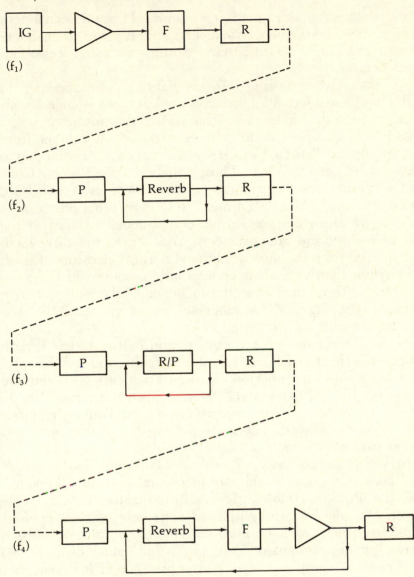

EXAMPLE 16. Continued

pulses, which was an idea not too far removed from Stockhausen's chain of subaudio impulses. Maxfield used the pulses to modulate the supersonic sounds, rather than treating them as sources of different timbres.

Vladimir Ussachevsky's "Wireless Fantasy" also appeared in 1960. Its principal sound sources consisted of wireless code signals produced from the old spark generators used to transmit messages in Morse Code. The sound sources included an excerpt from Wagner's opera "Parsifal," which was the first musical composition broadcast by Lee De Forest. Those who understand Morse Code will be able to discern coded abbreviations for "New York" (NY), "end of message" (AR), "good night" (GN) and other phrases.

Many of the purely electronic compositions realized at the Columbia–Princeton Studio in New York during the early 1960s were derived from the more traditional musical elements of pitch and rhythm than were their counterparts produced in Cologne. This may have resulted from the influence of the early concrète works of Luening and Ussachevsky, in which rhythmic and melodic elements predominate.

Mario Davidovsky, an Argentinian, and Bulent Arel, a Turkish composer, were among the first, besides Luening and Ussachevsky, to use the Columbia–Princeton facilities. Davidovsky's "Electronic Study No. 1" (1960) and Arel's "Stereo Electronic Music No. 1" (1960) both revolve around recurring motives. Timbral relations exist within these pieces, but not to the extent that they appear in the works of Stockhausen or Ligeti.

In Arel's "Sacred Service: Prelude and Postlude" (1961), synthesized gong and organ sounds are incorporated in the "Prelude," while the "Postlude" is totally derived from sine tones. As in Stockhausen's "Studie II", Arel employed extremely rapid successions of sine frequencies so that timbre and sonorous masses, rather than discrete pitches, are heard. The contrasting nature of these two movements is counterbalanced by the presence of low-frequency pedal tones in both sections which provides a structural link between the two.

Milton Babbitt, the composer and mathematician from Princeton University, is the codirector of the Columbia–Princeton Studio. His "Composition for Synthesizer" (1961) was also based upon pitch and rhythmic relations, but he chose more instrumental timbres than did Davidovsky. The electronic reproduction of piano and woodwind timbres was not easy for Babbitt to accomplish, but the task was facilitated by the RCA Mark II Synthesizer which the New York studio acquired in 1959.

The word synthesizer is often misused. In this text it denotes a multi-function machine possessing sound generators, modifiers, and mixers. Even though a synthesizer often duplicates similar equipment found in a "classical" electronic studio, it has many advantages over the latter. The individual modules are electronically compatible with one another; that is, each electronic circuit operates on and produces voltages within a predetermined range. This eliminates the need for additional circuits to compensate for a disparity among them. Each module has a permanent physical location, so that interconnections between modules are not problematic. An outstanding feature of the more recent synthesizers is their small size and portability, unlike the original RCA synthesizer. The Mark II occupies almost an entire wall at the Columbia studio. Although it was one of the first synthesizers to be practical for composers to use, it was sometimes difficult to operate.

Harry Olsen and Herbert Belar had completed their first synthesizer, the RCA Mark I, by 1955. Columbia University's newer model possessed some improvements over the original version. A typewriter-like keyboard was employed to punch holes in a moving paper roll. Punched paper rolls had previously been used in the rudimentary French synthesizer designed by Givelet and Coupleux in 1929, but the Mark II functioned on a binary number system, like a modern computer.

In a binary system there are only two numbers, 0 and 1. The Mark II was designed so that the operation of each component (sound sources and modifiers) was contingent upon specific binary information including, among other things, frequency, amplitude, and duration. Since composers numerically define these elements in the decimal system, they must be assigned a binary code. The encoded numbers are then punched in the paper roll, which is divided into five paired columns; one column signifies 0, and the other, 1. This information is conveyed to the appropriate circuits via electronic relays that are activated when sets of brushes, paired to correspond to the columns on the paper, pass over a punched hole. Although the electronic theory behind Givelet's and Coupleux's synthesizer foreshadows that of the Mark II, the former's application was restricted to control the pitch of eight oscillators.

The RCA synthesizer is more flexible, in that it both produces and modifies sounds.

The Mark II's sound sources included sawtooth and white noise generators, and provided for processing external sources like microphones and tape recorders. Some of the available modification devices included an amplitude modulator, filters, sixteen mixing amplifiers, a frequency glider for the production of glissandi, and resonators for amplifying or attentuating any of thirty frequency bands of a harmonic spectrum. The Mark II was therefore capable of controlling the frequency, envelope, harmonic spectrum, amplitude, duration, and temporal progression of sonic events; a formidable, though not ideal, system for the electronic production and control of sounds. Some of the synthesizer's disadvantages were its extraordinary size, complexity of operation, and the noise it made, which was partially the result of using tubes. Thanks to advances in technology and an emphasis on the miniaturization of equipment, these problems no longer exist.

The design of any synthesizer, including the types of modules and means of controlling them, dictates to some extent the character of the music produced. Babbitt's melodic and rhythmic motives, for example, were quite easily obtainable from the Mark II. This synthesizer could be programmed to automatically play a melodic or rhythmic series in various ways, including forward, backward, faster, and slower. It would have taken a composer much more time to accomplish these effects in a classical studio.

Another advantage of the Mark II was its ability to accurately control envelope contours without splicing. This not only saved time, but also afforded the composer a means of reconstructing the envelopes of musical instruments. This is yet another way to approach the timbral organization of a work, and has been used by many involved with computer music.

The same year that the Columbia–Princeton studio acquired its RCA synthesizer, the University of Toronto established an electronic studio under the direction of Arnold Walter. "Summer Idyl" (1960) by Walter, Harvey Olnick, and Myron Schaeffer was the first of several tapes for television to be realized by this trio.

The compositions realized at the R.T.F. studio during the early 1960s demonstrate a remarkable mastery of musique concrète techniques. Furthermore, the composers generally seem to have followed Pierre Schaeffer's concepts in dealing with timbre, that is, they produced new timbres by combining sounds of different qualities. These procedures emphasize the element of density. During this era many of the Paris composers devised structures contingent upon timbral and density relationships.

In two by the Yugoslavian composer Ivo Malec, "Reflets" (1961) and "Dahovi" (1961), the composer exercised great restraint in choosing the time of entry of each new sound. This determines density and timbral changes within each composition. The significant time span separating the entrances of different sounds assures their aural perception. Changes in density and timbre are reinforced by sustained and reverberated sounds, so that the piece's entire structure becomes clear to the listener. Although he used different technical procedures, Malec's formulation of musical structures closely resembles Stockhausen's, which articulate a continuum between two opposing poles.

A similar control of timbre by means of density relations is found in Luc Ferrari's "Tautologos I" (1961). The piece begins with chords stated in complex rhythmic patterns followed by contrasting new materials in the form of glissandi. The idea of contrasting two elements is developed to a greater extent in "Tautologos II" (1961), in which Ferrari isolates high and low sounds. This piece begins with predominately high sounds and much rhythmic activity, followed by a gradual transition to low, reverberated, and sustained sounds. Both kinds of sonorous material are combined at the end so that the outline of a high-low frequency continuum appears as one of the work's prime structuring principles.

Philippe Carson's "Turmac" (1962) resembles Pierre Schaeffer's noise études in the use of machine noises from a Dutch cigarette factory as sound sources. "Turmac" is divided into three sections. The first contains machine noises within which definite pitches were inserted. This was an ingenious method of adding timbral differentiations to what might be considered monotonous sounds; additional modifications were achieved by filtering.

Following a short pause, the second section commences with increased rhythmic activity which is abruptly curtailed at the beginning of the final section. At this point, isolated sounds are gradually juxtaposed to form increasingly dense sonorous masses of proportionally greater amplitude. Pierre Schaeffer has pointed to a structural correspondence based on Carson's control of amplitude in the first and last sections, both of which are characterized by a gradual crescendo. When the middle section is considered in this light, the conclusion appears to be a recapitulation of the opening, and reveals a structure founded upon amplitude relationships.

When the procedure of recapitulation is applied to short segments distributed throughout a composition, motivic repetitions such as those found in the works of Babbitt, Ussachevsky, and Arel result. Michel Philippot's "Etude III" (1962) evolves from a similar recurrence of motivic ideas, and emphasizes the restricted sound sources that characterized his first étude. In the third étude the motives are primarily formed from extensively modulated chordal statements, so that their timbre and pitch content become structurally significant.

In "Bohor I" (1962), Xenakis employed continuous repetition, thereby carrying the concept of recapitulation to the extreme. Like Carson's "Turmac," the sound sources reflect the first studies of Pierre Schaeffer. Xenakis limited his choice of sounds to a Laotian mouth organ and some Oriental jewelry. He was able to derive a variety of sounds by subjecting these sources to tape transposition. Low sustained sounds resulted from slowing down the tape of the mouth organ, while gong-like timbres were produced by applying a similar change of speed to the jewelry tape. When the sounds of the jewelry were sped up, crisp, metallic sequences resulted.

"Bohor I" is quite different from the pieces of Carson, Malec and other R.T.F. composers previously discussed. The hypnotic repetitions force the listener to pay close attention to the ensuing sounds. A similar situation occurred a few years later in Steve Reich's "Come Out." Both pieces are rather lengthy, and consist of relatively slow transitions of timbre and density.

Pierre Henry superimposed several structural plans in "Le Voyage" (1962), and produced another composition of formidable length. This piece was choreographed by Henry's friend and colleague Maurice Béjart. It was based on the *Tibetan Book of the Dead*, which contains a description of death and subsequent reincarnation. The book divides this cycle, the "Wheel of Life," into three stages. It provided Henry with a preliminary idea for his basic formal plan, which was eventually expanded to include seven sections, as indicated in Example 17. Henry enclosed the "Wheel of Life" (sections 2–6) within Breath I and Breath II, with breath symbolizing life.

The composer formulated additional structural levels on the original seven sections that involved timbre and duration. Breath I

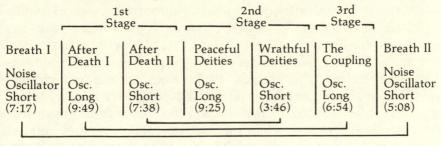

1st Stage		2nd Stage		3rd Stage		
Breath I	After Death I	After Death II	Peaceful Deities	Wrathful Deities	The Coupling	Breath II
Noise Oscillator Short (7:17)	Osc. Long (9:49)	Osc. Short (7:38)	Osc. Long (9:25)	Osc. Short (3:46)	Osc. Long (6:54)	Noise Oscillator Short (5:08)

EXAMPLE 17.   Pierre Henry, "Le Voyage"

and Breath II remain isolated from the body of "Le Voyage" because of the inclusion in them of noise masses, so that the "Wheel of Life" is articulated by timbre. On the other hand, Henry connected all the sections by employing oscillators as the sole sound source, so that within the timbral domain two other structural levels were produced. Both timbre structures follow and support the basic seven-section plan, but the organization of durations for each section counterbalances the form. The durations are paired as iambic, short-long, since there is no way to avoid the dissolution of the three stages because of the odd number of sections. Had the "coupling" been divided into two sections as the first two stages, the duration structure would have corresponded to that of the basic textural formal plan. Henry's choice of durations suggests an arch form. This was perhaps the best way he could symbolize the "Wheel of Life." The end (Breath II) is the beginning (Breath I), or reincarnation.

Sectionalization also characterizes "La Reine Verte" (1963), a tape composition in which Henry juxtaposed electronic and concrète elements. This piece was also choreographed by Béjart. The combination of instruments and voice with electronic sources, all enriched by textless vocal sonorities, produces timbral associations by tape manipulation and filtering. Structural relations among the sixteen sections result from the recurring timbres and thematic material. Piano, voice, and percussion provide sonorous points of reference, while thematic variants appear throughout the piece. Both timbral and thematic associations are especially evident in the paired movements: sections two and four ("La première reine" and "La deuxième reine"); sections three, five and twelve ("Les premiers insectes," "Les deuxièmes insectes," and "Les troisièmes insectes"); and sections eleven and thirteen ("Le premier funambule" and "Le deuxième funambule").

A more radical attempt to derive new timbres is found in "Gesang de Maldoror" (1966) by Rainer Riehn. This work was realized at the Studio for Electronic Music at Utrecht State University in the Netherlands. It incorporates "technical interference factors" to produce richer sounds. Riehn does not define technical interference, but we may assume that it consists of unwanted noises like hum, hiss, and feedback distortion that result from unsatisfactory amplitude settings while mixing and recording; these procedures, however, are intentional. The resultant distortion is reminiscent of Cage's tape collages because of rapidly changing timbres and extreme rhythmic complexity. The frequent use of repeated patterns is typical of motivic structure in the works of Philippot and Carson.

The Columbia–Princeton Center was one of the most important studios in America during the 1960s. Milton Babbitt continued to explore the possibilities of pitch, rhythmic and timbral controls available from the RCA synthesizer there. His "Ensembles for Synthesizer" (1963) is, like the "Composition for Synthesizer," an effort to produce instrumental-like sounds existing in complex pitch and rhythmic contexts not available from conventional musical instruments.

The Spanish composer Andrés Lewin-Richter, also working at the Columbia Studio, followed Babbitt's approach to timbral organization in his "Electronic Study No. 1" (1964). The ring modulation of two electronically generated pitches was the source of bell sounds, while a sine wave oscillator with appropriate envelope characteristics produced the effect of a pizzicato string bass. The principal structuring agent is a continuum extending between tension and relaxation, the tension characterized by rhythmic and timbral complexity, and the relaxation by more familiar sounds.

Rather than using electronic sources to produce instrumental sounds as Babbitt and Lewin-Richter had done, Ilhan Mimaroglu derived concrète-like sounds from electronic sources in his "Intermezzo" (1964) and "Agony" (1965), both of which were completed at the Columbia–Princeton Center. "Intermezzo" is particularly reminiscent of Pierre Henry's early musique concrète pieces, for Mimaroglu restricted electronic modification to ring modulation and mixing. Tape transposition and reversal, in addition to a great deal of splicing, provide additional correspondences between Mimaroglu's pieces and those of the pioneering R.T.F. composers.

Mario Davidovsky's "Electronic Study No. 3" (1965) displays the motivic structure that typifies his compositions. Rhythmic motives in the form of rapid pitch and noise sequences are contrasted against slower sustained sounds. Instrumental timbres including bell, woodwind, percussive, and string sounds, also appear. Davidovsky frequently treats particular timbres in a similar, recurring fashion so that not only the rhythmic, but also the timbral motives function as structuring elements.

Contrasts like those discussed relative to the rhythmic organization of Davidovsky's third study are the key structuring devices employed by Mel Powell in his "Second Electronic Setting" (1962). This was one of the first pieces realized at the electronic music studio established in 1962 at Yale University. The only sound source is that of an oscillator. Powell incorporated contrasts of register, timbre, density, and rhythm to separate individual parts or voices and to determine the overall structural plan. Register was divided into high and low frequencies, durations were defined as either sustained or short, and densities varied between a single pitch and chordal formations; timbral contrasts were achieved by changing the oscillator waveforms. Additional timbral gradations were obtained by filtering and modulation which yielded a complex structural organization similar to the earlier Cologne compositions.

A very refreshing electronic piece is "Lemon Drops" (1965) by Kenneth Gaburo. Realized at the Experimental Music Studio of the University of Illinois, "Lemon Drops" was derived from an electronic tone generator designed by Gaburo's colleague James Beauchamp. The tone generator's usefulness results from its flexibility of timbral control, and Gaburo was able to produce a variety of keyboard-like sounds with it. The rhythmic flow of "Lemon Drops" suggests jazz. This idea dates back to 1951 and Henry's "Tam Tam II." Like Mel Powell, Gaburo was a jazz pianist. During the late 1960s the use of electronics began to appear in jazz and rock groups.

Many new electronic devices such as Beauchamp's tone generator were developed starting in the mid-1950s, most of them in Germany and America. Harry Olson's and Herbert Belar's 1959 RCA synthesizer opened many new directions along these lines. In 1961, Harald Bode, the German engineer who had built equipment for the Cologne studio, wrote an article in which he described a new concept in equipment design, modular systems. The advantage of a modular system is that each electronic function, such as oscillator or ring modulator, is self-contained, and as many modules as desired can be put together into a single case. This makes custom design, a prime concern of most composers, possible.

Three years after the publication of Bode's article a young composer, Herbert Deutsch, asked Robert Moog, an engineer, to design and build some electronic equipment for him. Moog responded by building a voltage controlled oscillator (VCO) and a voltage controlled amplifier (VCA) in 1964. The following year Moog completed a voltage controlled filter (VCF). The idea of using control voltages to compose electronic music was a new one, and was not appreciated by composers until 1967.

Prior to this, the operation of electronic devices was controlled manually; a change in pitch or in amplitude, for instance, required the composer to turn appropriate dials, but this limits the speed, accuracy, and number of changes. A control voltage replaces manual control. Since an electrical voltage moves at a rate much beyond that of manual control, the speed of control voltages is of prime importance. Voltages can be accurately measured with a voltmeter; this degree of precision provides another advantage over manual control. Finally, any number of control voltages may be employed simultaneously to yield multiple changes. All of these factors save the composer an enormous amount of time in realizing a composition.

There are many similarities between a modern synthesizer and a "classical" electronic studio such as the WDR. Both contain sound sources and sound modifiers. The former consists of oscillators and noise generators, and the latter of ring modulators, filters, frequency shifters, envelope generators, and mixers. In the classical studio of the 1950s, these functions would be manually controlled, whereas with a synthesizer, one has the option of voltage control. Furthermore, many of the synthesizers are now portable, which makes them especially useful for live performances.

Control voltage applications are divided in two main categories, active and passive. The former consists of voltage sources that control individual modules; those typically found in a synthesizer are the keyboard, sequencer, and random voltage source. In addition, audio signals can be converted to active control voltages by means of frequency and envelope followers. A frequency follower converts pitch to a proportional voltage, whereas an envelope follower does the same to amplitude. If a composer wishes to retain, or store, a control voltage for later use, this is accomplished with a sample and hold device; it contains a memory circuit that releases a stored voltage when it is triggered either electronically or manually. Finally, the direction of a control voltage is reversed by a voltage inverter. The operation of passive voltage controlled modules depends upon the aforementioned voltage sources, and they consist of the VCO, VCA, and VCF.

Control voltage sources may be used to modulate, or transform, a VCO's frequency or amplitude. Frequency modulation (FM) is a periodic fluctuation of a tone's pitch, whereas amplitude modulation (AM) is a periodic fluctuation of a tone's loudness. (When the modulation rate is slow, electronic composers and engineers sometimes refer to FM as "vibrato," and to AM as "tremolo," although in singing they are the same.) Amplitude modulation is achieved by connecting an oscillator to a VCA and controlling the VCA by another voltage source. The VCA is turned off when no control voltage is present, because its amplitude is proportional to the amount of voltage applied to it. Example 18 illustrates the connections needed for the production of frequency and amplitude modulation.

Sound travels through air in the form of waves, and the waveform is a graphic representation of this movement. Oscillators can provide a few different timbres because of the multiplicity of available waveforms. Most oscillators produce five standard waveforms: sine, sawtooth, triangle, square, and pulse. In addition, a ramp wave, whose extremes are the sawtooth and triangle, exists; it is manually controlled only, and it differs from the sawtooth and triangle waves in respect to timbre. A graphic representation of

EXAMPLE 18. Frequency and amplitude modulation

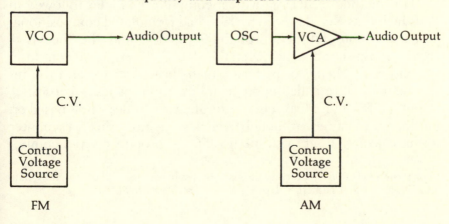

FM   AM

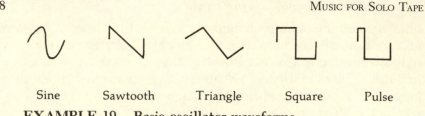

Sine   Sawtooth   Triangle   Square   Pulse

EXAMPLE 19.   Basic oscillator waveforms

these waveforms is given in Example 19. The variety of wave
shapes is dependent upon the harmonic content and the resultant
amplitude relationships of the upper partials of a fundamental
tone. (For a more detailed discussion of this topic see Part IV.)[1]

Even before synthesizers became commercially available there
was a growing interest, chiefly in the U.S., in the application of
computers to musical composition. The operation of a computer
consists of three stages: data input, data processing, and data output. Three distinct approaches to the compositional process that
involve these computer operations have evolved.

The first such use of a computer occurred at the University of
Illinois in 1957. Lejaren Hiller and Leonard Isaacson wrote a computer program that produced tables of numbers from the logic
operations existing within the program. These numbers were then
applied to traditional musical elements including pitch, duration,
and orchestration to produce the "Illiac Suite for String Quartet"
(1957). This composition is not electronic in the usual sense because a string quartet performs the piece. The computer's sole
function was to produce the score itself, with the compositional
process defined within the computer program.

This method of dealing with a computer was later followed in
Paris by Iannis Xenakis, who by 1959 had formulated compositional
processes upon statistics, probability theory, and the theory of
games. In this last instance, Xenakis states: "The musical composer
establishes a scheme or pattern which the conductor and the instrumentalists are called upon to follow more or less rigorously."
"Duel" (1958–9), for two conductors and two orchestras, is based on
the theory of games. Although Xenakis was not using a computer
for his calculations at that time, in 1962 he produced seven compo-

---

[1] For those interested in a further discussion of synthesizers, I recommend Chapters 3, 4, and 5 of Hubert S. Howe's *Electronic Music Synthesis*.

sitions in which the computer functioned in a manner similar to that employed in the "Illiac Suite." Two of these works are "Amorsima-Morsima" and "Stratégie, Jeu pour deux orchestres". In 1964 "Eonta" for piano and five brass instruments appeared; this too used the computer as a type of composing machine.

Similar work was carried out in Paris by film composer Pierre Barbaud and choral conductor Roger Blanchard in 1960. Their activities were based at the "Centre de Calcul Electronique de la Compagnie des Machines Bull," a computer manufacturing plant. In England during the early 1960s it was D. J. Champernowne, Stanley Gill and D. H. Papworth who pursued these objectives. In the Netherlands, Gottfried Michael Köenig developed computer composing programs in 1964 at Utrecht State University which resulted in his piece "Project I".

The second approach to computer-aided composition is what has become popularly known as computer music. In this medium the computer actually produces the sounds by means of a digital-to-analog converter (DAC). The input to the computer consists of numbers arranged in a specific order, frequently encoded on a deck of IBM cards, or sent directly to the computer via typewriter. The numbers represent such elements as types of sound sources, modifications, pitch, duration, amplitude, wave shapes, and envelope contour. It is then up to the computer to translate this numeric input into a binary system where only two values exist, 0 and 1. The principal advantage of the binary system, as opposed to the decimal system, is speed, for the computer needs to differentiate only two values, rather than ten. When the translation has been completed, the computer performs whatever functions have been indicated and transfers the results, still in binary form, to a magnetic digital tape or disk. At this point the tape or disk is sent through the digital-to-analog converter, where the binary (digital) information is converted to a succession of voltages; the voltages are an electronic representation (analog) of the binary information, and are recorded on a conventional tape recorder. The recorder's playback head translates the voltage fluctuations to audio signals.

Computer generated sounds were first produced at Bell Telephone Laboratories in Murray Hill, New Jersey in 1957. Max Mathews, director of the Behavioral Research Laboratory, was the chief exponent of the new method of sound production and control. Composers who followed Mathews's example were John Pierce, James Tenney, Jean Claude Risset, and Frederick Moore.

The research at Bell Labs was so extensive that by 1968 a light pencil had been developed that eliminated much of the tedious work of punching input data on IBM cards. With this pencil, any of the musical elements such as pitch and amplitude could be denoted by drawing a graphic representation of their contour. For instance, a rise in pitch would be indicated by an ascending line, but this same line could also be made to represent an increase in amplitude or any other function provided for in the program. Modifications of the computer programs initiated at Bell Labs were made at Princeton University in 1964 by Hubert Howe and the late Godfrey Winham, and at Stanford University by John Chowning.

The most recent advances in the area of computer music are the hybrid systems, in which the computer is used to control synthesizers or other analog equipment. Peter Zinovieff whose work was carried out in England beginning in 1968, was the pioneer in this field. The following year Max Mathews and Frederick Moore prepared their "GROOVE" program which used the computer to control a synthesizer.

Among the composers at Princeton University who were actively engaged in computer-generated sounds was J. K. Randall. His "Quartets in Pairs" (1964), whose duration is just over one minute, is quasi-instrumental in character. Its texture is contrapuntal, with each line characterized by a specific timbre which sounds like a flute or a plucked string, for example. Mel Powell had already employed this idea two years earlier in his "Second Electronic Setting," and many other composers working with computers as sound generating sources have become deeply involved with timbral possibilities. The computer is a viable tool for the construction of timbres because it provides the composer with complete control of the harmonic spectrum over a fundamental tone. Each of the upper partials can function independently by assuming a particular envelope contour and duration. This degree of flexibility is essential for the realistic reproduction or synthesis of instrumental timbres.

In the midst of all these electronic innovations many composers continued to deal with "natural" sounds, the most striking example being Pierre Henry's "Variations on a Door and a Sigh" (1963). The strict limitation of sound sources—a sigh, a musical saw, and a creaking door—in addition to Henry's rigorous application of tape manipulations are indicative of the composer's ability to transcend pure technique in favor of a "musical" effect. A number of other composers closely associated with Pierre Schaeffer at the R.T.F. have continued to use noise sources, including Philippe Carson and Iannis Xenakis. Henry's "Variations" is proof that the French tradition of musique concrète was still considered a viable compositional method at a time when attention was increasingly focused on purely electronic means.

François-Bernard Mache, who has been affiliated with the R.T.F. studio since 1958, realized a piece whose texture and sound sources closely resemble Xenakis's "Bohor I." Mache's "Terre de feu" (1963) is derived almost exclusively from metallic sources sped up to produce waterlike sounds and slowed down to resemble the striking of a gong. Like Xenakis's "Bohor I," this piece is characterized by continuous sonorous textures and smooth timbral transitions.

Mimaroglu's "Bowery Bum" (1964) is another example of a composer's rigorous restriction of sound sources. Mimaroglu is one of the few composers who persisted in deriving an entire composition from a single, concrète sound. His last works of this type are the "Preludes" (1967) and "Bal Des Leurres" (1973). Both the "Bowery Bum" and the "Prelude XI" are derived from the sound of the plucking of a rubber band transformed by filtering and tape manipulations.

In 1966 Karlheinz Stockhausen formulated the concept of "intermodulation." This was the logical extension of the previous methods of treating timbre as a structural determinant. Stockhausen's new concept may be regarded as a synthesis of earlier ideas, for intermodulation involves the "found object," characteristic of the French school, as well as procedures analogous to Stockhausen's own technique of additive synthesis.

Intermodulation results from the interaction of two or more sounds, wherein the melody, rhythm, amplitude, or timbre of one transforms similar properties of other sounds. It does not share any relationship with the collage that had been especially popular with John Cage and many of the earlier French concrète composers. There are many ways in which intermodulation can be realized, the most common of which is double ring modulation, as shown in Example 20. In this instance two oscillators supply the modulation frequency to the respective ring modulators.

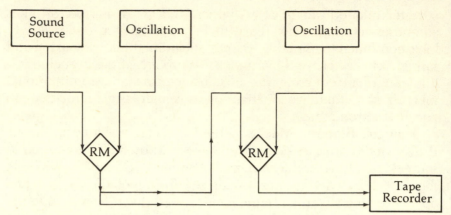

EXAMPLE 20.   Double ring modulation

A more sophisticated example of intermodulation could be obtained either by replacing the oscillators of the previous example
with rhythmic patterns from other melodies, or by electronically
generated rhythmic patterns. Whatever sonorous elements such as
pitch, rhythm, and timbre, are intermodulated, the result, Stockhausen maintains, is a higher unity. By developing the smallest
details of a piece in this manner, Stockhausen was able to construct
a macrocosmic structure.

The first composition to employ this technique was Stockhausen's own "Telemusik" (1966), the first of two works realized by
the composer at the Nippon Hoso Kyokai (NHK) radio in Tokyo.
"Telemusik," an attempt toward a universal music, is derived from
both folk music and electronically produced sounds. The folk elements were extracted from African, Amazon, Brazilian, Hunga-
rian, Spanish, Russian, Chinese, Vietnamese, Balinese, and
Japanese cultures, and intermodulated among themselves and electronic sources. Such processes produced results that retained certain characteristics of the original folk music, so that the end product established a continuum between the familiar and the
unknown.

In addition to sine and triangle oscillators, "Telemusik" incorporated an amplitude modulator, two ring modulators, three types
of filters, and four tape recorders. One of the tape recorders was
supplied with a variable speed control, and another was a special
six-track recorder, a unique feature of the NHK studio.

"Telemusik" is divided into thirty-two sections, each of which commences at the sounding of a Japanese temple instrument. The six temple instruments used are: Taku (high pitched wood block); Bokusho (wood block); Mokugyo (Chinese temple block); Rin (high pitched bell); Keisu (Buddhist metal chime); and four large temple bells. Stockhausen treated the instruments as large scale structural determinants, and the pitch of each instrument was associated with a specific durational range for each respective section. This is illustrated in Example 21.

In addition to relating instruments of high pitch to short sections, Stockhausen proportionately distributed the instruments among various sections based upon duration (Example 21). The number of short sections is greater than of long sections, which balances the total durations of all the sections: the shortest sections total 177 seconds as compared to the longest section of 144 seconds. The method of delineating sections by percussive strokes is characteristic of the Japanese Noh drama. This is a further indication of Stockhausen's desire to incorporate elements of Oriental culture into "Telemusik."

The illustration of intermodulation contained in Example 20 is basically what Stockhausen employed in "Telemusik." Modifications such as filtering and amplitude modulation usually occur between the two ring modulators, at the input of the first ring modulator and the output of the second. This configuration is referred to by Stockhausen as the "Gagaku-Schaltung"; more complex intermodulations are derived by ring modulation of the "Gagaku-Schaltung" with amplitude-modulated sine chords.

As may be expected, double and triple ring modulation produce extremely dense textures because of the multiplication of frequencies. In fact, the textures become so complex that any resemblance to the constituent folk melodies is lost. In order to alleviate this problem Stockhausen separated the output signals from both ring modulators. As Example 20 shows, the output from the first ring modulator is simultaneously sent to the second modulator and the

EXAMPLE 21.   Karlheinz Stockhausen, "Telemusik"

Duration in seconds	13-14	21-23	34-37	55-57	89-91	144
Instrument	Taku	Bokusho	Mokugyo	Rin	Keisu	Four temple bells
Number of sections	13	8	5	3	2	1
Pitch	High ←				→ Low	

tape recorder so that the sound is continuous. On the other hand, the second ring modulator's output is manually controlled so that its appearance is periodic, and is generally at a lower amplitude level. Additional control of the texture is maintained by the use of filters at appropriate points within this configuration. Since Stockhausen was working with a six-track tape recorder, the output from each ring modulator could be assigned a separate channel. During a performance, the spatial distribution of the loudspeakers, one for each track, would insure the desired separation between both ring-modulated segments. The final version of "Telemusik" is actually for only five tracks; the sixth channel was used solely during the realization process. Unfortunately, Tokyo is the only city where "Telemusik" may be heard in its original version, inasmuch as five tracks are needed for playback. Although much of the spatial effect is lost on a stereo recording, Stockhausen has made a special two-channel version of this piece in an attempt to retain that effect as much as possible.

Example 22 illustrates an exquisite combination of electronically generated sounds, time delay, and intermodulation. Two sine tones were recorded on each of six tracks, the whole rerecorded on channel V with a time delay of approximately .3 seconds, producing a reverberated chordal mass. The output of channel V was then recorded on channels I and IV with a .6-second time delay. All three outputs were ring modulated at B and recorded on channel III. At the same time, channel V's output was also ring-modulated at A, amplitude-modulated, and finally recorded on track II. This section is only thirteen seconds long, beginning at 0:21 in the composition. Within this short period Stockhausen had many timbral variants at his disposal by simply regulating the amplitudes of the oscillators and tape recorder.

"Hymnen" (1967), Stockhausen's next tape composition, was realized at the WDR. It is a work of epic proportions, presently comprised of four Regions, and lasting just less than two hours. The principal sound sources are national anthems from countries the world over, which brings "Hymnen" even closer than "Telemusik" to Stockhausen's goal of a universal music.

Each of the four Regions has two, three or four Centers which include the national anthems that undergo intermodulatory processes similar to those in "Telemusik". Like its predecessor, "Hymnen" is not a collage, for the degree of sonorous transformations extends over a vast continuum.

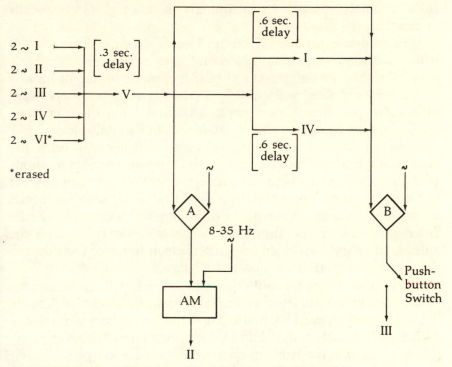

EXAMPLE 22. Karlheinz Stockhausen, "Telemusik"

Timbral relationships account for one of the structural plans Stockhausen formulated for "Hymnen". Example 23 depicts these relationships as they occur throughout the first Region. Stockhausen divided this Region into seven sections: Introduction, first Center, second Center-Antecedent, second Center, second Center-Consequent, Bridge, and Interlude. The progression between successive Centers—the "Internationale" (United Nations) and the "Marseillaise" (France)—is continuous. To these are added electronically generated sounds, short-wave receptions, Morse code signals, speech, children's screams, flood sounds, and rolls on a side drum. The electronic modifications of amplitude modulation, frequency modulation, ring modulation, filtering, and reverberation are freely applied to all of the sound sources. In addition, the national anthems are frequently fragmented, juxtaposed, or transposed by a variable speed recorder, which often results in a superficial resemblance to the tape collages of John Cage or the intricate splicing patterns characteristic of the early works of the R.T.F. composers. The national anthems were sung by mixed and male choruses, played by a military band and electronically generated.

The timbral structure of Region I can be seen in Example 23, with the gradual elimination of sound sources providing the basic plan. Stockhausen employed a similar technique in one of his first compositions, "Kontra Punkte" (1952). Ten instruments were grouped in pairs based on timbral similarities, and the successive elimination of each instrument established a structural level.

Each of the sections contained within the first Region is the result of timbral changes that are smooth because similar sonorous elements are retained between successive sections. Another aspect of Stockhausen's timbral organization is that of density. The initial sections of Region I generally exhibit thicker textures than the Interludes. A corresponding relationship also exists between the Introduction/first Center and the Interlude in terms of their overall durations, which are long–short.

Additional structural subtleties within the first Region, such as Stockhausen's insertion of a gambling casino episode, add to its dreamlike character. This particular digression occurs periodically within the Introduction and first Center, beginning with a croupier saying "Faites votre jeux messieurs-dames s'il vous plaît". Each time the croupier speaks, his voice is filtered, and appears to come from a distance. A few minutes later the croupier speaks again, followed by a play on the words "red," "rouge," "rot," and "rojo," treated in a 16th century polyphonic vocal style with a paradoxically medieval melodic contour. The four men's voices in this two-minute episode enhance the flashback to the tenth century, for they sound like monks performing Gregorian chant. The dream is over near the end of the first Center as the croupier announces "Messieurs-dames, rien ne va plus." The inclusion of such episodes makes the piece assume theatrical proportions. Perhaps this is what Stockhausen was referring to in his program notes for the world premier of this work: "Hymnen for radio, television, opera, ballet, recording, concert hall, church, the open air . . ."

Another composition utilizing a wide variety of sound sources is "Orient–Occident III" (1968) by Xenakis. This work is a revision of "Orient–Occident I" (1960), which initially existed in two versions. The original tape from which a second version for concert performance was derived was prepared for a film by Fulchignioni for

0:00	6:05	17:42	21:07	22:37	26:45	27:38	28:08
Introduction	1st Center	2nd Center-Antecedent	2nd Center	2nd Center-Consequent	Bridge	Interlude	
Morse Code	Male Chorus						
Short-Wave Mixed Chorus	Short-Wave Mixed Chorus			Children's Screams			
Speech Anthem Fragments Military Band	Speech Anthem Fragments Military Band	Side Drum Speech Anthem Fragments Military Band Flood Sound	Side Drum Anthem Fragments Military Band Flood Sound	Anthem Fragments Military Band Flood Sound	Flood Sound Electronic Sounds	Flood Sound	
Electronic Sounds	Electronic Sounds	Electronic Sounds	Electronic Sounds	Electronic Sounds			

EXAMPLE 23.   Karlheinz Stockhausen, "Hymnen," Region I

UNESCO. The duration of the latter version was reduced by almost half. The sound sources for this group of pieces consist of the results of a cello bow being drawn across cardboard boxes, metal rods, and gongs. Electric signals from the ionosphere were recorded and transposed to produce low roars, high cries, and glissandi, and a transformed excerpt from Xenakis's orchestral work "Pithoprakta" (1956), played at a slower speed, are also employed.

Luc Ferrari's "Presque Rien No. 1" (1970), subtitled "Daybreak on the Beach," is an environmental piece that utilizes the kind of sonorous elements found in John Cage's work: voices, birds, motors, footsteps, waves, bells, and so on. These sounds suggest a story. The chief difference between Ferrari and Cage is the pronounced absence of any electronic or tape modifications in Ferrari's composition.

"Presque Rien" evolves slowly. The gradual increase in the number of voices, the sounds of children playing, and automobile engines sounds like people arriving at the beach. About midway through the piece, a continuous, noise-like sonorous mass enters very softly. It gradually becomes louder, eventually masking the other environmental sounds.

By the mid-1960s composers were devising elaborate networks for sound modification much like those employed by Stockhausen. The configuration of equipment used for the realization of Josef Malovec's "Orthogenesis" (1966) is shown in Example 24. This work was originally intended for radio broadcast by the Czechoslovak Radio, Bratislava, at whose electronic studio "Orthogenesis" was produced. Electronically generated and modified sounds were recorded and played back on a special tape machine that contained four record and four playback heads. The output from each of the four heads was then individually modified by either filtering or feedback networks, after which it was reprocessed via a reverberation

EXAMPLE 24.   Jozef Malovec, "Orthogenesis"

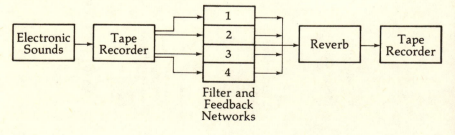

unit, and recorded. Both the technical processes and Malovec's desire to create large structural units by means of small, singular events reflect Stockhausen's compositional ideas. These concepts have come to pervade the works of many composers regardless of the equipment they use.

Eugeniusz Rudnik's "Dixi" (1967), realized at the Experimental Studio of the Polish Radio in Warsaw, is derived from the combination of oscillator-produced frequencies to form sound-blocks. As the timbre of these blocks is varied, a three-part formal plan is revealed, with the last section a transformation of the first. This transformation is achieved by means of tape and electronic modifications. The middle, and longest, segment is distinctly delineated from its neighboring sections by prominent octaves and noise bands, but the overlapping sections help to conceal the presence of the classical ABA form.

Timbral transformations occur as a continual process in Gottfried Michael Koenig's "Terminus II" (1967). An existing sound structure was subjected to electronic and tape modification processes in order to produce a variety of timbres, all of which are interrelated due to their common source. Koenig employed a more sophisticated method for controlling equipment in his "Funktion Grün" (1967). Voltage-controlled sound generators and modification devices were operated by a tape containing prerecorded control signals. Such methods not only provide greater accuracy, but also free the composer from the need to manipulate the equipment during the recording process. With the advent of hybrid systems in 1968, the control tape used in "Funktion Grün" could now be replaced by computer generated control signals, thereby adding greater flexibility and precision to this highly automated system.

In New York, Mimaroglu continued his work with instrumental sounds. His "Prelude No. II" (1967) employed an electronic organ that was modified by electronic processing devices in much the same manner as his other preludes. One of the many timbral changes that occur results in the sound of an electric piano. This is obtained by applying an appropriate envelope contour to the original organ sounds. Mimaroglu's more recent eleven-movement "Music for Jean Dubuffet's Coucou Bazar" (1973) is purely electronic in its derivation, aside from the last section, "Bal Des Leurres," which was discussed in the first chapter.

As I noted before, one of the prime interests of the composers at the Columbia–Princeton Center has been either the modification or the electronic synthesis of instrumental sounds. Pril Smiley's "Eclipse" (1967) is made up of electronically-produced and prerecorded percussion sounds, with both sound families undergoing extensive modifications. Timbre again serves as one of the principal structural determinants; the majority of the sounds are electronically generated.

The rise of electronic music studios in America was limited to a few locations, most notably to New York. One of the first studios, Louis and Bebe Barron's, was in operation as early as 1942. Although it was a private studio, a few other composers such as John Cage and Christian Wolff used these facilities during the early 1950s. By 1951, Otto Luening and Vladimir Ussachevsky had initiated the Columbia University Center, and four years later the choreographer Alwin Nikolais had set up a studio for the realization of tapes to accompany his dance company at the Henry Street Settlement Playhouse. Bell Telephone Laboratories in New Jersey, under the direction of Max Mathews, had begun producing tape pieces in 1957. By this time a small number of composers started to follow the Barrons' example by establishing private studios in New York.

Aside from a few efforts on the part of the film industry in California, there was essentially no successful attempt to establish an electronic studio outside the New York area before 1948, when two important centers arose in the mid-West, and one in California. The composers Gordon Mumma and Robert Ashley set up their private Cooperative Studio for Electronic Music (CSEM) in Ann Arbor, Michigan in 1958, and the University of Illinois Studio in Urbana was underway the following year under the direction of Lejaren Hiller. That same year, 1959, Morton Subotnick and Ramon Sender helped to establish the San Francisco Tape Music Center.

During the early 1960s many American universities began to build electronic music studios. They were frequently maintained by former faculty and graduates from those schools already possessing such studios. California has attracted quite a few musicians from the mid-Western studios, including Ken Gaburo, Olly Wilson, and Roger Reynolds. Gaburo's tape piece "For Harry" (1966) was one of his last compositions to be realized at the University of Illinois; he is currently teaching at the University of California at San Diego.

"For Harry" was dedicated to the American composer and instrument builder Harry Partch. Like most of Gaburo's tape pieces, "For Harry" is structured on rhythmic, timbral and pitch relationships.

Olly Wilson, presently teaching at the University of California at Berkeley, was the winner of the First International Electronic Music Competition at Dartmouth in 1968. His composition "Cetus" (1967) derives its structure from the transformation of relatively simple events into those of greater complexity, followed by a return to the original simplicity. An amplitude-modulated sine wave provides the basic melodic material, which is subsequently modified by ring modulation and filtering, resulting in more complex rhythms and timbres. This type of sectionalization based upon timbral or rhythmic relationships is among the most common ways of constructing an overall formal plan. It is easily employed regardless of the electronic devices used in the realization process.

Pauline Oliveros, a colleague of Ken Gaburo at the University of California, was initially affiliated with Morton Subotnick and Ramon Sender at the San Francisco Tape Center two years after its inception. Although much of her recent work has involved live electronics and theatre pieces, even her solo tape composition "I of IV" (1966) could be realized in live performance since it does not involve any tape editing or splicing. Her use of two tape recorders for the production of feedback loops and time delays is especially interesting. Its configuration is shown in Example 25.

Twelve oscillators were connected to a keyboard, amplified and reverberated. The signal was sent to channel 1 of the first tape recorder. The output of channel 1 was connected to the input of channel 2, while the output of channel 2 was sent back to the input of channel 1, thereby creating a double feedback loop with the first recorder. The second tape recorder was set in the playback mode while the recording tape was fed from the first recorder to the second machine. The two machines were physically separated,

EXAMPLE 25. Pauline Oliveros, "I of IV"

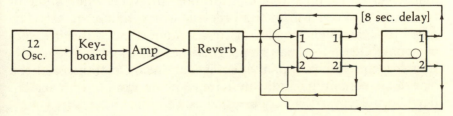

producing an approximately eight-second delay between their respective playback heads: 60 inches at 7½ ips or 120 inches at 15 ips. The outputs from channels 1 and 2 of the second recorder were finally connected to the inputs of channels 1 and 2 on the first machine, producing an eight second time delay of the double feedback loops. These methods of controlling timbre by regulating the resultant density of an initial sound via feedback loops and time delay have come to be widely used by musicians involved in live performance. Stockhausen, for example, employed a series of time delays in conjunction with a live performer in his "Solo" (1966).

In San Francisco during the early 1960s, Morton Subotnick and Ramon Sender began to consult an electrical engineer, Donald Buchla, about building some electronic equipment. It was just at this time that Robert Moog was designing equipment for Herbert Deutsch in Trumansberg, New York. The result of the West coast experiments was the Buchla Electronic Music System. When Subotnick temporarily moved to New York in 1966 to develop an Intermedia Program at New York University, he constructed an electronic music studio around this synthesizer.

Shortly after his arrival in New York, Subotnick received a commission from Nonesuch Records to produce an electronic composition specifically for a record. The result was "Silver Apples of the Moon," which he realized entirely on the Buchla system. In this piece, Subotnick frequently approaches the sounds of conventional instruments in much the same way that Milton Babbitt had done with the RCA Mark II synthesizer. Subotnick also deals with melody, harmony, and rhythm in a rather traditional manner, but because of the sequencer module in the Buchla synthesizer Subotnick was able to create a variety of rhythmic and melodic patterns which would have been practically impossible to accurately produce without the aid of voltage controlled devices.

The sequencer is a control voltage source which may be used to regulate voltage-controlled oscillators, filters, amplifiers, and the like. It consists of a number of points, or stages, at which voltages that have been manually preset are present. When they are activated, these stages run in the order in which they were set. The speed of the sequence is also manually controlled. After it makes one complete cycle, it can be programmed to repeat continuously. In order to produce a similar effect in a classical electronic studio, a tape loop containing individual frequencies would have had to have been prepared, a very time-consuming task.

Subotnick's next work, "The Wild Bull" (1968), was also a commission from Nonesuch Records. The sequencer again plays an important role, with one very inventive use of it illustrated in Example 26. A sawtooth oscillator is the sole sound source in this excerpt. It is connected to an octave filter bank, a filter that extracts frequencies within a range of successive octaves, such as 100–200 Hz., 200–400 Hz., and so forth. The most valuable aspect of this device is the inclusion of a separate output for each range, so that distinct timbral characteristics of any sound may be independently treated. In this piece, Subotnick selects four different segments of the harmonic spectrum above the fundamental tone produced by the source oscillator. These four frequency bands are then sent to a voltage-controlled mixer which, like the voltage-controlled amplifier, is turned off unless a voltage source is present. The amount of voltage applied to the mixer therefore regulates the amplitude of the audio signals.

Four envelope generators with individual settings for the attack, steady state, and decay times supply the necessary control voltages for the mixer. Each envelope generator controls one of the four frequency bands emitted from the filter bank. The sequencer pro-

EXAMPLE 26. Morton Subotnick, "The Wild Bull"

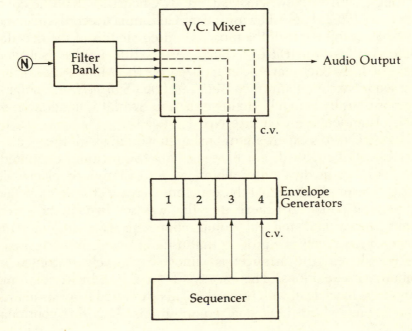

duces four voltages which serve as timing pulses to trigger or activate each of the envelope generators. If the speed of the sequence is set to its maximum, the four frequency bands appear to begin simultaneously, but as the sequencer rate is slowed down four individual attacks can be heard.

The result of this rather complex configuration is a very refined method for controlling the timbre of the original sawtooth frequency. Since the sawtooth wave is particularly rich in harmonic content, various segments of the harmonic spectrum may be separately controlled by the envelope generators, resulting in numerous possibilities for complex envelopes.

Although both the Moog and Buchla synthesizers enjoyed equal popularity among composers during the latter part of the 1960s, it was the Moog synthesizer that eventually exposed the record-buying public to electronic music. Walter Carlos, who had been using the facilities at the Columbia–Princeton Center in 1963, was responsible for this exposure. His first commercially recorded compositions incorporated live performers with prerecorded tape, but he had also produced solo tape pieces. In 1966 Carlos set up a private studio where he made electronic arrangements of the popular songs, "What's New, Pussycat?" and "Cherish," which he completed in 1967. The following year, Columbia Records released what has become one of the most overrated albums of the decade, Walter Carlos's *Switched on Bach*. As its title implies, selected works of J. S. Bach have been realized on the Moog synthesizer. The sequel to this album, *The Well-Tempered Synthesizer*, contains compositions by Handel, Monteverdi, and Scarlatti, in addition to Bach's Brandenburg Concerto No. 4.

While Carlos's expert craftmanship in working with the synthesizer cannot be denied, nor his sensitivity toward timbre ignored, this does not qualify either album as an example of electronic music. The implication that these albums were electronic music led the general public to believe that this was so. In fact, however, arrangements and musical composition are entirely different. Composition involves a process that usually treats all musical elements, whereas the arranger is almost exclusively restricted to timbral considerations. The variety of ways in which electronic composers have dealt with these elements stemmed from structural relationships within individual compositions. It is this continual process, including electronic considerations, that constitutes an electronic composition.

One of Carlos's best compositions, "Sonic Seasonings" (1972), again employs the Moog synthesizer. It is divided into four movements representing the four seasons, a kind of formal structuring also found in the works of Henk Badings and Pierre Henry. Carlos's ability to realistically synthesize the timbres of musical instruments is undoubtedly one of the major accomplishments of this piece; for, like Subotnick, Carlos favors a more traditional approach to the other elements of melody, harmony and rhythm.

Isao Tomita, a Japanese composer who specializes in music for television and film, followed in Carlos's footsteps. His album, *Snowflakes Are Dancing* (1974), contains arrangements of Debussy's most popular compositions performed on the Moog synthesizer. Pieces from the "Children's Corner Suite," "Suite Bergamasque," "Estampes," and the first book of "Preludes," are included in this album. Tomita's technical mastery of the equipment has enabled him to produce beautiful arrangements of Debussy's music, but again, this album does not qualify as electronic music.

Another such attempt has been made by Joseph Byrd, formerly of the United States of America group. His album, *A Christmas Yet To Come* (1975), consists of synthesized arrangements of traditional carols. The instrumental sonorities realized involve the original instruments employed in the particular historical periods from which the carols originate. These sounds are then used as a point of departure for subsequent timbral variations. Like the arrangements of Carlos and Tomita, Byrd restricts his modifications to tape delay, equalization, envelope control, and mixing. An equalizer, like the octave filter bank, is divided into successive frequency ranges, but the equalizer includes separate amplitude controls for each range. This permits both attenuation and amplification of selected frequency ranges.

These works are in a popular style in which harmonically complex modulations, or ring modulation, are absent. Entire compositions from earlier periods are reproduced and often subjected to slight timbral transformation. In contrast to this nondevelopmental process, Lou Reed, the former leader of the Velvet Underground, juxtaposes excerpts from rock and classical music to produce a formidable degree of distortion through modulation, filtering, and reverberation in his "Metal Machine Music" (1975). The sonorous content of this composition is reminiscent of

"HPSCHD" by Cage and the concrète segments of Stockhausen's "Telemusik" and "Hymnen"; the resultant modulations possess such harmonic complexity that the record grooves are wider than usual to yield a better frequency response.

Brian Eno is another rock star whose work has begun to extend beyond the boundaries of that medium. Educated in his native Great Britain, Eno has studied with Christian Wolff, and worked with Roxy Music, Robert Fripp of Yes, and the former Velvet Underground members Nico and John Cale. His rock music will be discussed in Chapter 9.

A sensitive and intelligent musician, Eno is not concerned with electronic effects as an end in themselves, but rather as structural determinants. Automated music is an extension of this idea. As Eno stated: ". . . I have gravitated towards situations and systems that, once set into operation, could create music with little or no intervention on my part." He applied this principle in his solo tape piece "Discreet Music" (1975), in which two melodic lines subjected to equalization, echo, and time delay, are the sole sound sources. Both melodies are slow and tonal; equalization creates instrumental sonorities; and the delay line permits textural variety, so that intervals and chords are produced. Because of its length, half an hour, "Discreet Music's" melodically repetitive nature becomes a pedal point, like Steve Reich's "Come Out." Although there are some interesting timbral and textural transformations, they also function as stationary reference points.

The monotony that could result from these melodic, rhythmic, timbral, and textural repetitions is offset by an extremely low playback volume. In discussing the low amplitude level, Eno suggests that "Discreet Music" be played softly, ". . . even to the extent that it frequently falls below the threshold of audibility." This attitude reflects John Cage's neo-Dada philosophy. The role of the composer/performer in this piece is more passive than in Eno's rock realizations, and the nature of the performance area directly influences the character of the work: a noisy environment produces an entirely different effect than does a quiet concert hall. This aspect of "Discreet Music" is beyond compositional control.

Charles Wuorinen is another young composer who has used the Columbia–Princeton studio. His Nonesuch commission "Time's Encomium" (1969) was awarded the 1970 Pulitzer Prize for music. Wuorinen first used the Columbia Studio in 1960 while he was a student there. In this two-movement work, the composer first derived his sound materials from the RCA synthesizer, processing these sounds with a conventional analog synthesizer. Wuorinen considers the initial section an exposition and the second movement a development of the first. As Babbitt did with the Mark II synthesizer, Wuorinen developed many instrumental-type timbres, particularly the keyboardlike sounds of the piano, harpsichord, and organ. The electronic synthesis of instrumental timbres was one direction taken by composers working primarily with synthesizers. The availability of voltage-controlled devices was certainly a determining factor in this, for the computer made it possible due to the precise control of the harmonic spectrum that it afforded the composer.

It is not difficult to hear the timbral transformations in Ussachevsky's "Computer Piece No. 1" (1968), in which concrète sources of a gong, an electronic organ and voice are used in combination with computer-generated sounds. The sound sources were not modified by the computer, but in an analog studio, and consisted of frequency shifting and reverberation. Frequency shifting is a simplified version of ring modulation. Rather than producing both sum and difference tones, a frequency shifter provides a separate output for each. The mixture of the sum and difference outputs results in ring modulation.

The "Computer Piece No. 1" follows a classical three-part formal plan, beginning with sustained sounds of continually changing timbres. In the second section these sounds are sped up, then followed by a brief recapitulation of the initial sustained sounds. The predictability of the ABA formal scheme is concealed by the insertion of a long silence between the last two sections.

Ussachevsky employed Max Mathews's and F. Moore's GROOVE program in "Two Sketches for a Computer Piece" (1971). Most of the sounds were produced on a keyboard connected to the computer, allowing for the possibility of live performance. The main purpose of the GROOVE program is to allow a synthesizer to be controlled by a computer. Other sounds were computer generated by a random function generator which, as its name implies, supplies an indeterminate series of electronic signals. Contrary to the "Computer Piece No. 1", pitch and rhythmic elements rather than timbre assume the most important structural functions.

J. K. Randall's "Quartersines" (1969) was totally realized on a computer, with the four sections of a sine wave providing a graphic derivation of pitches. Glissando patterns result from various transformations of a sine wave, shown in Example 27. This idea would be perfectly suited to the use of the light pencil developed at Bell Labs in 1968, the X-axis denoting duration and the Y-axis, frequency.

New Zealander Barry Vercoe is both a computer programmer and a composer. He is presently director of the Experimental Music Studio at M.I.T. His computer piece "Synthesism" (1969) is the product of two methods of dealing with pitch. The first entails the division of the octave into sixteen equal parts, resulting in four more pitches per octave than is customary in traditional Western music (although this procedure is not a new one). Such a slight departure from Western tuning systems is not always easily audible, particularly in the higher registers, which give the impression of being "out of tune."

The second technique involving pitch perception is first used at the beginning of "Synthesism," where bands of filtered noise are mixed with specific pitches. The process of filtering merely suggests a frequency range, whereas the degree of pitch perception is dependent upon the amplitude relationships between the noise and the individual pitches. Even though timbral relationships result from this process, it is Vercoe's control of pitch that establishes the primary structural levels. Amplitude and frequency modulations must also be viewed from this perspective.

The last composer I will discuss in this chapter is Charles Dodge, who began to use the computer facilities at Columbia University in 1967. Dodge has recently received a grant from the National Endowment for the Arts to compose an electronic opera for radio, utilizing synthetic speech. Additionally, he has been commissioned to do an electronic realization of Samuel Beckett's radio play "Cascando." Other composers associated with the

EXAMPLE 27. J. K. Randall, "Quartersines"

duration   (a)   (b)

Columbia–Princeton Center who have recently been recipients of similar grants include Ussachevsky, Luening, Babbitt, and Arel.

Dodge's "Changes" (1969) involves such an accurate simulation of musical instruments that it appears to be instrumental rather than computer-generated. It is for three instruments—keyboard, horn or bass, and percussion, and sounds very much like a "free" jazz improvisation. Subtle timbral changes provide the keyboard sounds of electric piano, organ and harpsichord. Additional timbres suggest a large array of percussion instruments as well as an alteration between the sounds of horn and electric bass. All these transformations result primarily from changes in filtering, envelope contour, and basic waveshape. Varying degrees of rhythmic complexity contribute to the overall structural design. The absence of a "solo" increases the authenticity of "Changes" so that it sounds like an example of the "avant garde" jazz style of such musicians as Cecil Taylor and Marion Brown.

J. K. Randall's "Quartersines" has shown how the computer is especially suited for the interpretation of geometric figures; the shape of a sine wave performed the function of pitch determination. "Earth's Magnetic Field" (1970) by Charles Dodge makes use of the computer in a similar manner by employing graphs of Kp indices. According to Dodge and Bruce Boller: "The designation Kp is derived from an abbreviated form of the German word for 'corpuscular.' " These depict the average level of magnetic activity for Earth; in this piece, they determine pitch, register, dynamics, and tempo.

Graphs of the Kp indices were developed by Julius Bartels, a German geophysicist. Bruce Boller, a solar-terrestrial physicist, Carl Frederick, a physicist in infra-red astronomy, and Stephen Ungar, an astrophysicist, provided Dodge with technical assistance in the preparation of his graph. The Nonesuch recording for which this piece was commissioned contains two different interpretations of the 1961 Kp indices, one on each side of the album. The first index was segmented to produce a diatonic succession of pitches over a four octave range, in a monophonic presentation. Dodge avoided a rather dull interpretation of the graph by varying the wave forms of the pitches, assigning envelopes of diverse characteristics to each pitch, and applying reverberation. The last two procedures contribute to a polyphonic texture resulting from the overlapping envelopes and reverberation times.

The second side of the album is polyphonic, the standard twelve divisions per octave replacing the previous diatonic organization. "Sudden commencements," or rapid changes of Earth's magnetic field, provide another interpretation of the Kp indices.

In two decades, tape composition techniques have been extended from basic tape recorder manipulations to include sophisticated computer sound generation and voltage-controlled synthesizers. Because there have been so many technical advances, it is easy to lose track of the specific compositional aesthetics of electronic composers. By 1953, with the establishment of the Cologne Studio, the basic sonorous elements and modification techniques employed in electronic music had been realized. Shortly thereafter, the Italian studio at Milan was founded. France, Germany, and Italy formed a nucleus about which electronic music revolved in Western Europe.

The R.T.F. studio in Paris has exerted the greatest influence on the works of Ussachevsky and Luening at the Columbia University Studio. In 1955, Americans made the first substantial technical contributions to electronic music. The first departure from the European electronic tradition was the RCA synthesizer, followed by the application of computer technology to electronic composition at Bell Telephone Laboratories in New Jersey. By the mid-1960's the appearance of the Buchla and Moog synthesizers firmly established the usefulness of control voltage applications in this medium. The convenience of synthesizers has exerted an enormous influence upon the practice of electronic music in America. The compact physical design, as well as the synthesizer's relative ease of operation, has stimulated many individuals and universities to establish electronic studios.

There are many advantages in working with a voltage controlled synthesizer, especially those of speed and automation. On the other hand, it is often difficult to maintain a precise control of sonorous elements without using volt meters and frequency counters. A composer working with voltage-controlled equipment often tends to rely on his ear rather than to follow a predetermined plan specifying exact envelope characteristics, filter frequencies, amplitude levels, and so on.

The RCA Mark II synthesizer offers a solution to this problem by providing an accurate means of controlling these functions. Since there is only one in existence, however, the basic problem remains. Computers offer a more practical solution, particularly the hybrid systems that maintain precision while allowing for the processing of external sources.

Discography

AITKIN, ROBERT
"Noesis," Folk.
FMS—33436

AREL, BULENT
"Electronic Music No. 1,"
Son—Nova 3

——————

"Music for a Sacred Service,"
Son—Nova 3

——————

"Stereo Electronic Music No.
1," Col. MS—6566

BABBITT, MILTON
"Composition for
Synthesizer," Col.
MS—6566

——————

"Ensembles for
Synthesizer," Col.
MS—7051

BADINGS, HENK
"Evolutions," Epic
BC—1118

——————

"Genese," Epic
BC—1118

BERIO, LUCIANO
"Momenti," Lime.
LS—86047

BOUCOURECHLIEV, ANDRÉ
"Texte II," BAM
LD—071

BYRD, JOSEPH
A Christmas Yet To Come,
Takoma C—1046

CAGE, JOHN
"Fontana Mix," Turn.
TV—34046S

——————

"Williams Mix," Avakian
JC—1

CARLOS, WALTER
"Sonic Seasonings," Col.
KG—31234

——————

Switched On Bach, Col.
MS—7194

——————

*The Well-Tempered
Synthesizer,* Col.
MS—7286

CARSON, PHILIPPE
"Turmac," BAM
LD—072

CZAJKOWSKI, MICHAEL
"People the Sky," Van.
C—10069

DAVIDOVSKY, MARIO
"Electronic Study No. 1,"
Col. MS—6566

——————

"Electronic Study No. 2,"
Son—Nova 3

"Electronic Study No. 3,"
  Turn. TV—S—34487

DOCKSTADER, TOD
"Eight Electronic Pieces,"
  Folk. FM—3434

DODGE, CHARLES
"Changes," None. 71245

———

"Earth's Magnetic Field,"
  None. 71250

**DUFRENE, FRANCOIS AND JEAN
  BARONNET**
"U47," Lime. LS—86047

EIMERT, HERBERT
Elektronische Musik,
  Wergo WER 60006

ENO, BRIAN
"Discreet Music,"
  Obscure 3

FERRARI, LUC
"Etude aux accidents,"
  BAM LD—070

———

"Etude aux sons tendus,"
  BAM LD—070

———

"Presque Rien No. 1,"
  DGG—2543004

———

"Tautologos I," BAM
  LD—072

———

"Tautologos II," BAM
  LD—071

———

"Tête et queue du dragon,"
  Can. 31025

"Visage V," Lime.
  LS—86047

GABURO, KENNETH
"Exit Music I: The Wasting of
  Lucrecetzia," None.
  71199

———

"For Harry," Hel.
  HS—25047

———

"Lemon Drops," Hel.
  HS—25047

HENRY, PIERRE
"Antiphonie," DUC—9

———

"Astrologie," DUC—9

———

"Entité," Lime.
  LS—86048

———

"La Reine Verte," Philips
  6332 015

———

"Le Voyage," Lime.
  LS—86049

———

"Tam-Tam IV," DUC—9

———

"Variations on a Door and a
  Sigh," Philips
  836—898 **DSY**

KAGEL, MAURICIO
"Transicion I," Lime.
  LS—86048

KOENIG, GOTTFRIED MICHAEL
"Funktion Grun,"
  DG—137001

"Terminus II,"
DG—137001

LE CAINE, HUGH
"Dripsody," Folk.
FMS—33436

LEWIN-RICHTER, ANDRÉS
"Electronic Study No. 1,"
Turn. TV—34004S

LIGETI, GYÖRGY
"Artikulation," Lime.
LS—86048

LUENING, OTTO AND VLADIMIR
USSACHEVSKY
"Suite from King Lear,"
CRI—112

MACHE, FRANÇOIS-BERNARD
"Terre de feu," BAM
LD—072 and Can.
31025

MADERNA, BRUNO
"Continuo," Lime.
LS—86047

MALEC, IVO
"Dahovi," Can. 31025

"Reflets," BAM LD—072

MALOVEC, JOZEF
"Orthogenesis," Turn.
34301

MAXFIELD, RICHARD
"Night Music," Odys.
32160 160

MIMAROGLU, ILHAN
"Agony," Turn.
TV—34046S

"Bowery Bum," Turn.
TV—34004S

"Intermezzo," Turn.
TV—34004S

"Music for Jean Dubuffet's
Coucou Bazar," Finn.
SR—9003

"Prelude No. II," Turn.
34177

"Prelude No. XI," Turn.
34177

MUMMA, GORDON
"Music for the Venezia Space
Theatre," Adv.
FGR—5

OLIVEROS, PAULINE
"I of IV," Odys.
32160160

PHILIPPOT, MICHEL
"Ambiance I," BAM
LD—070

"Etude I," DUC—9

"Etude III," Can. 31025

PONGRÁCZ, ZOLTÁN
"Phonothese,"
DG—137011

POUSSEUR, HENRI
"Scambi," Lime.
LS—86048

POWELL, MEL
"Electronic Setting I,"
Son—Nova 3

"Second Electronic
Setting," CRI S—227

RAAIJMAKERS, DICK
"Contrasts," Epic
BC—1118

RANDALL, J. K.
"Quartersines," None.
71245

"Quartet in Paris," None.
71245

REED, LOU
"Metal Machine Music,"
RCA CLP2—1101

RIEHN, RAINER
"Gesang de Maldoror,"
DG—137011

ROBB, J. D.
"Collage," Folk.
FMS—33436

RUDIN, ANDREW
"Tragoedia," None.
71198

RUDNIK, EUGENIUSZ
"Dixi," Turn. 34301

SAHL, MICHAEL
"Tropes on the Salve
Regina," Lyr.
LLST—7210

SALA, OSKAR
"Five Improvisations,"
West. 18962

SAUGUET, HENRI
"Aspect Sentimental,"
BAM LD—070

SCHAEFFER, MYRON
"Danse R 4 ÷ 3," Folk.
FMS—33436

SCHAEFFER, PIERRE
"Etude aux allures," BAM

LD—070 and Philips
6521 021

"Etude aux
casseroles," DUC—8 and
Philips 6521 021

"Etude aux chemins de fer,"
DUC—8 and Philips
6521 021

"Etude aux sons animés,"
BAM LD—070 and
Philips 6521 021

"Etude aux tourniquets,"
DUC—8 and Philips
6521 021

SCHAEFFER, PIERRE AND
PIERRE HENRY
"L'Oiseau RAI," DUC—9

SMILEY, PRIL
"Eclipse," Turn.
TV—34301

"Kalyosa," 2—CRI—268

STEPHEN, VAL
"Fireworks," Folk.
FMS—33436

"The Orgasmic Opus,"
Folk. FMS—33436

STOCKHAUSEN, KARLHEINZ
"Hymnen,"
2—DG—2707039

"Kontakte" (tape version),
DGG—138811

"Studie I,"   DGG—16133

"Studie II,"   DGG—16133

"Telemusik,"   DG—137012

SUBOTNICK, MORTON
"4 Butterflies,"   Col.
M—32741

"Sidewinder,"   Co.
M—30683

"Silver Apples of the
Moon,"   None.   71174

"Touch,"   Col.   MS—7316

"The Wild Bull,"   None.
71208

TAKEMITSU, TORU
"Water Music,"   RCA
VICS—1334

TAYLOR, KEITH
"Lumière,"   Varese   81001

TOMITA, ISAO
Snowflakes Are Dancing,
RCA   ARL   1—0488

USSACHEVSKY, VLADIMIR
"Computer Piece No. 1,"
2—CRI—268

"Experiment No. 4711,"
Son—Nova 3

"Metamorphosis,"
Son—Nova 3

"Piece for Tape Recorder,"
CRI—112

"Two Sketches for a
Computer Piece,"
2—CRI—268

"Wireless Fantasy,"
CRI—227

VARÈSE, EDGARD
"Poème Electronique,"
Col.   MS—6146

VERCOE, BARRY
"Synthesism,"   None.
71245

WALTER, ARNOLD, HARVEY
OLNICK AND MYRON
SCHAEFFER
"Summer Idyl,"   Folk.
FMS—33436

WILSON, OLLY
"Cetus,"   Turn.   34301

WUORINEN, CHARLES
"Time's Encomium,"
None.   71225

XENAKIS, IANNIS
"Bohor I,"   None.   71246

"Concret P-H II,"   None.
71246

"Diamorphoses,"   BAM
LD—070

"Diamorphoses II,"
None.   71246

"Orient-Occident III,"
None.   71246

CHAPTER THREE

MUSIC FROM VOCAL, ELECTRONIC, AND OTHER CONCRÈTE SOURCES

THE WAY IN WHICH A COMPOSER formally organizes a tape piece is often dependent upon his choice of basic sonorous materials. If these are predominantly electronic in origin, or if they proceed from "noise" sounds, it is likely that the structural design of the composition will be based primarily upon the perceptibility for the listener of particular elements and events like timbral transformations and motivic repetitions. The compositions treated in the previous chapter displayed these characteristics.

On the other hand, once the voice is included as a sound source, entirely different structural possibilities arise, as has been demonstrated in the first chapter discussion of works totally derived from the voice. The composer had the option of treating the voice solely as another timbral source, as Henry did in "Vocalise"; of relying on the meaning of the text, as in Philippot's "Ambiance II"; or of working within a continuum encompassing meaning and pure vocal sounds, as in Berio's "Thema" and Reich's "Come Out." This chapter will examine the situations that arise when both vocal and non-vocal sound sources are used.

"Symphonie pour un homme seul" (1950) was the product of the first collaboration between Schaeffer and Henry at the R.T.F. studio. It occupies a central position among the pieces produced at

86

the R.T.F. for several reasons. After realizing relatively short études for over a year, Schaeffer attempted to organize a work of major proportions, the "Symphonie" being the second such attempt. Its predecessor, a five movement "Suite pour 14 instruments," was the first piece to exceed a duration of twenty minutes. The "Symphonie" contains eleven movements with individual durations of between one and three minutes. It was the first musique concrète piece to be choreographed by Maurice Béjart and Jean Laurent, and was performed at the Théâtre de l'Etoile in 1955.

An extremely wide range of vocal sounds including speech, whistling, humming, shouting, laughter, and various types of breathing, was employed. In the eighth movement, "Apostrophe," the word "absolument" undergoes complete fragmentation followed by its reconstruction, a process which was to be evoked a few years later by Stockhausen in his "Gesang der Jünglinge". It also demonstrates the use of voiced timbral changes like those used in Henry's later composition "Vocalise". Similarly, the fourth section, "Erotica," contains breathing sequences and bursts of laughter, anticipating Berio's "Visage" by more than a decade.

These vocal materials were used in conjunction with prerecorded excerpts of orchestral music, percussion instruments, and prepared piano, in addition to the sounds of footsteps, knocking, and pops. At times a Cageian collage results, while at other times "Symphonie" appears to be a slowly evolving environmental piece that can be interpreted as the sonorous representation of one man's actions. Within this existential atmosphere brilliant flourishes, erratic rhythms played on the strings of the piano, the South American Beguine rhythmic pattern, footsteps, and all of the aforementioned vocal sounds coexist, providing close motivic connections throughout the entire composition. Most of the tape techniques employed are transposition and editing. "Symphonie" is far removed from Schaeffer's "noise" études, for the techniques are no longer an end in themselves.

The first collaboration between Luening and Ussachevsky, "Incantation" (1952), appeared immediately after the completion of their individual tape pieces derived from flute and piano sounds. In some respects this later piece resembles the "Symphonie pour un homme seul," especially in the use of a textless vocal part, conventional musical instruments, and frequent tape transposition. The instrumental sources were wind instruments and bells, usually accompanied by the addition of much reverberation similar to Luening's earlier flute pieces. Like Ussachevsky's and Luening's initial tape compositions, "Incantation" contains many passages that are played by the instruments and subsequently transformed by tape transpositions. Continual changes of speed result in glissando patterns, while amplitude modulation and reverberation contribute to the general unintelligibility of the vocal part, which is derived from a male chorus.

An elaborate structural relation between literary text and electronic sounds exists in Stockhausen's "Gesang der Jünglinge" (1956), for which the "Apocrypha" to the *Book of Daniel* serves as a basic text. Realized before "Kontakte" but after "Studie II," "Gesang der Jünglinge" reveals an additive approach in dealing with the basic sonorous elements, much like that employed in the two other pieces. "Gesang der Jünglinge," however, applies this process to the carefully chosen text.

Since Stockhausen employed a biblical source he was dealing with general knowledge. Therefore, the reversal of word orderings would not necessarily destroy the original meaning because listeners would automatically focus their attention upon the content of the word. This enabled the composer to recompose the text according to preestablished compositional determinants without sacrificing the fundamental message of the text. The late nineteenth century French poet Mallarmé had been the first to experiment with syntax by changing the logical word orderings within his poems. He referred to this process as transposition. Stockhausen and Berio were among the first electronic composers to utilize this technique.

Two levels of organization are operative within the textual sphere; they are based on timbre and speech. The formulation of relations among vowels and consonants was probably influenced by Stockhausen's study of acoustics and phonetics with Werner Meyer-Eppler at Bonn University. Stockhausen established the following timbre scales: vowels-consonants, dark vowels (u)–light vowels (i), and dark consonants (ch)–light consonants (s). Helmholtz had already carried out extensive experiments with vowels; Stockhausen's procedures reflect the physicist's results. Helmholtz established the pitch of vowels by using tuning forks, determining "u" as a lower frequency than "i." This corresponds to Stockhausen's vowel continuum.

The speech continuum of "Gesang" displays various degrees of textual comprehensibility which stem from Stockhausen's work with Meyer-Eppler in the area of information theory. Extremes of the speech continuum are defined by the syntactical and timbral treatment of words, the latter achieved by the division of individual words into syllables and phonemes. This degenerative process is followed either by the rearrangement of the constituent elements or by the insertion of foreign sonorous elements into the syllables and phonemes. Example 28 illustrates some of the possibilities afforded by this technique.

Both "Blitze" and "Scharen" occur in the text. The former can be divided into two syllables with electronic sounds inserted between them. "Scharen" is also comprised of two syllables, but the first, "scha," can be further subdivided into the unvoiced "Sc" and the aspirate "ha" sounds, resulting in three individual elements whose ordering can then be rearranged to produce synthetic words. Electronically generated sounds could also be employed to separate "Scharen" into three segments. The duration of these foreign sounds affects the comprehensibility of the word: a rather long electronic segment may destroy the connection between the syllables, thereby producing the illusion of two or more separate words.

Another method of deriving new words that is characteristic of the German language is simply to connect two or more words to form a longer word. By so doing Stockhausen was able to exercise even greater control over the syntax of the original text, for he could join words of diverse meanings resulting in word connections that did not appear in the "Apocrypha." Stockhausen has given the following examples of this technique: "Schneewind" (snowwind), "Eisglut" (iceheat), and "Feuerreif" (firefrost).

Finally, Stockhausen established a direct correlation between

EXAMPLE 28.   Karlheinz Stockhausen, "Gesang der Jünglinge"

Blitze———▶ Blit_____ ze———▶ Blit_(electronic sounds)_ ze

Scharen———▶ Sc_____ ha ___ ren———▶ Screnha
                                                       haScren
                                                       renScha
                                                       harenSc
                                                       renhaSc

Sc_(electronic sounds)_ha_(electronic sounds)_ren

Blitze = Lighting

Scharen = Hosts

vocal and electronically produced sounds. Vowels were represented by sine tones, consonants by noise bands, and plosives by impulses. Plosives are phonemes that possess a sudden attack and reach an amplitude peak. In addition, these families of sound could be intermingled to produce more complex relationships. This procedure is similar to Ligeti's method of determining linguistic functions by means of various sized noise bands in his tape piece "Artikulation."

By treating speech as pure sound and electronic sounds as speech, Stockhausen's basic sonorous elements not only became totally interchangeable, but timbre and textual comprehensibility served as functions of one another. In terms of structural significance, the composite elements were active determinants of the formal organization. This accounts for Stockhausen's need for very accurate means of controlling the basic sonorous materials, and for this reason, Stockhausen always defines his sound sources and processes of transformation prior to the actual realization of a composition. He begins with a single sonorous event from which an entire composition will follow. In order to facilitate further study of this piece a sketch of the recorded performance has been included in Example 29, including intelligible textual excerpts and approximate timings.

The same year that Stockhausen completed "Gesang der Jünglinge," Otto Luening finished his "Theatre Piece No. 2" (1956) for tape, piano, soprano, narrator, percussion, and wind instruments. This was the first composition since 1952 that Luening had not realized in collaboration with Ussachevsky. Although the "Theatre Piece" has not been commercially recorded in its entirety, the opening of the work, "In the Beginning," illustrates yet another method of treating the voice in the tape medium.

"In the Beginning" is for solo tape comprised of electronically produced sounds, instrumental sounds with tape manipulations, and a textless soprano voice that is not subjected to any transformations. Luening's use of the voice revolved around timbral considerations not only because of the absence of a text, but also because the voice appears only during the last third of the piece, articulating a major structural division at its entry. The opening is characterized by slow successions of sustained sounds with some motivic repetitions. The vocal part is made up of long, flowing melodies reminis-

0:00	2:47
Preiset den Herrn	Preiset den Herrn, Sonne und
ihr Scharen alle des Herrn	Mond—preiset den Herrn,
Werke	des Himmels Sterne.
ihn	aller Regen und Tau
und	den Herrn
über	preiset
alles	alle Winde

4:40	5:15	6:40
Preiset	Feurer und Sommers	Regens Fall
	glut—preiset den	Frost und Eis
	Herrn, kälte und	
	starrer Winter.	

7:38	8:28
Preiset den Herrn, Reif	Preiset
und Schnee-preiset	Licht und Dunkel
Nächte und Tage	Herrn
	über alles
	Frost und Eis
	ihr Scharen alle

EXAMPLE 29.   Karlheinz Stockhausen, "Gesang der Jünglinge"

cent of Luening's flute pieces from the early 1950s, for it incorporates traditional musical elements such as tonal centers, triadic formations, and scale passages.

Three extracts from Romuald Vandelle's "Crucifixion" (1960), realized at the R.T.F., also reflect a preference for instrumental sounds in combination with voice. As in "Gesang der Jünglinge," the voice serves both as a vehicle for meaningless speech and as a source of additional timbres. Each of the three sections contains a Latin phrase, each one clearly articulated only once. Subsequent vocal appearances are treated as functions of timbre.

"Trois visages de Liège" (1961) by Henri Pousseur is a three movement work of which only the last two sections employ the voice. The text is a selection of poems by the late Jean Séaux. Their rather clear presentation makes them comprehensible. Section I, "L'air et l'eau," is the product of heavily modulated electronic signals, filtered noise bands, and many glissandi. Ring modulation accounts for bell and gong sounds, a method of processing that occurs in each of the movements in order to provide a timbral connection among them.

The second section, "Voix de la ville," is derived from the voice, electronic sounds, and a pizzicato chord. It begins with the amplitude modulation of this chord, followed by ring-modulated sonorities and glissandi from the first movement. The voice is set apart from the electronic and concrète sounds by the addition of reverberation; the poems retain their intelligibility despite over-dubbings in the form of tape loops and collage techniques.

"Forges," the final movement, contains a predominance of modulated organ-like sounds; the voice is again reverberated. The poems are comprehensible even though they are sometimes treated in a collage style. The main function of the voice is not oriented toward timbral transformations; but structural links among the three movements are based upon timbral relationships among the electronic sounds. The most obvious sound is that of ring modulation. Glissandi patterns are also easily discernible although their presence is not as frequent as the ring modulated sonorities. Reverberation and elementary tape manipulations of the voice provide a high level of timbral unification between the two final movements.

As early as 1950, Schaeffer and Henry made use of vocal sounds such as breathing and laughter in the "Symphonie pour un homme seul." Although actual speech was not employed, meaning could still be gleaned from the non-speech sounds. For example, "Erotica" successfully conveys the feeling of sexuality that its title implies without recourse to explicit words.

This primitive aspect of language is recognized and used by all cultures. It was with this feature that Berio was concerned in his composition "Visage" (1961), realized at the RAI studio in Milan. The sound sources include voice, filtered noise bands, and oscillators frequently subjected to amplitude, frequency, and ring modulation.

Berio began by constructing a language based upon phonemes: Ă, Ē, Ō, U, D, G, K, R, S, and T combined to form syllables like SĂ, DĂ, DĒ, STĂ, DT, ST, and KER. These syllables were joined together to form meaningless words, and successions of words were used to produce nonsense speech. In addition to these linguistic elements' individual appearances, Berio employed the vocal inflections of crying, laughing, breathing, and screaming. Only one actual word appears; it is "parole," which means "words" in Italian.

With such a large, meaningless vocabulary at his disposal, Berio was able to portray the gamut of human emotions including pain, joy, sorrow, sexual desire, and indifference.

The formal organization of "Visage" consists of an exposition followed by four variations, as depicted in Example 30. The statement of the words "parole" or "parol" articulate the division between the exposition and the first three variations. The third and fourth variations are separated by an increasing density of texture

EXAMPLE 30. Luciano Berio, "Visage"

0:00	0:09		3:10		3:29
	syllables, inflections		cry → laugh		"PAROLE"

3:38	5:45	5:50	5:54
nonsense speech	"PAROL"	laugh	"PAROL"

6:04		7:19
syllables, inflections, laugh, wail → cry		AH
		< >

7:30	8:39	8:55	9:08
speech, inflections, laugh	cry	laugh	speech

9:26	9:44	9:52	10:00
laugh	"PAROLE"	speech, laugh	inflections, laugh

10:05	10:17	10:37	10:42	10:50
inflections	inflections	laugh	inflections	inflections

11:00	11:25	11:33	11:40	11:59
inflections	inflections	inflections	inflections	speech

12:30	13:07	14:43
inflections, speech	Duet → Trio	
	[E, OH, AH]	

15:09	15:36	15:50	20:20
Vocal Solo + Speech → Vocal Solo → Chorus			
[E, AH, OH, U]		[AH OH]	
		< > < >	

achieved by overdubbing the voice to produce duet, trio, and choral segments. Whereas the oscillator sounds occur throughout the composition, only the exposition and variations II and III contain the filtered noise bands, so that their absence reinforces the sectional divisions on a purely timbral basis. This secondary timbral structure is in turn supported by the individual durations of each section; the exposition and first three variations last between two and a half and three and a half minutes. Variation IV, however, goes on for seven minutes, twice that of any of the preceding sections. This longer duration reinforces the increasingly dense textures that appear in the last variation. The complex networks of structural relationships are therefore based primarily upon linguistic elements, accompanied by the secondary structural levels of timbre, density, and duration.

In contrast to Berio's process of developing a new language, the Egyptian composer Halim El-Dabh used the ancient Arabic ode "Majnum Leiyla" as the basis for the text of "Leiyla and the Poet" (1961). Two characters, a madman and a poet, try to convince Leiyla to follow two opposing paths. The sound sources employed in this piece include the two men's voices, an oscillator, and excerpts of mid-Eastern music performed on flute, percussion, and string instruments. As in "Visage," the prime structural level involves the text, with the poet's voice differentiated from that of the madman through the addition of reverberation. This distinction between the two characters also exists in the text, for the vocabularies and verb tenses used by the madman and the poet are distinct from one another.

The madman's text contains eight references to himself, usually in the form of the possessive adjective "my," accompanied by eight references to Leiyla. This provides an equal balance between himself and Leiyla. The text of the poet, however, contains fifteen references to himself, all involving the word "my," and thirty-three allusions to Leiyla. Eleven of these are statements of her name while the others are more poetic descriptions such as love, light, sight, desires, heart, and woman. The poet's text is not as self-centered as the madman's, nor are his feelings toward Leiyla as possessive.

The verbs in the madman's text, "shall succumb" and "will love," also support his possessiveness, whereas the poet always speaks in the present tense, employing only the verbs "free" and "love." Both texts begin with the statement of Leiyla's name. The madman ends with the phrase "my Leiyla," while the poet concludes by alluding to Leiyla as "a vision there yonder," putting her out of his reach. The self-centered and possessive character of the madman is epitomized by the manner in which he speaks Leiyla's name; an ominous glissando is inserted between the two syllables, as Leiy∧la.

El-Dabh incorporated this basic structure within a large, sectional formal plan as outlined in Example 31. The oscillator is present throughout most of the piece, but the statements of the initial oscillator melody are reserved for the beginning and conclusion. With the exception of the initial and final sections, mid-Eastern instruments also appear throughout the composition, producing simple thematic and timbral relationships among the nine sections.

The first entrance of the madman and the poet (0:18) contains unintelligible speech, a characteristic later applied predominantely to the madman. The madman also appears more frequently than the poet; this too emphasizes his possessive nature. Structurally, the entire composition revolves around the contrasting of two characters, chiefly on a linguistic level. Although sound sources other than the voice appear throughout the entire work, they do little to reinforce the vocal structure, but serve more to embellish the main material. The only exception to this is the reliance upon the oscillator melody to signify the beginning and end of the composition.

Not all composers dealing with the voice became involved with language and levels of comprehensibility, but the use of these elements as compositional determinants has become increasingly important in many recent tape compositions. Nonetheless, it is not surprising to find Bernard Parmegiani's "Danse" (1962) reflecting the vocal techniques and modifications of the earlier French composers like Pierre Henry. Parmegiani began working at the R.T.F. in 1959, after having spent five years as a television sound engineer. Most of his works are for television and film, his later compositions involving the combination of jazz ensembles with prerecorded tapes. "Danse" employs a textless voice modified by tape transposition and filtering, accompanied by sounds from conventional instruments.

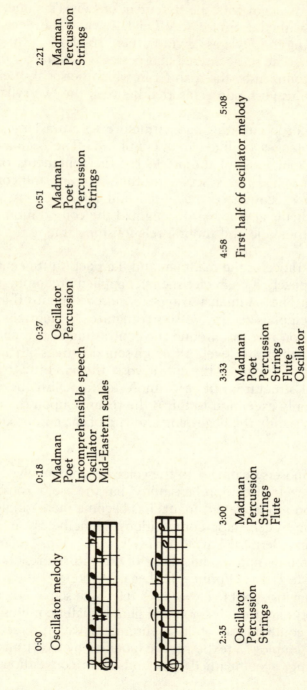

EXAMPLE 31. Halim El-Dabh, "Leiyla and the Poet"

Mel Powell's "Events" (1963), for three prerecorded voices and electronic sounds, is another example of a composition based upon a literary text; in this case, Hart Crane's poem "Legend." "Events" was one of the first works realized at the Yale University Electronic Studio which Powell had established the previous year.

In dealing with Crane's poem Powell did not dissect individual words as Stockhausen had done in "Gesang der Jünglinge." He did change the ordering of the words, however, placing them out of their original context, thereby producing new meanings and a novel interpretation of "Legend." Powell followed to some extent the progression of verses as they occur in the poem, but he emphasized the following words by frequent repetitions: "realities plunge," "silence," "kisses," "twice," "perfect cry," "relentless caper," "legend," and "silent," which is the concluding sound. These words often appear out of their original context, so that the overall effect is that of a collage. Reverberation is usually applied to the voices, causing the individual words to overlap. Overdubbing the vocal parts produces the sound of a massive crowd, and a total loss of intelligibility results.

In "Legend," there is a close relationship between the vocal and electronic sounds. Sometimes it takes the form of a dialogue between the two sources; at others, the filtered, reverberated oscillator frequencies assume a quasi-vocal character. Whereas "Thema" revolves primarily around timbral relationships based on the passage from Joyce, "Events" derives its structural plan from semantic relationships.

Semantics is of prime importance in Herbert Brün's "Futility 1964," produced at the University of Illinois. Brün did his first work in the electronic medium at the Cologne Studio from 1956 to 1958. He moved from there to the newer studio at Munich, and finally accepted a position at the University of Illinois in 1963.

A prerecorded voice reading the composer's poem, is combined with electronic sounds. Since textual comprehension was a major concern, Brün did not juxtapose electronic sounds with the recitation of the poem. Instead, he alternated each line of text with electronic segments. The composer thereby established two structural levels based upon the linguistic structure of the poem and the recurring electronic motives. The isolation of both sound sources insured textual intelligibility, which permitted slight vocal modifications. The addition of reverberation to the voice not only provided a timbral link with the electronic sounds, many of which were reverberated, but also allowed the final vocal fragments to overlap with the beginning of the electronic segments, producing a continuous texture.

A text concerned with the "futility" of verbally explaining the meaning of the accompanying electronic sounds dictated the choice of a dual structural plan in John Cage's "Indeterminacy." The text for this piece consists of Zen parables and personal anecdotes. "Futility 1964" combines two entities, a poem and an electronic composition. Their interaction, although not as extensive as Stockhausen's method of intermodulation, produces a higher degree of intelligibility than does intermodulation. Even though both procedures result in widely differentiated levels of complexity, the trend during the 1960s was to explore possibilities of interaction among sonorous elements.

The influence of Henry and Luening is again evident in "Vocalise" (1964) by the Israeli composer Tzvi Avni. He realized this piece at the Columbia–Princeton Center, and also worked at the electronic studio at the University of Toronto during that same year. "Vocalise" not only shares the same title as Henry's composition from 1952, but both pieces were derived from a textless voice articulating the syllable "ah." Luening's influence can be found in Avni's preference for long melodic vocal lines. Since there is no text, Avni's piece is centered around timbral relationships that result from the combination of vocal and electronic sounds. A timbral continuum is established between these two sound sources so that the application of filtering, modulation, and reverberation to the electronic sounds result in varying degrees of vocal simulation. Reverberation is the only electronic modification used in the voice part, but a choral effect is achieved by multiple overdubs of the solo voice. Both the electronic and vocal parts contain motivic repetitions, a unifying technique frequently employed by composers at the Columbia Studio.

J. K. Randall's "Mudgett: Monologues by a Mass Murderer" (1965) was the first computer composition realized at Princeton University in conjunction with the Columbia–Princeton Center. In addition to computer-generated sounds with their accompanying transformations, a prerecorded voice free from any electronic modifications is employed. Juxtaposition of the vocal parts is the only vocal alteration. At times, this contributes to a mild collage effect.

Only the first two movements of "Mudgett" have been completed, "Electronic Prelude," and "Toronto." The first one contains only computer generated sounds. Randall refers to the text as a "Collage of literary documents unconnected with the events which they have been compounded to narrate . . ." Herman Webster Mudgett was in fact a mass murderer whose real name was Dr. H. H. Holmes. He was executed in 1896.

The vocal part of "Toronto" contains long melodic lines, and when a second voice is superposed, it is differentiated from the previous voice by the combined use of speaking and singing: one voice speaks while the other sings. The character of the vocal parts creates an Expressionistic atmosphere reminiscent of Arnold Schoenberg's music in the 1930s. The treatment of the voice and electronic sounds is unexpectedly traditional, with the computer accompanying the vocal materials. This accompaniment not only assumes a periodic rhythmic design, but the resultant chordal combinations are sometimes quite tonal, and reflect the harmonic vocabulary of the early twentieth century. The computer actually duplicates the pitches of the voice to create an even closer relationship between those two parts.

Kenneth Gaburo incorporated jazz elements in some of his tape pieces realized at the University of Illinois. "Lemon Drops" is one such example. Another is "Exit Music II: Fat Millie's Lament" (1965). Both these pieces were completed in the same year. The use of voice in the latter work is strongly suggestive of the rhythmic patterns resulting from Steve Reich's employment of tape loops and phasing techniques in "Come Out." Gaburo initiated two separate rhythmic parts in "Fat Millie's Lament." One pattern was derived from percussive and bell sounds, the other from a textless voice, sometimes transformed by tape transposition. The rhythmic patterns reflect African and Latin jazz influences. They comprise the first part of the composition, and periodically undergo subtle rhythmic changes.

One of the most striking features of this piece which immediately attracts the listener's attention is the relatively low amplitude of the rhythmic patterns. Since the rhythmic variations are very slight, the very quiet entrance of an unaltered excerpt from Morgan Powell's big band composition "Odomtn," comes as a surprise. Gradually the big band sound completely masks the initial rhythmic sequences which retain their low dynamic level; but eventually "Odomtn" disappears. As the jazz excerpt fades out the rhythmic patterns regain their audibility, finally giving way to silence and the conclusion of the composition.

The structural organization of "Fat Millie's Lament" is primarily based upon continual repetitions of rhythmic ideas contrasted against a melodic fragment. Concurrent with this plan is the prevailing low amplitude level, disrupted during the jazz band segment, which establishes a high degree of correspondence between these two formal frameworks. Aside from Steve Reich's "Come Out," this piece is one of the few pieces to employ the voice as a source of rhythmic ideas rather than to establish timbral or semantic relationships.

Mimaroglu undertook to set a poem by the Turkish poet Orhan Veli Kanik in his "Prélude No. XII" (1967), which he realized at the Columbia Studio in New York. Electronic and transformed piano sounds occur throughout the composition, frequently creating some ambiguity as to the identity of the source due to subtle timbral modifications. A reverberated voice reciting Kanik's poem appears near the conclusion of the prélude, accompanied by concrète and electronic sounds. Any structure revolving around timbral relationships would seemingly be restricted to nonvocal sources, whereas the function of the voice is to read the text. Since the poem is read in Turkish, however, the listener who does not understand that language will probably be more aware of the sonorous qualities of the text. Although this does not necessarily indicate that the composer formulated the prélude's structure on this premise, a knowledge of Turkish would certainly provoke a different response from a listener so that the question of semantics as opposed to the pure sonorous quality of individual words arises here. The textual portion of Mimaroglu's prelude appears to share the same function as speech in Berio's "Visage." In the latter composition speech cannot convey specific meanings because of its synthetic construction; the results are the same, although for another reason, in Mimaroglu's piece.

Luigi Nono, in "Contrappunto dialettico alla Mente" (1968), incorporates elements found in earlier works of Stockhausen and Berio. The voices of four women and one man are combined with concrète and electronic sounds, while tape transformations and mixing contribute to the degree of speech comprehension, and changes of texture. Vocal elements interspersed with electronic sonorities yield additional speech permutations like those found in Stockhausen's "Gesang"; white noise, for instance, appears in conjunction with aspirate speech sounds. The voice is further extended by the use of laughter and other nonspeech elements. This reflects some of the methods Berio used in "Visage."

"Hymn of Creation" (1969) by Ralph Swickard demonstrates a novel method of establishing a direct correlation between the voice and electronic sounds. Electronic devices have been invented that convert the frequency and amplitude of an analog sound to correspondent control voltages. These devices are commonly referred to as frequency followers and envelope followers. Swickard applied these processes to the voice; the resultant control voltages operated voltage-controlled oscillators and filters. The entire composition was realized on the Moog synthesizer.

The narrator's text was derived from a hymn contained in the *Rigveda*, an ancient Indian religious manuscript. Vocal modifications include reverberation, ring modulation, tape delay, and juxtaposition of textual segments. The text remains comprehensible despite a multitude of transformations, although new word meanings do proceed from textual fragmentation and superposition.

A gradual dissolution of textual comprehension takes place in Alice Shield's "The Transformation of Ani" (1970), also composed at the Columbia–Princeton Center. The voice, accompanied by electronically generated sounds, undergoes the complete range of modifications including transposition, reverberation, ring modulation, and filtering. The text consists of an excerpt from the Egyptian *Book of the Dead*. This piece is constructed on the principle of sectionalization, with the divisions articulated by alternating the text with electronic and greatly modified vocal sounds.

"The Transformation of Ani" begins with modified vocal sounds, followed by a reverberated recitation of a textual segment that is entirely comprehensible and devoid of extraneous sounds. Its subsequent appearances, however, mark an increasing verbal fragmentation, and a greater emphasis on the techniques of tape transposition, juxtaposition, and the use of electronic sounds. The text's third and final entry displays the piece's most complex vocal textures, accompanied by many unintelligible textual passages. In spite of the piece's gradual progression toward incomprehensibility, semantics and timbre are treated separately. The former obviously is associated with the literary excerpts, while the emphasis on vocal transformations resulting in timbral differentiations is limited to those sections not involved with the transmission of the text.

This concludes our survey of solo tape compositions. Of particular significance is the number of pieces that employ either the human voice or musical instruments as sonorous sources, which indicates the existence of a sense of tradition among composers. The rise of musique concrète and electronic music—foreshadowed by Russolo, Varèse, and Cage—was the result of a growing awareness of all types of sounds. Although new techniques of sound modification extended composers' vocabularies tremendously, many could only proceed very cautiously due to their traditional musical training. It was not coincidental that Pierre Schaeffer's 1948 noise études were produced by a recording engineer.

The use of musical instruments or voice, provided the perfect point of departure in composers' search for new sounds. Since scientific method has shown that experimentation with known quantities will eventually lead to the unknown, it is not surprising to find new music following such a rational approach. Familiar sounds provided the basis for the work done at the two earliest centers of tape composition, Paris (1948) and New York (1951). When the Cologne studio was permanently established in 1953, the time for purely electronically generated sounds had come. Yet the most important composer to emerge from the German studio, Karlheinz Stockhausen, had received his initial exposure to this new medium at the R.T.F. The processes of additive synthesis he employed in his early studies were derived from the simplest electronic signal, the sine wave.

Even though a great deal of emphasis has been placed on the kinds of sound sources employed in a composition, it is their relation to one another that poses the first significant problem for the composer, for it is from these considerations that a structure will evolve. Timbre has assumed an increasingly important role within the electronic medium, and the search for new timbres has often resulted in an unusual treatment of melody and rhythm. The voice is probably the most volatile sound source because of its wide range of applications and structural possibilities. Phonetics, syntax and semantics have all been employed as structural determinants in tape compositions. When combined with electronic or other concrète sources, complex relationships are frequently established on more than one level of organization.

The ideal machine for use within the electronic medium may prove to be the computer. This is the belief of many composers, and there are substantial reasons to support their position. The increasingly lower cost of electronic parts has enabled a few manufacturers to offer computers in the form of kits. The speed and precision afforded by computers would be advantageous in both studio and live performance. Finally, most universities already possess computer terminals.

The type of equipment employed in the realization of a work does not automatically guarantee its success or failure, but does usually influence the composer's approach to the organization of his materials. Within the solo tape medium, the possibilities of formal organization are quite varied because of the wide range of available sound sources and the many ways of controlling and transforming these sounds. Part II will include the additional organizational procedures resulting from the presence of a live performer playing or singing in conjunction with a prerecorded tape.

Discography

AVNI, TZNI
"Vocalise," Turn. TV 34004S

BERIO, LUCIANO
"Visage," Turn. TV 34046S

BRÜN, HERBERT
"Futility 1964,"
Hel. HS—25047

EL-DABH, HALIM
"Leiyla and the Poet,"
Col. MS 6566

GABURO, KENNETH
"Exit Music II: Fat Millie's
Lament," None. 71199

LUENING, OTTO
"In the Beginning,"
2—CRI 268

LUENING, OTTO AND VLADIMIR
USSACHEVSKY
"Incantation," Desto
6466

MIMAROGLU, ILHAN
"Prelude No. XII," Turn.
TV 34177S

NONO, LUIGI
"Contrappunto dialettico alla
Mente," DGG 2543006

PARMEGIANI, BERNARD
"Danse," Can. CE
31025

POUSSEUR, HENRI
"Trois visages de Liège,"
   Col. MS 7051

POWELL, MEL
"Events," CRI—S227

RANDALL, J. K.
"Mudgett: Monologues by a
   Mass Murderer," None.
   71245

SCHAEFFER, PIERRE AND
   PIERRE HENRY
"Symphonie pour un homme
   seul," DUC—9

SHIELDS, ALICE
"The Transformation of
   Ani," 2—CRI 268

STOCKHAUSEN, KARLHEINZ
"Gesang der Jünglinge,"
   DG 138811 SLPM

SWICKARD, RALPH
"Hymn of Creation,"
   Orion 7021

VANDELLE, ROMUALD
"Crucifixion" (extracts),
   BAM LD—071

Part Two

Music for Performers and Tape

Progress in the physical and mechanical sciences determines a progress in art . . . .

Carlos Chavez, 1957

CHAPTER FOUR

MUSIC FOR VOICE AND TAPE

COMPOSITIONS THAT INVOLVE a live vocalist necessarily dictate structural relations different from those encountered in the preceding chapters. Electronic modification of the voice is impossible in this medium. The composer is therefore limited to two manners of textual treatment. The first is to follow the text as written, so that the semantics and syntax remain intact. The second involves either the dissolution of individual words into syllables and phonemes or the rearrangement of word orderings. Compared to compositions that employ recorded voice, both procedures establish various levels of meaning that offer a limited range of textual transformations.

The first compositions combining performers and electronic tape were written for conventional instruments. Edgard Varèse, who began to experiment with this idea in 1949, was one of the first to realize a composition, "Déserts," in this medium. During the early 1950's works by Badings, Varèse, Luening, and Ussachevsky appeared, all incorporating instruments with tape. By the following decade this new form of composition had been adopted by many composers, but it was not until 1958 that the voice received such attention.

John Cage produced the "Aria with Fontana Mix" in 1958 at the RAI studio in Milan. Completed the same year as Berio's "Thema," Cage's piece results from the juxtaposition of two compositions, "Aria" and "Fontana Mix." The latter work has been discussed in the second chapter. Indeterminacy pervades both the "Aria" and the tape collage; its text consists of words, syllables, vowels, and consonants from five languages: English, French, Italian, Armenian, and Russian. In addition, the vocalist is required to produce nonmusical sounds such as finger snaps and pops.

Cage did not want the text to be intelligible, and it is unlikely that anyone could sufficiently understand the five languages. Similarly, in "Vocalism Ai" of Toru Takemitsu, the Japanese word "ai" contains the same diphthong also found in Romance and Germanic languages. The degree of semantic confusion in "Aria" varies for the individual listener, so that each one can supply his own structural relations. This unique condition stems from Cage's preoccupation with the indeterminate procedures that permeate all aspects of the "Aria."

In the "Aria," Cage denoted ten different singing styles by various colors. The choice of styles is left to the discretion of the performer, so that the results are unpredictable, or indeterminate. Pitch and duration are graphically represented, but no dynamic indications are given. The "Fontana Mix" tape plays without interruption; the voice enters at approximate temporal intervals that are based upon a visual interpretation of the score.

Even though Cage employed a variety of languages as an obstacle to comprehension, all of them are contemporary. In contrast, Ussachevsky, in "Creation: Prologue" (1961), superposed Latin and Akkadian, the language of Babylon. He chose these languages in order to suggest an early civilization which symbolizes creation of the world. Ussachevsky was not concerned with semantics, and achieved a dramatic effect with the text, which he reinforced by the use of white noise at the beginning and conclusion of the composition. Slowly rising and falling envelope contours applied to the noise produce the impression of the sea and of creation.

Aside from a few programmatic electronic sounds, the remainder of the tape displays Ussachevsky's predilection for instrumental timbres. Silence is also incorporated to accentuate an a cappella choral style reminiscent of liturgical music from the Middle Ages and Renaissance. Many of the tape entries occur as periodic punctuations to enhance the overall dramatic effect maintained by the text.

Textual treatment in these works of Cage and Ussachevsky is similar to that found in compositions employing electromechanical modifications to recorded vocal materials. The most obvious manifestation of this phenomenon is an emphasis upon timbre rather than meaning. Milton Babbitt's "Vision and Prayer"

(1961), based on the poem by Dylan Thomas, contains a more conventional use of the voice. The text is not permutated, and its comprehensibility is maintained throughout the entire composition.

Dylan Thomas wrote "Vision and Prayer" in 1944 as part of his fourth book of verse, *Death and Entrances*, which was published two years later. It is a religious poem in two sections; one deals with physical birth, the other with spiritual birth. The most striking feature of the poem is its syllabic structure, which is presented in a format that foreshadows the concrète poetry that would appear in the next two decades. Each line of "Vision" is characterized by either the addition or the elimination of one syllable, which produced diamond and pyramid forms. The first section, "Vision", contains six verses of sixteen or seventeen lines each. The individual verses begin and end with monosyllabic words, while the intervening lines progressively increase in length by one syllable until a maximum of eight, nine or ten syllables is reached. At this point the process is reversed: the length of each line is progressively reduced by one syllable. "Prayer", the second half of the poem, incorporates the reverse procedure, so that the longest lines appear at the beginning and end of each verse.

Literary critics have ascribed two meanings to the diamond and pyramid shapes of the stanzas; both interpretations are supported by the content of the poem. The religious nature of "Vision and Prayer," in which the geometric forms are considered to be representations of a Communion cup or the Holy Grail, represents the first of these. The second is a secular interpretation of the shapes which depend upon the syllabic controls within each verse. This interpretation considers the linear expansions and contractions to be analogous to those of a woman in labor.

Babbitt's piece adheres to the syllabic structure of the poem on three levels: phrase length, tempo, and duration of verses. The most obvious parallel between the poem and the composition is the conformity of the vocal part to the linear divisions within each stanza. These divisions are articulated by musical phrases of varying lengths. The vocal writing is necessarily syllabic, and the successive lines of the poem are delineated by rests.

Textual contractions and expansions also determine the tempo and duration structures, both of which are organized within clearly established limits. Babbitt employs the following tempo scale to the quarter note: M.M. $\quarternote$ = 60, 75, 76, 80, 95, 100, 120, 125, 160 and

180. The durations of verses fall within a similar continuum defined in seconds: 108, 78, 77, 66, 65, 58, 57, 56, 50, 48 and 47. Example 32 illustrates the distribution of verses within these continua.

A tendency to organize stanzas into small groups of similar character is immediately apparent to the score reader, and two-thirds of the composition is treated in this manner. From this organization it is evident that the slow tempo markings are generally associated with longer sections (verses 1, 2, 5 and 12), whereas the faster tempo markings usually result in shorter sections (verses 4, 8, 9 and 10).

"Vision and Prayer" gradually proceeds from these slow, long sections to the quick, short sections, and concludes with a recapitulation of the piece's initial characteristics. Babbitt preserves the undulating nature of the poem by distributing the verses out of sequence within the tempo and duration continua, thus effecting a disjunct rather than smooth progression along these scales. A few carefully chosen vocal styles intensify this movement. The first verse is spoken and the second is dominated by *Sprechstimme*. A traditional singing style is subsequently employed until the final verse, in which *Sprechstimme* and speech are the sole elements.

The electronic sounds assume an instrumental quality reminiscent of Babbitt's earlier tape pieces. Rhythmic motives also recur. The piece's characteristic expansion and contraction is enhanced by their restriction to a few verses. Quick tremolos in the third, fourth, seventh and ninth verses illustrate this motivic repetition. Furthermore, these stanzas are related because they comprise the longest (verse 3) and the shortest (verses 4 and 9) sections. The composer's treatment of rhythmic motives as functions of duration enables him to extend the limits of the structural relationships that exist in the initial organizational plan.

EXAMPLE 32.   Milton Babbitt, "Vision and Prayer"

Tempo (M.M. ♩)	60	75	76	80	95	100	120	125	160	180
Verse	1, 12	5	2	7	3	6	4	9	8, 10	11

Duration (sec.)	108	78-77	66-65	58-56	50-47
Verse	3	1, 12	2, 5	6, 7, 11	4, 8, 9, 10

In the early 1960s, the electronic studio at the University of Illinois acquired a reputation as one of the most important studios in America. A wide range of interests—including Hiller's concentration upon computer applications and Kenneth Gaburo's involvement with phonetics and language—coexisted at the Urbana studio. "Antiphony III" for chorus and tape (1962), in which vocal and electronic sounds appear on the tape was among Gaburo's initial electronic compositions to be realized at Illinois. Consequently, Gaburo emerged as one of the first American composers to follow the vocal tradition established by Stockhausen and Berio during the late 1950s. "Antiphony III", derived from a poem by Virginia Hommel, employs vocal transformations that are reminiscent of "Gesang der Jünglinge," "Thema" and "Visage." The word orderings are changed and the words themselves reduced to phonemes, so that the sounds vacillate between meaning and nonsense. Tape transposition and reverberation are applied to the prerecorded voice, so that further emphasis is placed on vocal timbres.

The vocal part consists of speaking, whispering and singing. Some of the more obvious phonetic reductions are: pea(rl), whi(te), set(t), s(pe)c(k)s, sal(t), (s)al(t), a(gain), t(ime), (be)tw(een), t(wo), st(ill), ch(ill) and 't(il). The portions of the words enclosed in parentheses are not articulated; rather, they indicate the words from which the phonemes are derived. The frequent occurrence of "s" and "t" results in additional phonetic relations: s(e)t, s(peck)s, s(al)t and (be)t(ween). The isolation of "s" (specks) and "t" (time, two, between), in conjunction with their combination (still, salt, set), establishes timbral associations similar to those found in "Thema".

Gaburo applies these relations to electronic sounds by appropriately modifying noise sources. The "s" is obtained by filtering white noise, whereas modified and filtered noise with sharp attack characteristics produce the "t" sound. Noise formants associated with p(earl) and wh(ite) are derived from electronic sources in similar fashions. Analogous procedures were employed in "Gesang der Jünglinge" in order to establish timbral connections between the vocal and electronic sources.

Lejaren Hiller, in collaboration with Robert Baker at the University of Illinois, combined computer with voice in the "Computer Cantata" (1963). The "Cantata," Hiller's first major computer piece after the "Illiac Suite" (1957), employed the machine for the derivation of musical elements: pitch, duration, amplitude and timbre. Although Hiller had used similar procedures in the "Illiac Suite," in some sections of the "Cantata," he used the computer as an additional sound source.

The "Cantata" is in five main movements or strophes. Each of the first two strophes is preceded by a "prolog," and the last two are followed by an "epilog." Strophe III, the central section of the composition, is accompanied by both a "prolog" and an "epilog," to form a classical arch structure of eleven sections. The appearance of the voice is restricted to the five strophes. The text is based on computer generated sequences of English phonemes. Woodwind, brass, string, and percussion instruments, as well as the electronic Theremin or Ondes Martenot, are used periodically throughout the piece. The tape consists of three categories of electronic sounds: (a) sine, square, and sawtooth waves, (b) white and filtered noise, and (c) computer generated sounds. Such a wide variety of sound sources can produce many timbral differentiations.

Since a computer may be programmed to compose, that is, to determine pitch, duration, and so on, a knowledge of mathematics and logic operations is essential for the execution of such programs. Information theory and probability distribution are two valuable compositional tools for a composer who wishes to realize these processes. The choice of a multitude of timbral sources in the "Cantata" reflects a fundamental concept of information theory: as structural ordering increases the amount of information decreases. In the present example, timbre represents information. Repetition of timbral combinations, or a high level of structural ordering, results in a decrease of information. By employing a variety of sound sources, Hiller and Baker were able to control the amount of information disseminated to the audience. Information theory may be applied to any musical element, including pitch, duration and amplitude.

Probability distribution, frequently used by Xenakis, derives from mathematical formulae that determine the number of times an event should theoretically occur within a given time period. Probability theory determines the chance that, for example, a particular melodic pattern may appear within a composition. There is a greater probability that arpeggiated triads will occur within a Mozart sonata than in a motet by Machaut. Like information theory, probability distribution may be applied to any musical element.

As previously mentioned, Hiller and Baker structured the eleven sections of the "Cantata" in the arch form. The composers applied to the strophes a probability distribution of pitches derived from an excerpt of Charles Ives' "Three Places In New England." In the "Prolog" to Strophe I and the "Epilog" to Strophe V Hiller and Baker—continuing to draw upon preexisting compositions as sources of organizational procedures—employed durational scales like those found in Oliver Messiaen's "Modes de Valeurs et d'Intensités" (1948). A progression of note durations was obtained by incrementing successive degrees of the duration scale by one sixteenth note, e.g., ♪, ♪, ♪., ♩, ♩♪, ♩., etc., or by one-third of a triplet, e.g., ♪, ♩, ♩ and ○. Organization of the "Prolog" to Strophe II and the "Epilog" to Strophe IV was based upon the compositional processes used by Pierre Boulez in "Structures for Two Pianos" (1952), which is a totally serialized work. Computer generated sounds, whose frequencies are obtained from equal-tempered tuning systems of nine to fifteen pitches per octave, constitute the sonorous material of the "Prolog" and "Epilog" to Strophe III. The pitch durations are essentially the same as those of the other "Prologs" and "Epilogs." Example 33 illustrates the complete arch form of the "Cantata."

The phonemic structure of its text resembles the vocal part of Berio's "Visage," for both pieces create a unique language. Although it is acceptable to construct a synthetic language to be used in a text, the composer who wishes to do so must possess a thorough knowledge of phonetics. Since he seldom does, the most common procedure among composers is to use a traditional text which can then be syntactically transformed.

Charles Hamm, a former colleague of Hiller's at the University of Illinois, utilized "Canto XLIX" of Ezra Pound for his piece "Canto" (1963). Completed the same year as the "Computer Canta," "Canto" includes tape and soprano, speaker, flute, clarinet, saxophone, prepared piano and percussion. The classical arch form, although it is only implied in the structure of the poem, governs the formal organization of the work.

The most striking feature of the poem is the inclusion of a series of Chinese words near the end. Pound had been interested in Chinese culture since 1909, so the appearance of these elements in his "Canto XLIX" (1948) is not surprising. In Hamm's piece, the Chinese segment is treated as the pivotal point of the structural organization. The arch form is articulated by alternating the phrases of the poem between the speaker and the singer throughout most of the first stanza. This is followed by the increased juxtaposi-

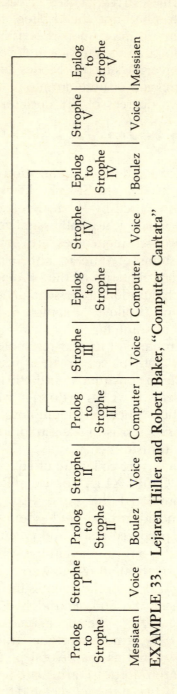

EXAMPLE 33.   Lejaren Hiller and Robert Baker, "Computer Cantata"

tion of the vocalists, which culminates in dense textures at the Chinese section. A return to the initial format in the final stanzas completes the arch form.

With the exception of the opening and closing verses, the composer freely rearranges the sequence both of words and of phrases, sometimes superposing textual elements to such an extent that all intelligibility is lost. The Chinese segment is a collage, and additional emphasis on the words is supplied by their appearance on the prerecorded tape. In spite of these textual modifications, much of the poem is comprehensible. The voices usually predominate, and the instruments are treated as accompaniment.

In 1963–4, Milton Babbitt produced "Philomel" for voice and tape on which he included speech and electronic sounds. "Philomel" is derived from a poem by John Hollander. Since the poet conceived of the work in "musical" terms, he included in it the operatic elements of recitative and aria. In addition, Hollander employed alliterative and onomatopoetic techniques which resulted in a sonorous similarity between "Philomel" and Berio's "Thema". The following are examples of these procedures, taken from the beginning of the poem: Eeee . . . , Feee . . . , Feee . . . l; true trees . . . true tears . . . trees tear . . . Tereus; feel . . . filaments . . . feeling . . . felony . . . Philomels.

The performer delivers the text in a traditional manner. Babbitt incorporates singing, speaking and *Sprechstimme* as he did in "Vision and Prayer," and the poem again remains intact and comprehensible. The tape contains a commentary on the text, and a recorded voice supplies textual fragments that are occasionally modified by tape transposition, echo, overdubbing and electronic modulation.

These electronic sounds typify Babbitt's use of the RCA synthesizer: they are instrumental in nature, and generally incorporate precise pitches. Non-pitched percussive (drum-like) and filtered noise sounds appear when the emphasis of the poem is on despair, terror and the errors of the Gods. Other electronic sounds (string-, woodwind-, and brass-like) assume the role of an orchestral accompaniment.

As he did in "Vision and Prayer," Babbitt closely adheres to the formal organization of Hollander's "Philomel." The poem is the center of attention while, as previously noted, the taped voice functions as a commentary. The myth of Philomel is of Greek origin, and the relationship between performer and prerecorded solo voice reflects one element of ancient Greek drama. Another ingredient of Greek drama is recitative, here treated by Babbitt as *Sprechstimme* and normal speech.

Kenneth Gaburo, in "Antiphony IV" (1967), also combines live and taped voice. Additional electronic sounds are recorded on tape, and piccolo, bass trombone and string bass extend the non-electronic timbral resources. As in "Antiphony III," Gaburo deals with language on a phonemic level: he groups phonemes according to their characteristic sounds. Relationships are established among phonemes and pitch, amplitude, duration and timbre to reveal sonorous and technical similarities with the vocal compositions of Stockhausen and Berio. Differentiation between live and taped sounds is accomplished by physically separating them within the performance area.

Compositional controls applied to basic linguistic elements characterize many electronic pieces produced during the 1960's. However, Hiller did not use these techniques in his theatre piece, "An Avalanche" (1968). The piece is based on a text by Frank Parman, and includes a pitchman (speaker), prima donna, player piano, percussionist and a prerecorded tape of quotations from Henry Miller, Frank Lloyd Wright, Frank Parman, John Cage, Louis Aragon (Dada Manifesto) and Lenin. "Avalanche" is divided into three sections; the first and last function as introduction ("Getting Ready For It") and reprise ("Cleaning Up The Mess").

Individual structural schemes are applied to the four performance parts and the tape, but the organization of tempi serves as a foundation upon which all the structural levels are built. The main part of "Avalanche", section two, is subdivided into twelve thirty-second segments characterized by gradual acceleration at the rate of M.M. $\downarrow$ = 12, i.e., $\downarrow$ = 60, 72, 84. . . . 192. In the percussion part, for example, the metronomic changes correspond to the stylistic changes: from slow rock to slow blues, slow fox-trot, cha-cha, medium fox-trot, bossa nova, medium rock, polka, medium jazz, rhumba, fast rock, and fast jazz.

The part of the prima donna contains two structures. First, the modulation by ascending half-steps at the beginning of each of the twelve sections reinforces the underlying pattern of tempo changes. Second, a succession of ten arias, each lasting thirty-six seconds, is superposed on the tempo structure. Each aria is delineated by an individual singing style, in the same procedure employed by John Cage in "Aria."

Formal organization increases in complexity throughout the player piano part, where thematic content, amplitude, and density are treated as functions of duration. Unlike the previously established twelve-division tempo scale of the percussion part, the player piano score is composed of eighteen sections, each one twenty seconds long. The piano plays nine autonomous melodic lines that are polyphonically treated, so that successive melodic entrances produce corresponding increases in density. Intervals of entry are equally spaced at forty seconds; that is, they occur in two of the eighteen sections. The first piano line, played throughout the entire piece, therefore contains eighteen twenty second segments. The second melodic line enters forty seconds later and contains only sixteen segments. Each successive line contains two segments less than its predecessor, which results in a uniform increase of density from one to nine parts.

Melodic fragments extracted from standard symphonic literature are randomly distributed among the twenty second segments. Similarly, the amplitude is changed every twenty seconds. The durational ordering of small sections within the piano part regulates thematic occurrences, amplitude and density.

The prerecorded tape of spoken excerpts enters at one minute intervals, but the entries are not synchronized with the periodic changes of tempo that occur every thirty seconds within the percussion part. The tape first appears at $0:20$, and the subsequent entries are at $1:20$, $2:20$, $3:20$, $4:20$ and $5:20$. Individual durations of the taped excerpts are not subject to any compositional controls but obviously must be less than one minute long.

The text of the pitchman opens with statements concerning the cultural explosion and mixed media, which are seen as products of socio-economic changes within American Society. He speaks of the "average," civic minded American who actively supports the erection of Urban Centers as a means of eliminating slum areas. The Civic Theatre, where these new concepts will replace the old artistic standards, is the immediate result of these activities. Civic Theatres are subsequently referred to as "New Art factories." The federal government's resistance to the cultural explosion is the catalyst for the American Cultural Revolution.

The structural organization of "Avalanche" is depicted in Example 34. It is truly polyphonic, and the multiplicity of texts

Time	0:00	0:30	1:00	1:30	2:00	2:30	3:00	3:30	4:00	4:30	5:00	5:30	6:00
Tempo ♩=	60 slow rock	72 slow blues	84 slow fox-trot	96 cha-cha	108 med. fox-trot	120 bossa nova	132 med. rock	144 polka	156 med. jazz	168 rhumba	180 fast rock	192 fast jazz	
Aria	1 ——→	2 ——→	3 ——→	4 ——→	5 ——→	6 ——→	7 ——→	8 ——→	9 ——→	10			
Key	C	D♭	D	E♭	E	F	F♯	G	A♭	A	B♭	B	
Tape	1 ——	2 ——		3 ——			4 ——		5 ——		6 ——		
Piano													

EXAMPLE 34. Lejaren Hiller, "An Avalanche"

suggests the thirteenth century motet, in which two texts, Latin and French, were often juxtaposed. Further distinction between the texts was achieved by the use of contrasting subject matter, religious and secular. A polyphonic texture was maintained by relating the two vocal lines to a third, instrumental part. In addition to coexistence of two distinct vocal melodies, languages and textual materials, the texts were frequently arranged so that selected words from one text were associated with those in the contrasting text to yield new meanings. Due to the dual nature of the subject matter, the new word associations were often comical or satirical, which was an effect that the composer intentionally created.

Similar correspondences appear in "Avalanche": multiplicity of texts, four languages (English, French, Italian and German), contrasting subject matter, structural relations between the textual parts and percussion based upon tempo changes, and new, unexpected word associations. Some of the resultant interrelationships between the texts of the pitchman, prima donna and prerecorded excerpts are shown in Example 35.

The theatrical proportions of "Avalanche" are common to many pieces, not necessarily electronic, which were composed from the mid 1960's onward. Although not all these pieces are intended as commentaries on contemporary society, they are

EXAMPLE 35. Lejaren Hiller, "An Avalanche"

Pitchman	Prima Donna	Prerecorded Tape
look this way	mine eyes	
American tradition	Hallelujah	
acoustical controls	God, King of Kings	
federal & state funds as Slum Clearance	ha-ha-ha-ha...	
city managers		manifest in Vivaldi
artistic		Italian troubadors
asymmetric interior		poetry, music
Animal tradition	Toréador	plus de littérateurs
Private Initiative	songe (dream)	plus de religions
artistic achievements	combattent (fighter)	plus de proletaire
Americans	oeil noir (black eye)	plus de bourgeois

nonetheless an outgrowth of changing social, political, economic and aesthetic values within the post-World War II generation. Although this phenomenon is not peculiar to the twentieth century, it does give some indication of these composers' consciousness and of their attitudes toward "art."

Like "Avalanche," "The Nude Paper Sermon" (1968–9) by Eric Salzman is a theatre piece comprised of an actor, a Renaissance consort, chorus, and electronic tape. The Renaissance instruments are racket, dulcian, recorder, gemshorn, krummhorn, korthalt, shawm, rauschpfeife, viola da gamba, lute and portative organ. "Three Madrigals" by John Ashbery and "The Nude Paper Sermon" by Steven Wade constitute the text. Electronic sounds from oscillators and noise generators make up a thin textured accompaniment; these sounds are always treated as secondary to the vocal and instrumental parts.

Most significant, however, are the ways in which "The Nude Paper Sermon" may be performed. It exists in two versions, as a live theatre piece and as a recording. The composer proceeded to organize the piece as a series of separate events recorded on individual tracks. The tracks were mixed to produce a two channel recording, a typical commercial recording industry procedure. "The Nude Paper Sermon," a commission from Nonesuch records, was realized expressly for this medium.

The text is also handled like that of "An Avalanche." Conversations, speeches and songs are juxtaposed in such a way that only isolated words and phrases retain their intelligibility. Again, humorous and satirical word associations frequently result. Conversely, the choral settings of the Ashbery "Madrigals" are in the sixteenth century style, so that the Renaissance seems to have been transported to the twentieth century via the recording medium. Salzman considers this phenomenon to be a positive effect that the record industry has had upon music. Smooth timbral transitions are generally maintained, and the sermon, delivered by the actor, functions as a point of reference around which all the parts gravitate.

The clear, formal organization of Ralph Swickard's music can be seen in his "Sermons of St. Francis" (1968), for narrator and tape. Sectional divisions based upon timbral repetitions and combinations constitute the basic structural level. The text is comprehensible and the tape appears as an accompaniment. A low, sustained pitch marks the beginning of "Sermons," and the first section is characterized by the predominance of low frequencies. The Moog synthesizer is the sole source of sounds (some of which approximate instrumental timbres of strings, winds and percussion), and of modifications.

A contrasting section follows, in which high frequencies occur most often. Reverberated and modulated textual excerpts, juxtaposed with the discourse of the narrator, appear with electronic sounds on the tape. The final section incorporates both high and low frequencies from the preceding sections, but the prerecorded voice is limited to a single reverberated fragment. Recapitulation of the opening timbres concludes the piece. Repetition of timbral combinations and the use of instrumental timbres are representative aspects of Swickard's work at the Columbia–Princeton Center in 1964.

Vocal transformations by electro-mechanical processes in compositions for vocalist and tape—a technique originally employed by European composers in Cologne, Milan and Paris—are often replaced by extensive manipulation of the text's phonemic structure, as we have seen in the works of Gaburo and Hiller. The inclusion of a live performer within the electronic medium is another important direction in which composers moved during the 1950's, thereby helping to eliminate one of the critics' major complaints about the new music: they said that concert hall performances that consisted only of tape recorders and loudspeakers produced a traumatic effect upon most audiences, who are conditioned to expect the presence of live performers. For this reason many composers considered music for tape to be more appropriate for radio broadcast than for performance in a concert hall. By combining performers with tape, composers broadened the popular appeal of electronic music to traditionally oriented audiences and critics alike.

Discography

BABBITT, MILTON
  "Philomel," AR 654083

"Vision and Prayer," 2—CRI 268

BADINGS, HENK
"Armageddon," Point. 101

CAGE, JOHN
"Aria with Fontana
Mix," Main. 5005

GABURO, KENNETH
"Antiphony
III," None. 71199

"Antiphony
IV," None. 71199

HAMM, CHARLES
"Canto," Hel. HS—25047

HILLER, LEJAREN
"An Avalanche,"
Hel. HS—2549006

HILLER, LEJAREN AND ROBERT
BAKER
"Computer
Cantata," CRI S—310

SALZMAN, ERIC
"The Nude Paper
Sermon," None. 71231

SWICKARD, RALPH
"Sermons of St.
Francis," Orion 7021

USSACHEVSKY, VLADIMIR
"Creation:
Prologue," Col.
MS—6566

CHAPTER FIVE

MUSIC FOR INSTRUMENTS AND TAPE

COMPOSITIONS FOR VOICE AND TAPE are likely to be structured upon textual or linguistic elements, whereas the substitution of the voice by instruments requires other methods of formal organization. The alternation between instruments and tape establishes timbral and textural associations that function as components of a large structural scheme. Edgard Varèse was the first to attempt to combine these two sonorous categories. His symphonic work "Déserts" (1949–54) was the result. Tape sounds establish timbral relations with the orchestra by the presence of modified instrumental sonorities subjected to filtering, reverberation, and modulatory processes. Electronically produced and concrète sounds appear in conjunction with each other, so that differentiation of the taped materials provides additional sonorous relations.

"Déserts" is divided into seven segments that are dominated by orchestral instruments that appear almost twice as often as taped sounds; they last approximately 14.5 minutes as compared to 8.5 minutes. The significance of the instrumental sections is further demonstrated by an arch framework: orchestra, tape, orchestra, tape, orchestra, tape, orchestra. The initial and final instrumental parts last about three minutes each, whereas the durations of the second and third orchestral sections are in great contrast: seven and a half minutes to one. Balanced durational units are also found in the tape part, composed of similar lengths of two, three and a half, and three minutes. The absence of significant temporal differentiation within the taped sections helps to articulate the structural importance of the orchestral segments, which exhibit real temporal variation.

Whereas "Déserts" isolates live from recorded sounds, "Capriccio for Violin and Two Sound Tracks" (1952) by Henk Badings combines both elements, and the tape assumes the accompanying role of an orchestra. As in his solo tape compositions, Badings derives instrumental timbres from purely electronic sources; in this instance, twelve oscillators. Percussion, string, and piano timbres, in addition to bell sounds produced by ring modulation, account for the majority of the electronic materials. Filtering and reverberation are used sparingly, while tape transposition generates motivic patterns repeated throughout the piece. Even though emphasis is placed upon the violin, there is a great deal of motivic interchange between the performer and the tape. Similar methods of organization are frequently found in works of the Columbia–Princeton composers, who were the first to combine instruments with tape in America in the early 1950's.

Otto Luening and Vladimir Ussachevsky collaborated on three pieces of this nature: "Rhapsodic Variations" (1953–4), "A Poem in Cycles and Bells" (1954), and "Concerted Piece" (1960). "Rhapsodic Variations," for orchestra and tape, was the first work of this kind to be produced in America. Like Badings's "Capriccio," thematic and motivic repetitions constitute a primary structural level in which canonic techniques, conventional tape manipulations, and extensive exchange of materials are treated as functions of melody rather than of timbre. Instrumental sounds are transformed by tape manipulations, while artificially reverberated flute melodies are reminiscent of Luening's "Fantasy In Space" (1952).

Explicit reference to earlier compositions appears in "A Poem in Cycles and Bells," also for orchestra with tape. Similarities to the "Variations" exist in the style of instrumental writing and thematic organization, while "Fantasy In Space" and "Sonic Contours" generate taped materials, and the melodies of both these pieces are sometimes presented by the orchestra. As in "Variations," the tape in "Poem" coexists with the instruments.

Luening and Ussachevsky's final joint project, "Concerted Piece," is once again for orchestra and tape. Not only is there a great deal of exchange between the two sources, but refined timbral associations are generated by the electronic synthesis of gongs, bells, and keyboard instruments. Another electronic source that appears near the end of the piece is a noise generator; while ring modulation, filtering, reverberation, and tape transposition occur throughout the composition. Compared to their earlier electronic works, "Concerted Piece" displays greater continuity between orchestra and tape by means of timbral relations.

Luening produced another piece for orchestra and tape, "Synthesis" (1962), which he organized around motivic recurrences and timbral shifts. Short tremolo figures on a single pitch characterize the orchestra and tape parts, while the taped material also consists of repetitive melodic fragments subjected to envelope variation. The timbral scheme is given in Example 36, which also shows sectionalization. Both orchestra and tape are apportioned essentially equal durations for their initial entries, which constitute practically the entire composition. The remaining minute and ten seconds originates from a comparatively rapid timbral transformation, in which the return of the orchestra serves as a coda.

By the mid 1950's composers were extensively exploring timbral relations between instruments and tape, and a clearly defined alternation between sources began to disappear. "Rimes pour différentes sources sonores" (1958–9), by Henri Pousseur, exemplifies this procedure. "Rimes" was his first work to incorporate performers with tape, and was among the first pieces realized at the Brussels electronic studio. Prior to his development of that studio in 1958, Pousseur had worked in Cologne (1954) and Milan (1957), where he produced tape pieces derived solely from electronic sources.

Pousseur's prefernce for electronically generated sounds is evident in "Rimes," despite the appearance of modified percussion instruments at the beginning. Amplitude, frequency and ring modulation, filtering, and reverberation are applied to white noise and sine tones, while tape transposition transforms instrumental timbres. "Rimes" is in three parts: in the first two, the tape is contrasted against small groups of instruments, whereas the appearance of only the full orchestra in the final part compensates for the absence of taped sounds. The motivic associations between the tape and the instruments demonstrate procedures previously followed by Henk Badings in the "Capriccio" such as flutter tonguing and tremolo to correspond to amplitude modulation.

EXAMPLE 36. Otto Luening, "Synthesis"

0:00		3:44		6:26		7:09		7:18		7:36
Orchestra		Tape		Tape + Percussion		Percussion		Orchestra	

The homogeneous textures that appear in "Rimes" are present as well in "Volumes" (1960), for twelve-track tape and chamber ensemble, written by François-Bernard Mache. Like "Rimes," this is Mache's first composition to employ instruments and tape, and was realized at the R.T.F. in Paris. Divided into three movements, "Volumes" is scored for seven trombones, two pianos, and percussion. The instruments are transformed by tape manipulation and filtering to produce a prerecorded tape. Close timbral associations result from the concentration on instrumental sounds, and the sonorous mixtures alternatively emphasize performers and tape. "Volumes" ends with blocks of sound that undergo continual timbral transformations accompanied by the reappearance of previously stated motivic fragments.

Luciano Berio employs similar recording techniques in "Différences" (1958–9), realized at the RAI in Milan. Live flute, clarinet, viola, cello, and harp begin the piece, while a prerecorded tape of these instruments appears midway through the work. Tape transposition, filtering, and modulatory processes were carried out by the composer during preparation of the tape, resulting in thicker textures and spatial effects; filtering causes the ensuing sounds to seem to come from a distance. The latter process is like that used by Stockhausen in his treatment of the voice of the croupier in the casino sequence of the first region of "Hymnen."

With the exception of Badings and Berio, composers prior to 1960 preferred to utilize orchestra or large instrumental ensembles in combination with tape. They did so because of a desire to establish sonorous connections between live and tape sounds, and the greater the number and variety of available instruments, the greater the possible resultant sonorities. Conventional instruments can be orchestrated to resemble electronic and concrète sounds, and the latter can be modified to approximate orchestral timbres. This situation did not change appreciably until the appearance of "Kontakte" (1959–60), the second version of which includes piano and percussion in conjunction with the original electronic tape.

Stockhausen did not reduce the number of available timbres in "Kontakte" by limiting the instrumental sources, although this might appear to be the logical result of it. By dividing percussive sounds into six categories, "musical" metal, "noise" metal, "musical" wood, "noise" wood, "musical" membrane, and "noise" membrane, the composer achieved an extensive timbral range complemented by the piano. Effects derived from the latter include tremolo, trills, clusters, grace notes, and the damper pedal techniques, of ½ and ⅓ pedal. In employing only two performers, Stockhausen was able to explore instrumental, as well as electronic, sonorous possibilities.

There are many associations between live instruments and tape, and they manifest themselves on structural levels: pitch, amplitude, rhythm, and timbre. Electronic and instrumental sounds are blended so that their autonomy is replaced by their interchangeability within a timbral continuum that ranges from dull to bright. Instrumental characteristics are given to taped elements through envelope control and filtering; while percussion and piano, due to their inherently rich harmonic content, assume the nature of electronic sounds when played in a nontraditional manner. For example, piano clusters in low registers lose pitch perceptibility and assume a noiselike nature; piano sonorities obtained from either extreme range may produce quasi-electronic effects. The gong provides a close correspondence to ring-modulated oscillator signals, while membrane percussion are electronically derived from filtered noise with an appropriate envelope contour.

After "Kontakte" appeared, many electronic composers began to employ small instrumental ensembles, or even a soloist, with prerecorded tape. Among the first to do so were the Columbia–Princeton composers Otto Luening, Charles Wittenberg, Walter Carlos, and Mario Davidovsky, some of whom adopted a neoclassical approach to electronic composition. Luening's "Gargoyles" (1960) is for violin and electronically-generated tape, and is structured on a melodic-rhythmic idea of descending pitches in a triplet configuration. Motivic interchange pervades the composition, formally organized as a series of solo tape and violin segments, in which an occasional superposition of sources occurs. The sections that include both violin and tape treat the latter as an accompaniment; these sections are characterized by chordal formations, rhythmic patterns and countermelodies. In addition to typical electronic sources and modifications, Luening extensively utilizes tape manipulations to alter the taped sounds. Although "Gargoyles" is chronologically closer to "Kontakte" than to Badings's "Capriccio," neo-classic stylistic traits link these pieces by Luening and Badings.

Thematic relations function in a similar fashion in two early works of Walter Carlos, "Dialogues for Piano and Two Loudspeakers" (1963) and "Variations for Flute and Electronic Sound" (1964). Both pieces are relatively short, made up of quick timbral contrasts between tape and performer. "Dialogues" is permeated by motivic repetitions that appear in rhapsodic fashion, one instance of which is shown in Example 37. The tape introduces this motive at 2:13, followed by its restatement by the piano. Its subsequent appearances occur on the tape at 2:56 and 3:14, with the rhythm slightly modified.

Tapes for both compositions are purely electronic, and are treated as sources for thematic and accompanying materials. "Variations," as its title implies, is divided into seven sections, a theme and six variations. Like Badings's and Luening's pieces, these works of Carlos also reflect a neo-classic approach. The retention of conventional elements such as melody, harmony, and preconceived formal schemes, enabled traditionally trained composers to more easily transfer compositional techniques to the electronic medium.

Mario Davidovsky avoids literal thematic repetitions among the performers and the tape in his early "Synchronisms." In "Synchronism No. 1" (1963) for flute and tape, there are close timbral associations between the two sources, for filtering and amplitude modulation provide close approximations of flute sonorities. Because of its pitch structure, the tape functions either as an accompaniment to the flute or in a solo capacity.

"Synchronism No. 2" (1964), for flute, clarinet, violin, cello, and tape, is constructed in a similar manner, incorporating timbral relations between the instruments and the tape. Pitches in extremely high registers, simultaneously played by flute and clarinet, are reminiscent of Stravinsky's "Symphony of Winds." They also resemble electronically-produced sounds, as do the col legno string passages. The latter group of sonorities are percussive in nature, and appear as electronically-generated sounds on the tape, in which rhythmic elements predominate.

Percussive sounds electronically generated by filtered noise with

EXAMPLE 37. Walter Carlos, "Dialogues for Piano and Two Loudspeakers"

sharp attack characteristics provide rhythmic complexities for the tape part of "Synchronism No. 3" (1965). An abundance of such special effects within the cello part, as col legno, sul tasto, pizzicato, glissandi, sul ponticello, and harmonics, result in quasi-electronic sonorities, thereby establishing reciprocal timbre structures between the cello and the tape. Unlike the earlier "Synchronisms," the third piece does not contain any solo tape passages, so that symmetry between live and taped material is maintained. Example 38 illustrates the structural relations of the three "Synchronisms," based upon the appearances of instruments and tape.

From this example, it is clear that Davidovsky employed almost identical formal plans in the first two pieces (Exx. 38a and b), whereas the scheme of "No. 3" (Ex. 38c) entails classical symmetry and periodicity, and is a refinement of the other plans. The third work also contains greater emphasis on nonelectronic materials, while the tape is more prominent in "No. 1." Davidovsky's tendency to concentrate on instrumental, rather than electronic, sounds reflects the attitudes of Mimaroglu and the R.T.F. composers.

An extreme application of this idea can be found in "Times

EXAMPLE 38. Mario Davidovsky, "Synchronisms Nos. 1, 2, and 3"

0:00	0:14	1:29	1:49	2:18	2:36	3:54	4:06
Flute	Flute	Flute	Flute			Flute	Flute
	Tape		Tape	Tape			Tape

"No. 1" (a)

0:00	2:17	3:03	4:16	5:00	5:19	5:38
Instruments	Instr.	Instr.	Instr.		Instr.	
	Tape		Tape	Tape	Tape	

"No. 2" (b)

0:00	1:24	2:23	2:38	2:53	3:49	4:24	4:48	4:51
Cello	Cello	Cello	Cello	Cello	Cello	Cello	Cello	
	Tape		Tape		Tape		Tape	

"No. 3" (c)

Five" (1963) by Earle Brown, who was an associate of John Cage at the Barron studio in New York during the early 1950s. "Times Five" was composed at the R.T.F. in Paris. It is dominated by instrumental sonorities: harp, violin, cello, trombone, and flute play in combination with a prerecorded tape that is derived from tape-manipulated segments of previously recorded instrumental excerpts. An approximation of piano, organ, vibes, and gong sounds result, so that there appear to be more instruments than there really are, which in turn allows for the construction of more complex textures. The whole assumes orchestral proportions.

Additional timbral subtleties are produced by such instrumental effects as string harmonics, sul tasto, glissandi, knocking on the instruments' wood, and speaking. The juxtaposition of high-pitched string harmonics yields sounds that resemble ring-modulated oscillators. "Times Five" is in open form. Constant repetition of the pitch G is distributed among the instruments and tape throughout the first half of the piece. Continual timbral transformations of G ensue, and serve as a type of tonal center about which the beginning of the work revolves. The absence of this pitch from the remainder of "Times Five" creates an open form.

Since composers are usually competent performers, and since composing involves an ordering of sonorous events, it is not surprising to find composers who are good improvisers. Bach's fugal improvisations are a classic example, but the practice of improvisation can be traced to Greek antiquity. Similarly, inprovisational techniques have regained their importance in the twentieth century, and are used in practically all forms of contemporary music. As noted previously, Ken Gaburo and Mel Powell are both composers and jazz pianists. Rock guitarist Frank Zappa is a composer, as are jazz musicians Charles Lloyd, John Lewis, and Andrew Hill. These musicians exemplify an important development in contemporary Western music, the amalgamation of classical music with jazz and rock. Furthermore, many musicians today, regardless of the idiom within which they compose or perform, undergo similar educational processes, so that the inclusion of electronic techniques in jazz and rock is a logical outcome.

Electronic composers began to experiment with the jazz idiom in the early 1950s, as can be seen in works by Frenchman André Hodeir. There are few such compositions from this period, however, and there was not a definite trend in this direction until the next decade. In 1962, jazz pianist-composer Bob James prepared tapes in collaboration with experimental composers Robert Ashley and Gordon Mumma, to accompany his trio. "The Wolfman" (1964), a six minute tape collage by Ashley, was superposed with the trio, which plays a blues song in a straightforward jazz style. Frequently covered by tape sounds, the ensemble fades in and out. The tape is concrète, and contains speech modulated to the point of distortion by racing-car motors.

An emphasis on diverse instrumental timbres characterizes Ashley's "Untitled Mixes" (1965) and Mumma's "Peasant Boy" (1965), both performed by the Bob James trio. The instruments are treated such that the ensuing sounds resemble those of accompanying concrète tapes. Interior piano sounds, glissandi and harmonics on the string bass, and a wide range of percussion instruments, maintain this effect, while the tape contains conventional musique concrète manipulations. "An On" (1965) by Barre Phillips, the trio's bassist, employs similar instrumental and tape techniques, although the relations between trio and tape display a closer dialogue than in "Untitled Mixes" and "Peasant Boy."

Another jazz musician to combine instruments with tape is George Russell, a composer, theorist, and pianist. His book, *The Lydian Chromatic Concept of Tonal Organization*, is a valuable guide to improvisation; it is based on the union of medieval modal theory with modern harmonic practice. From the 1950s on, Russell has been one of the major exponents of "third stream" music, an idiom in which jazz style is often replaced by classical compositional techniques and structures. The absence of a constant rhythmic pulse is a predominant characteristic of this music, as evidenced in compositions by Russell, Charles Mingus, Gunther Schuller, and Ran Blake. These developments were instrumental in the evolution of "free" jazz in the 1960s.

Russell continues his association with classical music in the "Electronic Sonata for Souls Loved by Nature" (1969), in which a jazz sextet plays with a prerecorded tape derived from concrète and electronic sources. He refers to the tape as "pan-stylistic," for fragments of all types of music appear in both their natural and electronically modified states. This concept is closely allied to Stockhausen's ideas of universality, and a high degree of similarity exists between works by these two composers.

Russell's way of relating instruments and tape is reminiscent of

Davidovsky's "Synchronisms." The emphasis is on the combination, rather than the separation, of the sonorous families. The use of such instrumental effects as flutter tonguing further establishes timbral associations within the composition. Both jazzlike tunes and improvisations in a free style are accompanied by the tape, and comparatively little time is allotted to solo instruments or tape alone, so that a homogeneous texture is produced.

Comparable, although less sophisticated, uses of electronic and tape manipulations first appeared in rock music in 1957. David Seville and the Chipmunks employed tape transposition to vocal parts, from which cartoonlike voices resulted. Seville, the group's only singer, derived four-part harmonies by overdubbing his voice at the recording studio. Examples of these techniques appear in the songs "Witch Doctor" (1957) and "The Chipmunk Song" (1958).

The Chipmunks are an isolated example of electronically-influenced rock prior to 1966. In that year, the California-based Beach Boys released "Good Vibrations" (1966) and "She's Goin' Bald" (1967). The Beach Boys' use of the theremin, tape transformations and commercial recording studio techniques, followed by the Beatles' *Sergeant Pepper's Lonely Hearts Club Band* (1967), initiated the era of electronic rock.

"A Day in the Life," from the *Sergeant Pepper* album, includes tape reversal and transposition, loops, and extensive splicing. The next Beatles album *Magical Mystery Tour* (1967), also incorporates tape reversal of both instruments and voices in "Flying" and "Blue Jay Way". The former album influenced the production of a similar one by the Rolling Stones, *Their Satanic Majesties Request* (1967), which appeared only a few months after *Sergeant Pepper*. Prepared piano, oscillator, tape echo, transposition, and reversal are combined in "2000 Light Years From Home," which contributed to a sharp, new distinction between live performance and recording studio situations. Rock bands had traditionally promoted their albums by performing selections from them in concert, but the employment of tape transformations made this procedure increasingly difficult. Consequently, some of the music from this period was accessible only on record.

A more elaborate use of electronics was made by the Grateful Dead, a California-based group that sometimes performed with prerecorded tape. "That's It for the Other One" (1967–68, *Anthem of the Sun*) concludes with a tape segment that consists of the following sounds and modifications: gong, bells, organ, piano, percussion, chimes, oscillators, white noise, filtering, modulation, and tape manipulations. In this instance, the tape serves as an interlude between successive songs. The timbral connections between performers and tape proceed from vocal modifications that include tape delay and phase shifting, and the inclusion of organ, prepared piano, harpsichord, kazoo, timpani, bells, gong, chimes, and finger cymbals in the nonelectronic portion of the song. Although the electronic applications in "That's It for the Other One" were more complex than those used by the Beatles and Rolling Stones, the Grateful Dead could perform this piece outside of a recording studio because most of the transformations appeared on tape, and required a minimum of coordination between performers and tape.

Vocal modifications accompanied by a prerecorded tape appear in "What's Become of the Baby" (1969, *Aoxomoxoa*). The tape contains sounds and transformations similar to those employed by the Grateful Dead: conventional instruments, oscillators, white noise, filtering, modulation, and tape manipulation. In this instance, however, the group maintains a closer structural association with the tape. The solo voice is amplitude- and frequency-modulated by taped elements—generally subaudio pulses—while the text remains intelligible. The additional vocal modification of phase shifting produces filtering and time delay effects so that two voices, rather than one, appear to be present. Phase shifting is a special effect achieved by mixing a sound with a delayed version of itself, and then varying the delay time. Vocal phase shifting is also employed in "Rosemary" (1969, *Aoxomoxoa*), a simple song with only acoustic guitar accompaniment. The Grateful Dead does not restrict the application of electronics to prerecorded tape; they are also involved with live electronic modifications like tape delay, phase shifting, and feedback. These techniques will be discussed in Chapter 7.

Frank Zappa and the Mothers of Invention were instrumental in the evolution of the new rock style. Their *Uncle Meat* (1967–68) album displays musique concrète techniques. Tape transformation of voices reproduces David Seville's Chipmunk effect, while occasional filtering supplies additional timbral interest. Zappa was initially exposed to these techniques when he purchased a recording studio in California. Experimentation with tape recorders and associated equipment resulted in the application of recording studio effects to the repertory of Zappa's newly formed group.

The importance of the Mothers centers around their use of electro-mechanical transformations structurally employed to reinforce the satirical content of their songs. Another rock group, the Velvet Underground, incorporates these techniques in a similar fashion in "The Murder Mystery" (1969). Two spoken monologs are juxtaposed on separate channels, and differentiated by polymetric groupings of three against four, 4/4 ♩♩♩ vs. ♩♩♩. These segments alternate with superposed vocal solos on individual tracks, in which contrast is maintained by using a female and a male singer instead of complex metrical associations. Conventional rock music supplies the background for the polyphonic duet, which is reminiscent of "An Avalanche" by Lejaren Hiller. The influence of R.T.F. techniques can be heard at the conclusion of "The Murder Mystery," where the piano passages are combined like the voices, on separate channels. One track contains unaltered material, while the other produces the same sounds in reverse.

The technique of isolating sounds on individual channels occurs in "Several Species of Small Furry Animals Gathered Together in a Cave and Gróoving with a Pict" (1969), by the British rock group Pink Floyd. Two tape loops are played on separate tracks, while a third loop appears on both channels. "Several Species," composed of loops, vocal tape transposition, and reverberation, is an epilogue to "Grantchester Meadows," a song ornamented with simulated bird songs.

A tape collage provides background material for Pink Floyd's "The Narrow Way" (1969). The opening is characterized by reversed taped sounds played at high speeds, by fast rewind on the tape recorder. The collage consists of spliced fragments and loops subjected to reverberation, tape transposition, and reversal. Tape transposition of percussion appears in "The Grand Vizier's Garden Party" (1969), and a similar treatment of the piano occurs in "Sysyphus" (1969), Part III.

Similar utilization of musique concrète procedures characterizes the work of Ron Gessin and Roger Waters. Waters, a member of Pink Floyd, assisted Gessin in the composition of a sound track for the film "The Body". The subsequent album, *Music from "The Body"* (1970), relies on those tape techniques employed by Pink Floyd and earlier musique concrète composers. Rhythmic patterns are derived from spliced fragments of breath, hand claps, belches, baby sounds, and piano; while the second section is a song accompanied by guitar, white noise, and birds. Further timbral contrast is provided by the third movement, in which a duet between violin and cello is not subjected to manipulations of kind.

Thick textures composed of overdubbed guitar, tape transpositions, and reverberation, constitute the final section.

Gessin's next album, *As He Stands* (1970–72), demonstrates many of the same techniques found in "The Body": tape transformation, filtering, and reverberation. More complex modifications like amplitude and ring modulation, are applied to a piano and a cymbal; they appear less frequently than the aforementioned processes. Tape delay and phase shifting, although seldom used, help to maintain timbral diversity within a sectionalized format. A variety of sound sources, speech, wind, fire, piano, banjo, cymbal, organ, and electronic bagpipes, supply additional timbres.

The rock groups discussed here were among the first to employ prerecorded tapes as part of an overall structural design. Although the early endeavors by the Chipmunks, the Beach Boys, and the Beatles were primarily products of recording studios, later ones made possible live performance in conjunction with prerecorded tape. Since the late 1960s, however, rock and jazz ensembles have become increasingly involved with portable synthesizers, and have thereby eliminated the need for tape playback equipment. These developments will be discussed in Part III, Live Electronics.

When Morton Subotnick temporarily moved to New York University in 1966, he established an electronic studio there. His first composition realized at N.Y.U., "Prelude No. 4," for piano and electronic tape, was produced on their Buchla synthesizer. The next piece from that studio was "Quartet No. 3" (1966) for string quartet and tape, by Leon Kirchner. This was followed by "A Mitzvah for the Dead" (1966) for violin and tape, by Michael Sahl.

Kirchner's quartet displays structural relations between instruments and tape like those in Davidovsky's "Synchronisms." The taped sounds generated on the Buchla system are purely electronic. Percussive sonorities appear most frequently at the beginning and end of the quartet, while pitch patterns produced on the sequencer occur throughout most of it. Also like Davidovsky's work, instruments dominate the piece's texture, and the tape fulfills the role of accompaniment. The importance of the taped sounds increases toward the middle of the composition, followed by recapitulation of the opening sonorities near its conclusion. The only solo tape passage, the penultimate section, is a brief restatement of sequencer patterns. Although the timbral nature of the quartet is predominately stringlike, the employment of harmonics, pizzicati, glissandi, col legno, and tremolo supply quasi-electronic effects that establish sonorous associations between the performers and the tape.

By sectionalizing "A Mitzvah for the Dead," Sahl could define distinct levels of timbral organization in a progression from combined to solo sources. The first two movements present both violin and tape, and the taped elements include both natural and modified violin sounds, in addition to excerpts from other compositions. The third movement, for solo tape, is a combination of electronic sources, brass fanfares, and instrumental excerpts. The final section is for solo violin; timbral and textual relations are reduced to their least complex forms.

The innate resonant qualities of piano and percussion instruments, in addition to the inharmonic overtone structure of gongs and cymbals, have attracted electronic composers since 1948. Lejaren Hiller employed these instruments in "Machine Music" (1964) and "Suite for Two Pianos and Tape" (1966), both pieces realized without the aid of computer at the University of Illinois studio. The former is divided into eleven sections formally organized upon timbral and textural relations. Example 39 illustrates the divisions that result from the distribution of piano, percussion, and tape.

Like the form schemes Hiller usually follows, "Machine Music" is constructed upon symmetrical textural and density relations. The sixth movement is the pivotal point about which all possible combinations of instruments and tape occur. There are seven possibilities: (1) piano alone; (2) percussion alone; (3) tape alone; (4) piano and percussion; (5) piano and tape; (6) percussion and tape; (7) piano, percussion, and tape. The first half of the piece, movements I to V, follows a density distribution of three, one, two, one, and one sources, whereas the second half, sections VII to XI,

EXAMPLE 39.   Lejaren Hiller, "Machine Music"

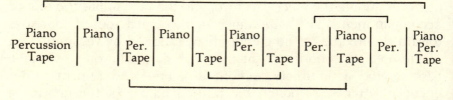

reveals a retrograde succession of densities, one, one, two, one, and three sources. The second and fourth movements (solo piano) correspond to the eighth and tenth (solo percussion), and are balanced by the inclusion of one solo tape appearance at movements V and VII. Each half of the composition contains one duet for instrument and tape, but central section VI consists of an instrumental duet.

A wide range of concrète and electronic sources are employed, including harmonic tone generator, white noise, oscillators, percussion instruments, and speech. The last section incorporates a modulated and filtered voice statement of the title in reverse: "Redrocer epat lennahc owt snoissucrep onaip rof cisum enihcam." Tape manipulations are accompanied by filtering, ring, amplitude and frequency modulation; subaudio pulses are used for frequency modulation; tape loops are ring-modulated by sine tones; beating is derived from oscillator frequencies separated by a few Hertz; and gong timbres are generated by ring-modulated oscillator tones.

Hiller's next composition, "Suite for Two Pianos and Tape" (1966), an excerpt from the theatre piece "A Triptych for Hieronymus" (1964–66), is for slide projections, dancers, actors, antiphonal groups of instruments, and tape. Electronic and concrète sources are subjected to electronic and tape transformations, but the pianos are treated traditionally. The tape appears both as accompaniment and solo, so that the juxtaposition of diverse sounds produces complex textures that sometimes result in a collage. Divided into three main parts, the suite is segmented into additional short sections, each of which entails a satirical depiction of a specific topic. "Animal Dance," for instance, includes lone animal sounds followed by modulated variations as an accompaniment to the pianos. As its title suggests, "Vox Humana" evolves from normal and transposed vocal sonorities in combination with electronically-generated sounds. The final section, "Intrada," is the most complex, consisting of voices, screams, noise, and oscillators subjected to filtering and modulation.

The collage effects that characterize many electronic compositions realized at the University of Illinois during the mid 1960s, are also present in Salvatore Martirano's "Underworld" (1965). Written in a "free" jazz style, "Underworld" is scored for tenor saxophone, two string basses, four percussion, and tape. The replacement of keyboard instruments or guitar by additional percussion and two string basses is typical of the jazz ensembles led by such musicians as Ornette Coleman during this period. "Underworld" parallels the use by Robert Ashley and Gordon Mumma of prerecorded tape in jazz.

After he completed "Suite for Two Pianos and Tape," Hiller resumed his work with computers. "Computer Music for Percussion and Tape" (1968) is derived from Strophes I, II, and IV of the "Computer Cantata" completed five years earlier. Three movements ("Decisively," "Briskly," and "Lyrically") correspond to the aforementioned strophes; the same tape is used in both pieces. Oscillator tones provide timbral contrast, while filtered noise, pops, and clicks correspond to percussion instruments.

"Algorithms I" (1968), Hiller's next computer-generated composition, employs a large instrumental ensemble that consists of flute, clarinet, bassoon, trumpet, harp, violin, cello, string bass, percussion, and tape. In this piece, like others by Hiller, the computer determined the compositional processes and generated the sounds. As a result, four versions of "Algorithms I" were made, derived from changes in computer programs or, more accurately, subroutines. A subroutine is a short, self-contained program that comprises part of the main program; complex programs often include a number of subroutines. A division into three sections is accompanied by different compositional principles. "The Decay of Information," section 1, and "Incorporations," section 3, are products of stochastic and probability theories; whereas section 2, "Icosahedron," is serialized. Stochastic theory is related to the principle of causality, in which all elements freely evolve towards a stable state. Incidentally, Hiller defines an icosahedron as a "geometrical object with 12 apices and 20 faces of three and five sides arranged symmetrically in three dimensions around a focal point." Since only the first and fourth versions have been commercially recorded, our discussion will be restricted to these.

The tape of both versions is of an instrumental character, so that aural separation of the two sound categories is difficult. Section 1 involves a gradual decrease of information from 100% to 50%, with the computer programmed to execute logical operations based on information theory and related processes. The decrease of information is maintained by the repetition of sonorous events. Slight modifications within sound synthesis routines are perceptible in the second section; version I distributes the percussive sounds over two channels so that the source appears to travel between the loudspeakers; while version IV applies subaudio amplitude modulation to those same sounds. The third movement of version I treats the instruments as electronically-produced sounds by employing effects such as string glissandi; version IV does not rely upon glissandi to such an extent. The internal flexibility of the computer program is so precisely controlled that the general characteristics of "Algorithms I" are the same in all versions. The composition has not been split into four segments, but may rather be heard from four perspectives.

The computer execution of compositional processes that consequently determine sonorous elements results in a highly integrated structure. A composer must be able to provide the computer with a logical progression of events and choices analogous to what goes on in his mind during the preparation of a musical composition. As John Cage points out, "it is the machine that will help us to know whether we understand our own thinking processes." The capacity of computers to function in this manner prompted Cage, in collaboration with Hiller, to use a computer for the realization of "HPSCHD" (1967–9).

In order to produce harpsichord and computer-generated sounds, "HPSCHD" requires up to seven harpsichords and fifty-one electronic tapes, combined in any way to produce a variety of performances. Each tape encompasses a range of five octaves, each one equally divided into successively smaller intervals, from five to fifty-six tones, from which fifty-one tapes are derived. The tones' micro-tonal properties are applied to duration and timbre. An example of the latter involves the electronic simulation of a harpsichord, characterized by an attack followed by a nonuniform decay rate. Minute timbral variations are made by modifying the rates of decay and the points where they change. Example 40 is a graphic representation of a few of these possibilities.

EXAMPLE 40. **Timbral variation of harpsichord envelope**

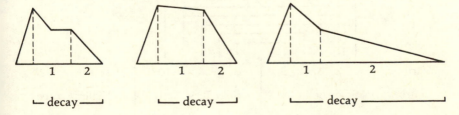

Aside from the first harpsichord solo, which is a transcription of the computer output for twelve divisions per octave, the six remaining solos are individual arrangements of preexisting compositions. Mozart's "Musical Dice Game" (K. 294d) supplies material for the second solo. The third is composed of passages from Mozart's piano sonatas, and the following one is derived from the juxtaposition of unrelated treble and bass parts from the sonatas. Solos five and six are similarly related, and include musical sources chronologically chosen from works of Beethoven, Chopin, Schumann, Gottschalk, Busoni, Schoenberg, Cage, and Hiller. The seventh solo can contain any of Mozart's music played in any manner.

The superposition of autonomous works was not new to the composers of "HPSCHD," but their methodologies do differ. Cage maintains indeterminacy in his music by using a philosophical tool, the *I Ching Book of Changes.* Conversely, Hiller achieves similar results from the application of mathematical laws, probability theory, and statistical distribution. Regardless of a composer's aesthetic, if he is totally aware of the logical sequence of his thought processes, a computer program that will accurately perform these operations can be written.

Because computers require a logical progression of events in order to function properly, and since limited data storage space is available, composers frequently realize their work in composite segments. These sections are often used as structural determinants for the completed composition. J. K. Randall's "Lyric Variations" (1968) for violin and tape consists of twenty variations grouped according to timbral characteristics. The piece's formal scheme is shown in Example 41.

Ternary and binary timbre structures, the latter of which contrasts solo textures against violin and tape combined, can be heard as a result of the distribution of sources. A symmetrical grouping of

EXAMPLE 41.   J. K. Randall, "Lyric Variations"

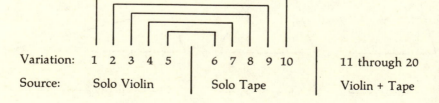

Variation:	1 2 3 4 5	6 7 8 9 10	11 through 20
Source:	Solo Violin	Solo Tape	Violin + Tape

variations also appears in the binary form, whereas the ternary structure consists of variations one to five, six to ten, and eleven to twenty. An additional internal balance among the first ten variations, one and ten, two and nine, etc., establishes fundamental associations between violin and tape, while the second half of the piece, variations eleven to twenty, is a transformation of variations one to ten.

During the late 1960s, Stockhausen formed a small ensemble for the performance of live electronic music. His disillusionment with sine tones and purely electronic sources had led him to incorporate a voice in "Gesang," followed by performers with tape in the second version of "Kontakte." By the time he was writing "Telemusik" and "Hymnen," Stockhausen's concerns had changed. The inclusion of excerpts from preexisting compositions not necessarily his own, which he would then electronically and mechanically modify, produced a new universal music. "Opus 1970" (1969) includes both performers and previously written music. The former are members of his ensemble: piano, electric viola, electronium, and tam-tam; fragments of Beethoven's music, edited and transformed by Stockhausen, yielded a set of concrète tapes whose appearances are regulated by the performers. Filtering, modulation, reverberation, tape transposition, and splicing are employed to create the effect of short-wave transmissions like those previously encountered in "Telemusik" and "Hymnen." The result is not a collage because the tape entries exist in relation to the performers.

A current trend among composers is the inclusion of prerecorded instrumental sounds in combination with performers. "Ricercar á 5" (1966) and "Ricercar á 3" (1967) by Robert Erickson utilize this technique to produce homogeneous timbral relations between the soloist and the tape. The first "Ricercar," for trombone and tape, employs four prerecorded trombone parts. Similarly, "Ricercar á 3" includes two prerecorded string bass tracks in conjunction with a performer. "Labyrinth" (1969), by Kenneth Heller, also incorporates prerecorded and manipulated cello sources played simultaneously with solo cello.

Davidovsky's recent compositions evidence this technique. Whereas his initial "Synchronisms" contrasted electronic sounds against instruments, his later compositions employ instrumental sonorities to achieve a timbral continuity somewhat lacking in his earlier pieces. "Synchronism No. 5" (1969), for percussion and tape, blends taped and live sounds so that it is practically impossible to aurally detect the first tape entry. A similar situation occurs in "Synchronism No. 6" (1970), for piano and tape. Variety is achieved by the electronic modification of instrumental sonorities, which helps to eliminate the sectionalization characteristic of the first three "Synchronisms."

The further use of prerecorded instrumental sounds to achieve timbral consistency can be found in works by Bielawa, Mimaroglu, Kupferman, and Kolb. Herbert Bielawa's "Spectrum" is for concert band and tape. The multitude of timbres present within the ensemble simplified the procedure of electronically synthesizing instrumental sonorities, so the composer contrasted these timbres by including taped piano sounds. Since piano is not normally included in a concert band, its use as a complementary timbral source is particularly effective.

Mimaroglu requires a substantially greater number of performers in "Sing Me A Song Of Songmy" (1971), for jazz quintet, reciters, chorus, string orchestra, Hammond organ, and tape. Centered around the atrocities of war, "Songmy" contains Turkish and Vietnamese poems, quotations from an essay by Kierkegaard, and musical excerpts from an étude of Scriabin and "A German Requiem" by Brahms. Sectionalization, accompanied by a variety of instrumental and tape combinations, allows each of the ten sections to exist as separate entities, while recurring timbres establish structural associations among movements. These timbres are illustrated in Example 42.

Although the textures vary, they are evenly distributed throughout the piece. The central sections are not as dense as the opening and concluding movements; this indicates a large-scale organization of the piece's formal structure. The trumpet and tape appear most frequently, while the organ is restricted to complex textures. Except in the first and final movements, the reciter is always accompanied by the chorus; the orchestra always plays in combination with the tape. Each instrumental and tape grouping occurs only once; and, except for the seventh section, there is always a timbral connection between successive movements. Finally, the segments dominated by trumpet with tape, five and ten, include taped and processed trumpet sounds. Such a careful choice

Quintet Orchestra Reciter Tape	Trumpet, Sax., Piano Orchestra Reciter Tape	Quintet Orchestra Reciter Tape Chorus Organ	Quintet Orchestra	Trumpet	Orchestra	Quintet Orchestra Reciter Tape Chorus Organ	Trumpet Orchestra Reciter Tape Chorus	Trumpet Reciter Tape
			Chorus	Tape	Tape			

EXAMPLE 42. Ilhan Mimaroglu, "Sing Me A Song Of Songmy"

and distribution of sonorous elements demonstrates the extent to which timbral associations can articulate intricate formal schemes.

An ingenious use of flutes provides a wide range of tonal shades for Meyer Kupferman's "Superflute" (1971), in which high, middle, and low registers are outlined by piccolo, C flute, and alto flute. The soloist plays only the C flute, while instruments of extreme range are prerecorded and manipulated on tape. The use of thematic materials, in addition to unaccompanied flute sonorities, recall Luening's early concrète pieces.

Barbara Kolb's "Solitaire," for piano and prerecorded vibraphone, consists of contrasting sonorities. A two-channel tape contains individual vibraphone parts subjected to echo and filtering. As in "Superflute," as many as three-part textures are available.

The electronic transformation of instruments is less frequently found in works of a similar nature by Jacob Druckman. "Animus I" (1966), for trombone and tape, is dominated by the latter, which is composed of both trombone and electronic sounds. The concrète source is filtered, modulated, and transposed, but it is overshadowed by electronically-generated percussive and pitched sounds. Timbral unification is achieved by correlating trombone effects with electronic modifications and sources: flutter tongue = amplitude modulation, mute = filtering, blow through the mouthpiece = noise. Aside from the opening trombone solo, and a passage approximately halfway through the piece, the tape is always present.

A textless voice, percussion and tape constitute the sonorous elements in "Animus II" (1968). The taped vocal part is comparable to Berio's "Visage" in the linkage of speech inflections to form nonsense words. Animus II differs from "Animus I" in two respects that concern taped sounds and their relation to performers. First, Druckman makes little attempt to associate electronic materials with percussion or voice with regard to timbre. Second, the tape does not dominate the piece's texture as it did in the first "Animus." The latter situation created an evenly balanced texture reinforced by the distribution of percussion on stage and in the audience.

"Synapse → Valentine" (1969), a two-movement work by Druckman, completely separates the tape from the string bass soloist. The first section, "Synapse," contains such stringlike sonorities as pizzacati and glissandi, although the movement is dominated by a variety of electronically-generated sounds. "Valentine," which is distinguished by a multitude of performance techniques, creates timbral associations with synapse. In addition to performing the standard string effects of double stops, col legno, pizzicato tremolo, trills of various speeds, and knocking on the body of the instrument, the bassist is required to whisper and sing, either in conjunction with, or in imitation of, musical passages. This use of the voice is frequently found in recent solo literature, particularly in Kenneth Gaburo's compositions. The variety of vocal sounds, enhanced by instrumental effects, evokes the feeling of electronic sources that are not even present. Both "Animus II" and "Synapse → Valentine" display an increased subtleness of timbral structure.

Similar vocal techniques periodically appear in "In No Strange Land" (1968) by Donald Erb. A virtuoso piece for trombone, string bass, and tape, this composition integrates electronic and instrumental sounds by its extensive use of imitative thematic elements. The tape is quasi-instrumental, while vocal and instrumental effects yield electronic analogues. The four sections are stylistically differentiated by melodic contour and tempo, but share in the equal distribution of instruments and tape. Fragmented lines permeate all but the second movement, derived from glissandi; whereas sustained tones are introduced during the final segment. A fast opening movement is contrasted by three successive slow sections, the last of which fluctuates momentarily between slow and fast tempi. Clearly delineated stylistic traits mark the first three sections, and the fourth possesses characteristics of the preceding parts.

Vocal techniques are also important in my own piece, "Exit" (1970), for trumpet and tape. The objective was to produce a multitude of sonorities, not necessarily analogous to electronic ones, from a single performer, while an electronic tape provides continuous background material. In order to achieve this effect, the following techniques are employed: tapping the bell of the trumpet with fingernails and the mouthpiece; blowing through the mouthpiece; lightly slapping the mouthpiece with the palm of the hand; pedal tones; humming specific pitches while playing others to produce modulation; tremolo; use of cup and straight mutes; flutter tonguing; and playing in a traditional manner. Such a variety of non-trumpet timbres appears throughout the beginning of the piece that a substantial interval elapses before the trumpet is clearly defined as the instrumental source. Finally, in order to reinforce the initial goal, the usual soloist-tape temporal relations are reversed.

Because of its continual presence, the tape functions as soloist; whereas the trumpet entries ornament the electronic sonorities. These inverse proportions help to articulate the desired timbral ambiguities.

Another means of deriving a variety of sonorities from a soloist is employed by Karl Korte in "Remembrances" (1971). The performer is required to play a different instrument in each of three movements, in which register is associated with tempo. The first section, for alto flute, is slow; moderate to fast tempi correspond to the C flute in the second movement; and the piccolo is employed in the very fast conclusion. Kupferman's "Superflute" used the flute family for similar reasons. Unlike "Superflute," however, Korte's composition incorporates purely electronic tape as opposed to prerecorded flute.

Relatively few orchestral works with tape have appeared since the mid-1960s. This is due in part to the additional rehearsal time needed to synchronize a large ensemble with tape. Morton Subotnick's "Laminations" (1970) is a rare attempt to fill this void.

Elaborate instrumental techniques are employed in "Laminations." Example 43 provides a list of these effects in the woodwind, brass, and string parts. The resultant timbres are extended by combining two techniques, such as glissando sul ponticello, and flutter

EXAMPLE 43. Morton Subotnick, "Laminations"

Woodwind effects	Brass effects	String effects
rattle keys	pedal tones	col legno
flutter tonguing	flutter tonguing	sul ponticello
clap hands	clap hands	play behind bridge
snap fingers	snap fingers	harmonics
blow air through instrument without producing pitch	mute	mute
	slap mouthpiece	tremolo
	pronounce "sss" into mouthpiece	glissandi
		pizzicato
		slap body of bass
		hit string with fingernail

tonguing tremolo. The ensuing sounds are not always electronic, but there are many timbral correspondences between the orchestra and the electronic tape. They include tremolo = amplitude modulation, flutter tonguing = modulation, muting = filtering, and blowing through the mouthpiece = white noise. In addition, a large battery of percussion instruments serves in both categories.

Since the orchestra and tape are in continual dialogue, Subotnick chose appropriate electronic sounds to complement the instrumental sonorities. Sliding electronic pitches appear with orchestral glissandi; rhythmic punctuations on tape correspond to finger snaps, accelerandi and ritards; synthesized horn clusters are superposed with instrumental horn clusters; and white noise is present with finger snaps, air blown through the instrument, and the pronunciation of "sss" into the mouthpiece. Subotnick fully developed these timbral resources, and the resultant associations between orchestra and tape allow for a single-movement composition of substantial length.

Compared to the solo tape pieces discussed in Part I, the addition of live performers to tape enhances the timbral palette. There are greater possibilities for more intricate structural relations, and the listener is more involved than he would be if the music came only from loudspeakers. If, as many composers believe, solo tape works are most suitable for radio and records, then the introduction of performers to the tape medium is not a logical extension of that medium, but is rather a necessity for composers. The final stage of this evolutionary process, live electronics, is the topic of Part III.

Discography

ASHLEY, ROBERT
 "The Wolfman," ESP
 1009

———

 "Untitled Mixes," ESP
 1009

BADINGS, HENK
 "Capriccio," Epic
 BC—1118

BEACH BOYS
 Smiley Smile, Cap.
 T—2891

BEATLES
 Magical Mystery Tour,
 Cap. MAL—2835

———

 *Sgt. Pepper's Lonely Hearts
 Club Band*, Cap.
 MAS—2653

BERIO, LUCIANO
"Différences,"   Philips
839.323   DSY

BIELAWA, HERBERT
"Spectrum,"   Cornell
University   1

BROWN, EARLE
"Times Five,"   BAM
LD—072

CAGE, JOHN AND LEJAREN
HILLER
"HPSCHD,"   None.
71224

CARLOS, WALTER
"Dialogues,"   Turn.
TV 34004—S

"Variations,"   Turn. TV
34004—S

DAVIDOVSKY, MARIO
"Synchronisms Nos. 1, 2, and
3,"   CRI—SD 204

"Synchronism No. 5,"
Turn. 34487 and
2—CRI—SD   268

"Synchronism No. 6,"
Turn. 34487

DOCKSTADER, TOD
"Omniphony I,"   ORLP—11

DRUCKMAN, JACOB
"Animus I,"   Turn. 34177

"Animus II,"   CRI—SD
255

"Synapse → Valentine,"
None. 71253

ERB, DONALD
"In No Strange Land,"
None. 71223

ERICKSON, ROBERT
"Ricercar a 3,"   Ars Nova
AN—1001

"Ricercar a 5,"   DGG
0654—084

ERNST, DAVID
"Exit,"   Orion   ORS—7294

GESSIN, RON
As He Stands,   RON
28B   (available from
Gessin, Headrest,
Heathfield, Sussex,
TN21   8TU)

GESSIN, RON AND ROGER
WATERS
Music from "The Body,"
EMI SHSP   4008

GRATEFUL DEAD
Anthem of the Sun,   Warner
Bros. WS   1749

Aoxomoxoa,   Warner
Bros. WS   1790

HELLER, KENNETH
"Labyrinth,"   Orion
ORS—7021

HILLER, LEJAREN
"Algorithms I" (versions I and
IV), DGG 2543—005

"Computer Music for
Percussion and
Tape," Hel. 2549006

"Machine Music," Hel.
HS—25047

"Suite for Two Pianos and
Tape," Hel. 2549006

KIRCHNER, LEON
"Quartet No. 3," Col.
MS 7284

KOLB, BARBARA
"Solitaire," Turn.
TV—S 34487

KORTE, KARL
"Remembrances," None.
H—71289

KUPFERMAN, MEYER
"Superflute," None.
H—71289

LUENING, OTTO
"Gargoyles," Col. MS
6566

"Synthesis," CRI S—219

LUENING, OTTO AND VLADIMIR
USSACHEVSKY
"A Poem in Cycles and
Bells," CRI—112

"Concerted Piece," CRI
S—227

"Rhapsodic Variations,"
Lou. 545—5

MACHE, FRANÇOIS-BERNARD
"Volumes," BAM
LD—071

MARTIRANO, SALVATORE
"Underworld," Hel.
HS—25047

MIMAROGLU, ILHAN
"Sing Me A Song Of
Songmy," At.
SD—1576

MUMMA, GORDON
"Peasant Boy," ESP—1009

PHILLIPS, BARRE
"An On," ESP—1009

PINK FLOYD
Ummagumma, Harv.
STBB—388

POUSSEUR, HENRI
"Rimes," RCA VIC
S—1239

RANDALL, J. K.
"Lyric Variations," Van.
C—10057

ROLLING STONES
*Their Satanic Majesties
Request*, Lon. NPS—2

RUSSELL, GEORGE
"Electronic Sonata for Souls
Loved by Nature," Fly.
Dut. FD 10124

SAHL, MICHAEL
"A Mitzvah for the Dead,"
Van. C—10057

SCHWARTZ, ELLIOTT
"Fantasy," Adv. FGR—7

STOCKHAUSEN, KARLHEINZ
"Kontakte," Wergo 60009

"Opus 1970,"
DGG—139461

SUBOTNICK, MORTON
"Laminations," Turn.
TV—S 34428

"Prelude No. 4," Avant
1008

VARÈSE, EDGARD
"Déserts," Col.
MS—6362 and
2—CRI S—268

VELVET UNDERGROUND
The Velvet Underground,
MGM 2353—022

WITTENBERG, CHARLES
"Electronic Study No. 2,"
Adv. FGR—1

ZAPPA, FRANK
Uncle Meat, Bizarre
(Reprise) 2024

Part Three

Live Electronics

Music was born free; and to win freedom is its destiny.
Ferruccio Busoni, 1907

CHAPTER SIX

TAPE RECORDERS IN LIVE
PERFORMANCE

THE APPLICATION OF ELECTRO-MECHANICAL PROCEDURES in live performance began relatively late, ten years after Pierre Schaeffer's initial musique concrète pieces. These procedures can be broken down into four categories: tape recorders in live performance (1958–9), amplification/modification in live performance (1960), live electronic ensembles (1966), and synthesizers in live performance (1967). In order to facilitate a discussion of these forms, each will be treated in a separate chapter, in chronological order.

Mauricio Kagel was the first to use tape recorders for live performance. In "Transición II" (1958–9), for piano, percussion, and two tape recorders, the pianist plays on the piano's keys while the percussionist plays on its strings, soundboard, and rim. By using tape recorders, Kagel attempted to unite past, present, and future. This involved the concept of repetition. The performers play in the present. As segments are recorded, they become part of the future; but when they are played back, they exist in the past. The solution of this philosophical problem determines the formal structuring of the piece.

The score consists of thirty-five loose pages divided into three structures (A, B, and C) composed of nine, seven, and five sections respectively. The resultant versions, made up of any number of sections, must not be less than ten minutes in duration. The first tape, which is produced by recording sections from B and/or C prior to performance, can be modified, as in Berio's "Différences," or it can be used for simple reproduction without any transformation. Having prepared this tape, the performers may not play any of the prerecorded sections during the concert. The second tape contains recorded fragments of the performance, excluding the sections that involve the first tape. These excerpts are made into loops, but may not be manipulated or electronically transformed. The length of the taped sections must be at least one-third of the total length of the performance.

Although the formal scheme of "Transición II" is founded on repetition, this was an element that had been consciously avoided by Kagel and other post-World War II serial composers. Kagel solved this problem by excluding repetitious fragments and patterns from the entire score. He further recommended that the performance tape include superposition of various sections.

A more intricate playback system is required in "Solo" (1965–6), which immediately precedes "Telemusik." This work of Stockhausen is for melody instrument with feedback, and requires four assistants in addition to a soloist. Segments of the performance are recorded on a two-channel tape and juxtaposed through a specially designed feedback device, with or without additional electronic modification. The result is then played back during the performance with tape delay over two speaker systems.

Timbral variety is achieved by requiring the performer to employ four different timbres of his choice, derived from the use of at least two instruments and/or modification devices such as filters and modulators. Noises, referred to by Stockhausen as "coloration," are also produced by the soloist to yield additional sonorities. The expansion of timbral resources is needed in order to maintain as nonrepetitive a texture as possible, similar to the situation in "Transición II."

Example 44 depicts the configuration of equipment essential to the performance of "Solo." A directional microphone, connected to a stereo tape recorder, registers the performance. The tape passes six moveable stereo playback heads, with individual amplifiers, en route to a second recorder that serves as take-up reel for a tape loop. The output from the six playback heads is split and simultaneously sent back to the first recorder and switching panel. The latter is connected directly to amplifiers with level controls, and the ensuing sounds projected by four loudspeakers. Because the playback heads are movable, the delay times are variable, depend-

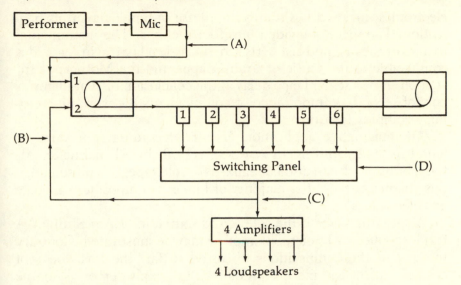

EXAMPLE 44. Karlheinz Stockhausen, "Solo"

ing on which of six versions of "Solo" the performer chooses to play. A further control of the delay material is effected at the switching panel, where playback heads are manually selected.

Four technical assistants are responsible for the following operations: amplitude control of microphone (A), amplitude control of feedback (B), amplitude control of playback (C) and switching of playback heads (D). The score indicates relative amplitude levels to the first three assistants; short periods of silence interrupt the recorded material sufficiently often to isolate the soloist from the playback sonorities, subsequently avoiding a literal repetition of melodic elements. Stockhausen suggests that when the soloist is not playing, "Recorded sounds should sometimes be very soft to give the impression of coming from a distance."

Great timbral and textural flexibility are inherent in "Solo," whereas fragmented melodic repetitions provide adequate structural relations between performer and tape. Time delays of up to 45.6 seconds produce Wagnerian-like prolongations of thematic elements, while short temporal intervals create Impressionistic sonorous masses. Finally, the listener hears three distinct sound sources: the soloist, the tape delay (channel 1), and the delayed feedback (channel 2).

Lucas Foss's "Paradigm" (1968), for percussion, electric guitar, unspecified high, middle, and low register instruments, tape, and electronics, makes a less sophisticated use of tape delay in its final section. The piece is divided into four sections. The instrumental writing of the first and last parts is neo-classic à la Stravinsky, and is comparable to the music of Frank Zappa and the Mothers of Invention. A two-second tape delay at the conclusion of "Paradigm" is only of secondary importance; it complements the work's increasingly complex textures.

An imaginative application of basic recording procedures is found in "I Am Sitting In A Room" (1970) by Alvin Lucier. Although this work can also be realized for solo tape, it is presented in this chapter because the majority of Lucier's compositions involve live electronics.

A speaking voice is the sole sound source in "I Am Sitting." A text is supplied by Lucier, but another may be substituted. Contrary to most of the compositions discussed so far, the text does not critically affect the piece's structure, but simply serves as source material. No electronic modifications occur, so that only a microphone, tape recorders, and a playback system are needed.

The realization of "I Am Sitting" is simple, but the results are astonishing. After the spoken text is recorded, it is played back and recorded again, this time with a microphone, to produce a second generation tape, which is in turn played back and rerecorded to yield a third generation tape. This process of recording prerecorded statements with a microphone may be carried out indefinitely, and Lucier suggests that the recording environments be changed to afford greater timbral variety. The version for solo tape consists of splicing successive tapes in chronological order, but the composer does not give instructions for real time performance; this is left to the discretion of the performers.

The commercial recording of this work includes a sampling of nine readings from a total of fifteen. During the second reading, a mild feedback on the phonemes "s" and "c" is already detectable, and consequently, high, ringing sounds are produced. Hollow, distant sounds, increased reverberation, and feedback characterize the next two parts, while speech begins to lose intelligibility in the fifth reading. Continuous feedback has destroyed all semblance of speech by the seventh section, so that only the rhythm of the original speech remains. "I Am Sitting" progressively assumes an electronic nature, in which actual pitches result from resonant frequency characteristics of the recording area.

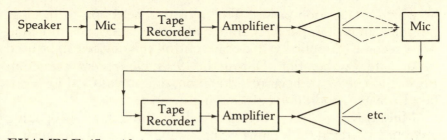

EXAMPLE 45. **Alvin Lucier, "I Am Sitting In A Room"**

An elaboration of this process, shown in Example 45, is an instance suitable for live performance. Any number of microphones, tape recorders, and playback systems may be employed; the present example inherently produces tape delays of less than one second between successive generations. This can easily be avoided by turning amplifier levels on and off; this helps to minimize excessively thick textures. However, Lucier does not prohibit this situation. He merely states: "Make versions that can be performed in real time." Further timbral variants can be derived from the judicious placement of loudspeakers and microphones within the performance area, taking advantage of reflective surfaces such as walls, hallways, and low ceilings.

The electrification of instruments, the appearance of synthesizers, recording studio techniques and Dr. Timothy Leary's psychedelic experience are at least partially responsible for the rock revolution of the late 1960s. With the exception of jazz pianist Bob James, the use of tape delay systems in jazz groups did not appear until acid rock was established. The title tune from the *Bitches Brew* (1968) album of trumpeter Miles Davis not only utilizes tape delay, but also incorporates jazz and rock elements. This is usually referred to as "fusion" music.

A delay system like that used in "Solo" is not feasible for most commercial groups because of the spatial requirements for the physical separation of playback heads. The electronics industry has attempted to compensate for this by developing the "echoplex," a compromised version of Stockhausen's delay network. The echoplex is portable, and consists of a series of adjacent playback heads by which a tape loop passes. The individual selection of heads is possible, but the temporal separation of events cannot be more than a few seconds. Supplied with decay control, this device can be used to simulate reverberation. During the 1950s, composers referred to this technique as artificial reverberation, and it was used in "Fantasy In Space" and others of Luening's works.

Miles Davis's "Bitches Brew" uses delay throughout its opening section. Contrapuntal fragments, cascading runs, and arpeggiated triads supply diverse textural possibilities, in this instance from solo trumpet, that have profoundly influenced recent jazz musicians. Don Ellis achieved similar effects in "Open Beauty," in which an echo chamber is combined with tape delay. An unaccompanied trumpet solo results in duets and trios, and a decay time of four to five seconds reinforces the trumpet choir effect. Electric pianos and an echoplex appear in "His Last Journey" (1971) by Joe Zawinul, formerly Miles Davis's pianist. As in the other examples, a slow tempo and repetitive melodic fragments yield the best results.

The incredible vocal artistry of Polish singer Urszula Dudziak, combined with tape delay and reverberation, reveal Dudziak as a very exciting performer. Her most obvious influences have been Miles Davis, Ella Fitzgerald, and Luciano Berio. The melodic contour and "scat" singing style stem from Davis and Fitzgerald, while the textless songs, vocal inflections and timbral transformations from change of mouth positions can be traced to "Visage." Since she has a four octave range, Dudziak need not rely on electronic modifications for additional resources. This is apparent in the album *Newborn Light* (1974), where a subtle application of tape delay and reverberation is employed in "Dear Christopher Komeda," "Ballad," "For Pia," and "Chassing," this last a canon for solo voice. The synthesizer is seldom used; and "Randi and Bamse" provides an instance of vocal filtering and amplitude modulation.

The almost exclusive restriction to tape recording techniques of the compositions covered in this chapter suggests that they be categorized as live musique concrète. Although these same procedures appear in the works to be discussed in the following chapters, the use of additional electronic modifications is substantially greater in them. Chapter seven will investigate the application of amplification and electronic transformation processes.

Discography

DAVIS, MILES
Bitches Brew, Col.
GP—26

DUDZIAK, URSZULA
Newborn Light, Col.
KC—32902

ELLIS, DON
Electric Bath, Col.
CS—9585

FOSS, LUCAS
"Paradigm," DGG
2543—005

KAGEL, MAURICIO
"Transición II," Main.
5003

LUCIER, ALVIN
"I Am Sitting In A Room,"
Source Record No. 3

STOCKHAUSEN, KARLHEINZ
"Solo," DGG 137—005

ZAWINUL, JOE
Zawinul, At. SD 1579

CHAPTER SEVEN

AMPLIFICATION/MODIFICATION
IN LIVE PERFORMANCE

By 1960, COMPOSERS UNDERSTOOD electronic modulatory devices, but left the engineers to deal with the problem of improving amplifier designs. These latter concentrated on optimal fidelity in order to insure quality recording and transmission. Musique concrète and electronic composers demanded especially sensitive equipment, because of the sonorous nature of their sources.

John Cage has introduced important concepts in his music and his writings, notably the use of chance operations as determinants of compositional structures. His work has not been restricted to abstract ideas, however, for Cage was one of the first composers to explore the compositional possibilities of amplification (as was noted in the Introductory discussion of "Imaginary Landscape No. 2," which employed an amplified coil of wire). A more recent piece of this nature, for live performance, is "Cartridge Music" (1960), which is an outgrowth of "Imaginary Landscapes," "Williams Mix," and "Fontana Mix." As the title indicates, "Cartridge Music" stems from phonograph cartridges and contact microphones placed on piano strings and other objects. Volume and tone controls are regulated to amplify, transform, and distort "small sounds." The choice of sound sources makes "Cartridge Music" another example of live musique concrète.

Indeterminacy prevails in most of Cage's works, which do not indicate the type of sounds employed, or the number of performers needed. The realization of these pieces takes the form of versions produced by performers who must assume an active role in the compositional process. Cage and the pianist/composer David Tudor are responsible for the commercially recorded version of "Cartridge Music," and Tudor amplified a piano for a realization of Cage's "Variations II" (1961). Contact microphones were placed on the piano and phonograph cartridges on its strings; a variety of objects were inserted into the cartridges to activate the strings. The piano keys are never played in a conventional manner, so that all sounds are related to piano timbre only by degree. Successive sonorous events, separated by long time intervals, possess conspicuously long durations which result from a delicate control of feedback. Feedback also produces periodic oscillations and filtering effects, both of which enhance the piece's timbral qualities.

The realization by Cage and Tudor of "Variations IV" (1964) involves the placement of microphones outdoors to obtain sounds from traffic and pedestrians. Although a resemblance to musique concrète does exist, it does not go beyond Cage's choice of sound sources. Unlike the indeterminate factors in Cage's music, the concrète composers, particularly Pierre Henry, invariably subject their sonorous elements to strict formal schemes. The essence of musique concrète, then, is not solely the physical attributes of sound, but a compositional methodology. These reasons also account for the ideological differences between early French and German tape composers.

Another aspect of "Variations II and IV," which is their electronic format, is also indeterminate. Since Cage specifies neither the sound sources nor the number of performers, it logically follows that electronic devices and microphones need not be employed for any given version of a piece. Once again, the choice is made by the performers, and obviously depends on individual musical background and taste.

A series of realizations of similar works by Cage, Earle Brown, and Sylvano Bussotti was prepared by percussionist Max Neuhaus in 1964 and 1965. "Fontana Mix—Feed," for which a partial configuration is presented in Example 46, results from feedback loops derived from contact microphones placed upon various percussion instruments. These instruments are positioned in front of loudspeakers, so that the sounds they emit cause a chain reaction. The vibration of the microphones activates the instruments, whose sound is then picked up by the microphones and played through the loudspeakers.

The duplication of this network creates continuous, multiple

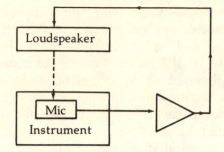

EXAMPLE 46.   John Cage and Max Neuhaus, "Fontana Mix—Feed"

feedback oscillations; that is, pitches and aperiodic microphone vibrations produce contrasting rhythmic activity. The following elements allow for timbral variety: the amplitude of the loudspeakers, which is controlled by the performer; the room acoustics; the spatial relation between the microphones and the loudspeakers; microphone placement; and the choice of instruments.

The score of Earle Brown's "Four Systems" is comprised entirely of horizontal lines of various thickness and length. Neuhaus chose four amplified cymbals as sources, with their decay characteristics and timbre dependent on the presence of feedback. In this instance, minimal feedback avoids the appearance of oscillations, so that the textures are not compounded by extraneous pitches. Timbre is controlled by the regulation of feedback amplitude, and density is variable between one and four sources.

Neuhaus extended microphone applications in "Coeur pour batteur—Positively Yes," by Sylvano Bussotti. Greatly amplified cymbal and tamtams, positioned among other percussion instruments, vibrate sympathetically with instrumental sounds transmitted by loudspeakers. The derivation of timbral variants and the increased duration of individual sonorous events proceed from these sympathetic vibrations. Additional sounds, obtained from the amplification of body movements and from incidental vocal utterances, supply rhythmic and timbral subtleties. Feedback is again utilized to generate periodic oscillations and to increase the durations of instrumental events.

Neuhaus's realizations of these works demonstrate the creative application of feedback within a structural context. The inherent dangers of distortion or of piercing, high frequencies that arise from feedback have been eliminated in these performances, which indicate the resources available from standard sound systems. The absence of synthesizers and electronic devices is not noticeable, for so many other effects are available. A knowledge of acoustics and recording techniques is essential for the execution of these ideas, which are also useful within the tape medium.

Cage's "Solos for Voice 2" (1966) displays novel methods of vocal amplification, for the composer indicates that contact microphones are to be attached to the throat and lips of each singer. There is no text; only phonemes, syllables, and speech inflections reminiscent of tape pieces by Berio, are used. Unintelligible speech is complemented by many vocal glissandi, and is transformed and distorted by reverberation, filtering, and modulatory devices. A multitude of timbres retain audible relations because of the imaginative placement of contact microphones.

Although this is a departure from his tape collages and "Variations IV," the realization of "Variations II" by David Tudor employed similar timbral continua. Cage does not discourage this type of timbral organization by not specifying sound sources. It is, in fact, implied, if a limited number of sources are used. Significantly contrasted versions may result from choices made by performers; Cage supplies only a general framework within which the role of performer is elevated to that of composer. The opportunity for individual expression can be seen as a manifestation of the philosophical influence of Zen Buddhism on Cage.

The Japanese composer Toshi Ichyanagi derived vocal material from glissandi in "Extended Voices." The glissandi are of various speeds and lengths, as in "Solos for Voice 2," but Ichyanagi extended the vocal ranges by requiring the singers to play slide whistles. The introduction of nonvocal elements increases timbral variety and establishes associations with an accompanying electronic tape. The glissandi are contrasted against sustained tones in addition to the taped sounds, whereas extensive electronic modulation applied to the chorus provides further timbre control. The predominance and regulation of glissandi patterns reveal linear characteristics of some compositions by Xenakis that are sonorous analogs of geometric and architectural forms.

Amplification of acoustic instruments and the use of feedback by rock groups began in the mid-1960s. The Velvet Underground, which comprises organ, electric guitar, electric bass, percussion, and vocalists, included electric viola as early as 1965, when they were enlisted by Andy Warhol to perform in his "Exploding Plastic Inevitable." This was a multi-media show including music, dancers, film, lights, and slide projections. The lyrics centered around sex and drugs, and were accompanied by feedback from the electric viola on such songs as "Heroin." Feedback and the use of a fuzz box, a modulatory device that produces distortion, appear in "Run Run Run" and "European Son." These effects, often carried to extremes, convey the feelings of the psychedelic experiences in which young audiences were involved during the late 1960s.

The late guitarist Jimi Hendrix incorporated similar electronic techniques in his trio. "Purple Haze" (1967) displays the use of much reverberation and of a fuzz box; feedback is employed in "Manic Depression (1967); filtering effects appear in "Can You See Me," "All Along the Watchtower," (1968) and "Crosstown Traffic"; and "Red House" applies tape echo effects to voice and guitar solos. Like the Velvet Underground, many of Hendrix's songs deal with sex and drugs, as does "Purple Haze," which maintains a chaotic atmosphere by excessive modulation and distortion.

The Velvet Underground and Jimi Hendrix were based in New York, but San Francisco, and especially Haight-Ashbury, was the West Coast center for the new rock. The Grateful Dead, among the most influential groups from this area, treats feedback with a subtlety that equals the electronic realizations of Tudor and Neuhaus.

Smooth, gradual timbral alterations derived from a fuzz box, a reverberation unit, and from feedback, distinguish "Dark Star" (1968) from pieces by the Underground and Hendrix. The Dead treat texture and instrumental color as compositional elements; timbral associations determine the structure just as much as melody, harmony, and rhythm. The periodic recurrence of these elements significantly contributes to development in their long compositions. The introduction of delicately controlled feedback near the conclusion of "Dark Star" exemplifies its usefulness as both a timbral and a rhythmic source. The amplitude is adjusted so that continuous oscillations are barely avoided, and feedback can accentuate upper partials through the addition of metallic sounds that correspond to the rhythmic articulation of the instruments.

A unique improvisation, "Feedback," extends these techniques to their extreme. The resultant effects include flutelike, oscillator, and bell sonorities; noise masses; simulated ring modulation and tape reversal; all produced from feedback regulation. Reverberation and filtering effects enhance the feedback possibilities and assist in a gradual evolution of textures like those found in "Dark Star". The Grateful Dead is one of the few groups to have succeeded in treating feedback as something more than a shocking or psychedelic effect.

The British counterpart to these American groups is the Soft Machine, which was among the first to work with a light show, the Sensual Laboratory of Mark Boyle. Although they consider their music to be avant-garde jazz, the Soft Machine calls it rock to attract an audience. Their first U.S. appearance was in 1968 at the jazz series sponsored by the Museum of Modern Art in New York.

"Wah-wah" (filtering) and fuzz (modulation) are the predominant electronic modifications found in the Soft Machine's early pieces. "Joy of a Toy" (1968, *Soft Machine*), for instance, maintains timbral consistency by the application of guitar "wah-wah" throughout the entire song, while guitar fuzz and "wah-wah" combined with vocal "wah-wah" appear in "Lullabye Letter" (1968, *Soft Machine*). "Hibou, Anemone and Bear" (1969, *Soft Machine II*), the third of ten pieces from "Rivmic Melodies," includes guitar fuzz and vocal tape delay. The delayed voice is much softer than the original part, which gives the impression of excessive reverberation. Recent music by the Soft Machine relies upon synthesizers for the production of electronic effects. It will be discussed in Chapter 9.

Whereas classical composers incorporated electronic devices to transform sounds in their search for different timbres, many early rock groups relied on electronics for extramusical reasons. This situation could only have arisen out of musical ignorance on the part of rock groups, for electronic techniques had been in use for two decades in Paris, Cologne, and New York. Rock musicians have since become increasingly aware of electronic composers. For example, Frank Zappa has often mentioned his admiration for Edgard Varèse; and members of Yes, a British rock group to be discussed in a later chapter, have acknowledged the influence of Mimaroglu, Stravinsky, and Stockhausen. The constant exchange of ideas among electronic, rock, and jazz musicians may create a new medium. Further discussion of this topic is included in the following chapters.

Stockhausen was among the first European composers to engage in live electronic music with his "Mikrophonie I" (1964). Logical paths of development are particularly evident in his music:

"Mikrophonie I" embodies the extension of the concepts involved in the realization of the instrumental version of "Kontakte," i.e., the combination of instrumental with electronic sounds. "Kontakte" is the first example of this process, but the electronic elements are confined to prerecorded tape. The dualism between electronic and instrumental music is resolved in live performance for the first time in "Mikrophonie I."

A large tam-tam, two microphones, two filters with potentionmeters (variable resistors) for amplitude control, and a sound reproduction system, are required for the performance of "Mikrophonie I." Two performers activate the tam-tam while two others pick up the resultant sounds with microphones connected to individual filters. As in the works of Cage, the amplification of the tam-tam reveals normally inaudible upper partials, significant in this instance because of the inherently complex inharmonic spectrum of that instrument.

Many variables contribute to timbral diversity, and a continuum is formed with the tam-tam as its focal point. Both the material (wood, metal, etc.) of the striking object and the manner in which the tam-tam is made to vibrate, produce different results. The distance between the microphones and the tam-tam affects perception of the source's spatial location, complemented by a rhythmic movement of microphones. Finally, the obvious transformations obtainable from filter response and amplitude settings give Stockhausen control of pitch, register, timbre, spatial location, rhythm, and amplitude. The composer has effectively transferred the majority of classical studio controls to another medium, that of live performance.

Stockhausen continued to work with live electronics in his next compositions, "Mixtur" (1964) and "Mikrophonie II" (1965), both of which are involved with the ring modulation of instrumental or vocal sonorities. "Mixtur" employs an orchestra divided into five categories: woodwind, brass, string (arco), string (pizzicato), and percussion, of which the first four are separately ring-modulated by sine tones (Example 47). Three groups of percussion instruments, each consisting of cymbal and tam-tam, are amplified by contact microphones and transmitted over individual loudspeakers.

As in "Mikrophonie I", Stockhausen attempted to unite instruments with electronics in live performance, but "Mixtur" is derived from reversed techniques. Whereas the former evolves from the subtractive process of filtering, "Mixtur" proceeds from ring mod-

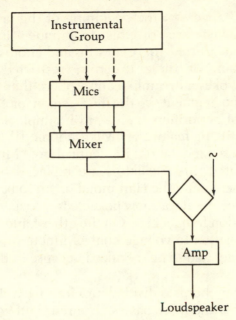

EXAMPLE 47. Karlheinz Stockhausen, "Mixtur"

ulation, an additive technique that yields pitches foreign to the harmonic spectra of the modulated instruments. Since timbre is dependent upon overtone structures, any alteration of their inherent harmonic content generates new instrumental timbres. Shifting oscillator frequencies to the subaudio range, below 16 Hz., allows for rhythmic transformations; the ring modulator functions as an amplitude-modulating device.

"Mikrophonie II" (1965), for Hammond organ, choir, and ring modulators, is the most significant of Stockhausen's electronic composition from this period. It not only refines the techniques used in earlier live electronic pieces, but it possesses a nucleus of the elements from which "Telemusik" and "Hymnen" were derived.

The second "Mikrophonie" stems from "Gesang der Jünglinge"; both entail the synthesis of vocal and electronic music. The medium of "Gesang" is tape, while "Mikrophonie II" is performed live; the relationship between these two is like that of "Kontakte" and "Mikrophonie I." "Mikrophonie II" contains additional associations with "Gesang," for it is derived principally from *Einfache Grammatische Meditationem*, a treatise on the manipulation of syntax by Helmut Heissenbüttel. Moreover, prerecorded excerpts from "Gesang" appear at the beginning of the latter work: this is Stockhausen's first use of this technique. Fragments from "Momente" and "Carre," for orchestras and chorus, are also heard. The presentation of these excerpts, restricted to a separate loudspeaker, evokes a dreamlike atmosphere that foreshadows the gambling casino segment in the first region of "Hymnen." The configuration of performers is given in Example 48.

The most striking feature of "Mikrophonie II" is the role of the organ. The ring modulation is identical to "Mixtur," but here manually-operated sine oscillators are replaced by electronic organ. Stockhausen found the Hammond organ to be a more efficient electronic source, for it was now possible to alleviate the problem of tuning modulation frequencies. On the other hand, the organ is not automatic in relation to voltage control functions; in addition, extreme frequencies had to be sacrificed because of the organ's range limitation.

The chamber chorus is divided into four parts, two groups each of three sopranos and three basses. The resultant vocal transformation often resembles the distortion in "Telemusik" and "Hymnen." Traditional organ timbres rarely appear because that instrument

EXAMPLE 48. Karlheinz Stockhausen, "Mikrophonie II"

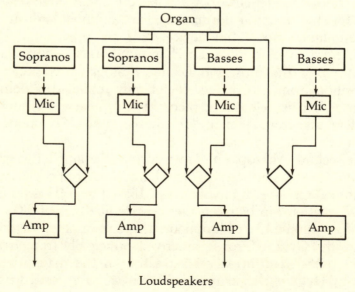

Loudspeakers

controls vocal modulation. The mixing of the voice with transformed derivatives is accomplished by regulating loudspeaker amplitudes, while the placement of the loudspeakers within the performance area enhances this association.

With the exception of "Mixtur," Stockhausen's live electronic compositions proceed from single sound sources. In "Mantra" (1970), two pianos are ring-modulated by sine tones. The pianists play on the keys, but are also required to play a set of tuned antique cymbals. The electronic techniques found in "Mantra" are not revolutionary, since identical procedures were employed by Stockhausen in earlier pieces in which the use of electronics was closely associated to major structural designs.

The concepts embodied in "Telemusik," Stockhausen's first composition to display his fascination for Oriental culture, reappear in "Mantra." The title refers to an ancient Indian belief in sounds that enable one to attain higher levels of consciousness. Antique cymbals functionally analogous to the Japanese temple instruments in "Telemusik," announce the commencement of new sections. Finally, "Mantra" is permeated by repetitive elements that suggest meditation.

The mantra is a series of thirteen pitches divided into four groups or limbs, each note articulated in a different manner; a pause separates successive limbs. Stockhausen's formal plan of thirteen sections is therefore derived from the mantra, in which each pitch generates an entire section. Excessive repetition of the mantra proceeds from intervallic expansion; seconds become thirds, thirds become fourths, and so on. The basic mantra and accompanying note forms are illustrated in Example 49.

These motives, often expanded intervallically, recur throughout the piece. Ring modulation by subaudio sine frequencies produces periodic repetitions characteristic of the initial pitch of the series, so that there is a close association between natural and modulated piano sonorities. Sine tones corresponding to the mantra progression are also ring-modulated with piano; and each of the thirteen sections is modulated by a particular pitch from the mantra to form timbral and structural relations among the individual sections. Complex wave forms are produced by ring modulation of the piano with sine frequencies that are not integer multiples of the piano tone; that is, inharmonic partials are generated to yield new timbres. Additional timbral subtleties proceed from Stockhausen's directive that "ring modulated sonorities should be slightly louder

1. A   "periodic repetition"

2. B   "accented at the end"

3. G♯   "normal"

4. E   "upper and lower neighbor tones"

5,6. F,D   "tremolo; last note occurs with chord"

7. G   "accented at beginning" (retrograde of No. 2)

8. E♭   "chromatic connection"

9. D♭   "staccato"

10. C   "nucleus for aperiodic repetition, i.e., Morse code"

11. B♭   "nucleus for trill"

12. G♭   "sforzato"

13. A   "arpeggiated connection"

EXAMPLE 49.   Karlheinz Stockhausen, "Mantra"

than natural piano sounds." Compared to "Mikrophonie II" and "Mixtur," a greater degree of cohesion between ring modulator and live sounds exists in "Mantra"; the result is a composition of greater length and increased resemblance to classical studio organizational procedures.

From a performance standpoint, using minimal electronic equipment is feasible because of coordination problems and the use of external patch cords. Synthesizers, to be discussed in subsequent chapters, are a solution. When synthesizers are not present, however, ring modulators, filters, feedback, and delay units offer the greatest versatility for electronic transformation. Ring modulation of amplified and prepared piano in "Accidents" (1967), by Larry Austin, demonstrates another application of limited electronic resources.

A piano is prepared by scattering flat, circular, shell wind chimes over the strings, on which at least sixteen contact microphones, phonograph cartridges, etc., are randomly placed. The sounds are ring-modulated and transmitted over a network of two to six loudspeakers. The sustaining pedal is always depressed to permit the maximum string vibration, sympathetic vibration, and reverberation effects characteristic of piano sonorities. Timbral variation, provided by ring modulation, is predominantly in the form of rapid repetitions, produced by subaudio modulatory frequencies. Higher modulatory pitches yield typical gonglike timbres, while glissandi continually transform the piano. Feedback, when employed, may be ring-modulated to obtain a remote reference to piano interior sonorities. At the discretion of the performer, prerecorded tape may accompany a live performance. In this instance, taped materials can be derived from performance excerpts, or a tape can be obtained from the composer.

A novel method of sound production is required of the pianist. The keys are to be depressed without sounding, which is a physical impossibility in performance. Sounds, or "Accidents," consequently appear; they are then amplified and ring-modulated. Projections of the score are flashed on a wall and a series of mirrors reflect exaggerated actions by the performer. The combination of electronics with visual elements is also found in the works of Roger Reynolds, a colleague of Gaburo, Oliveros, and Erickson at the University of California at San Diego.

"Ping" (1968), a multi-media composition by Roger Reynolds, includes flute, piano, harmonium, cymbal, tam-tam, ring modulator, tape, photocell sound distributor, two slide projectors, and film or live dancer projected over closed-circuit television. The sound distributor sends a sound to various loudspeakers by means of a moving light source that shines on a series of photocells; the intensity of the light regulates the sound's amplitude. The work originates from *Ping* by Samuel Beckett. The text is arbitrarily divided into three sections and displayed by slide projectors. Sectionalization is accomplished by the distribution of pitches, relative amplitudes, and employment of ring modulation, the latter illustrated in Example 50.

Rather than modulating instruments with electronic signals, Reynolds substitutes harmonium, cymbal, and tam-tam for oscillator frequencies, thereby modulating the instruments among themselves. Unlike, for instance, the procedures followed by Stockhausen, this method introduces more complex timbres because of the comparatively richer harmonic content of percussion instruments than of sine tones. Switches enable modulator inputs to be varied instantaneously, while the output is transmitted to loudspeakers by means of the photocell sound distributor. The first and third sections of "Ping" contain ring-modulated flute sonorities; the piano is modulated during the second segment to effect formal structural divisions.

EXAMPLE 50. Roger Reynolds, "Ping"

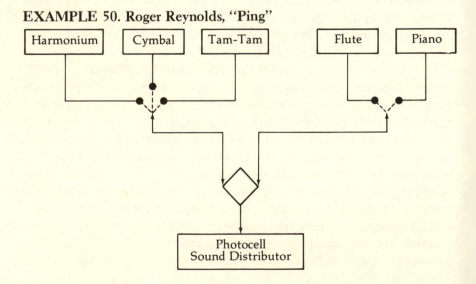

The control of pitch also helps to determine the timbral characteristics of the modulated elements, for both cymbal and tam-tam are played by drawing a bow across their edges. Specific pitches can be obtained in this manner, and the percussionist must experiment with these instruments prior to performance so that he will be able to produce pitches within the formal structure. Five pitches (C, C#, D, F, and F#) constitute the first section, whereas a complementary series of seven notes (D#, E, G, G#, A, A#, and B) make up the final part, with both these segments characterized by modulated flute. The middle section is contrasted by the presence of three chords that contribute to an increased timbral complexity derived from modulated piano sonorities. The ring-modulated textures of the second section display close associations to the bowed cymbal and tam-tam because the sounds are produced on the interior of the piano, and the bowed instruments often yield stringlike effects. Finally, the photocell sound distributor routes modulated and taped sounds to any of four loudspeakers. This device is light-sensitive; its amplitude is relative to the proximity of light sources.

Conventional instruments, ring modulator, oscillator, and tape appear in "Traces" (1969), also by Reynolds. In this instance, piano, flute, and cello are ring modulated by an oscillator, so that generally homogeneous timbres proceed from instrumental effects such as flute double-stops, or multiphonics, and piano interior, like the sonorities in "Ping". A six-channel tape composed of concrète and electronic elements enhances the timbral associations among the live sounds; it is analogous to the function of the two-track tape in Reynolds' previous works.

Jacob Druckman combines prerecorded tape and clarinet with feedback in "Animus III." The timbral homogeneity characteristic of his earlier pieces for instruments and tape recurs, maintained by the inclusion of modified vocal and clarinet elements on tape. In addition to obvious timbral similarities resulting from extensive use of the clarinet, there is frequent motivic imitation between performer and tape. A reliance on tape transposition obscures the comprehension of meaningful speech, so that the vocal elements extend, rather than delineate, the clarinet sonorities. The clarinet feedback further enhances the association between soloist and tape; movement within the timbral continuum is smooth, like the realizations of Tudor and Neuhaus.

Regardless of their stylistic diversities, the compositions treated in this chapter share an essential characteristic. The electronic modification of source materials is simple compared to transformations employed in a studio realization. The lack of electronic complexity does not detract from these pieces, but rather enforces timbral associations that in turn contribute significantly to structural relations. The restriction to ring modulation, for example, provides sonorous traits of a universal nature, so that any sounds subjected to this process assume common timbral characteristics. The same is true of filtering and feedback. The works presented in the following chapter are based on similar procedures, are distinguished by being products of ensembles specializing in the performance of live electronic music.

Discography

AUSTIN, LARRY
  "Accidents,"   Source Record
  No. 2

BROWN, EARLE
  "Four Systems,"   Col.
  MS—7139

BUSSOTTI, SYLVANO
  "Cœur pour
    batteur—Positively Yes,"
  Col.   MS—7139

CAGE, JOHN
  "Cartridge Music,"   Main.
  5015

———

  "Fontana Mix—Feed,"
  Col.   MS—7139

———

  "Solos for Voice 2,"   Odys.
  32160156

———

  "Variations II,"   Col.
  MS—7051

———

  "Variations IV,"   Ev.   3230

———

  "Variations IV" (excerpts),
  Ev.   3132

DRUCKMAN, JACOB
  "Animus III,"   None.
  71253

GRATEFUL DEAD
  Live/Dead,   Warner Bros.
  2 WS—1830

HENDRIX, JIMI
  The Jimi Hendrix
  Experience,   Reprise
  RS—6261

ICHYANAGI, TOSHI
  "Extended Voices,"   Odys.
  32160156

REYNOLDS, ROGER
"Ping,"   CRI   SD—285

"Traces,"   CRI   SD—285

SOFT MACHINE
Soft Machine,   Probe
CPLP—4500

Soft Machine II,   Probe
CPLP—4505

STOCKHAUSEN, KARLHEINZ
"Mantra,"   DGG   2530208

"Mikrophonie I,"   CBS
32—11—0044

"Mikrophonie II,"   CBS
32—11—0044

"Mixtur,"   DGG   137012

VELVET UNDERGROUND
*The Velvet Underground and
Nico,*   Verve   V6—5008

CHAPTER EIGHT

LIVE ELECTRONIC ENSEMBLES

IMPROVISATION IS CLOSELY ALLIED to composition, but it is distinguished by its spontaneity, an attribute considered essential by many contemporary composers. After World War II, John Cage, Earle Brown, Morton Feldman, David Tudor, and Christian Wolff explored improvisational techniques in their compositions, using procedures that often stemmed from aleatoric or indeterminate operations. Although a score was prepared, its interpretation was left up to the performers; thus, a new form, that of group composition, evolved. Electronic works that involve this approach are Cage's "Variations" and Brown's "Four Systems," discussed in the forgoing chapter. The presence of a score, despite its flexible interpretational possibilities, provides performers with a frame of reference from which they can proceed.

Cage and his followers began to work along these lines during the 1950s, but it was not until the next decade that composers attempted to eliminate the score entirely. Larry Austin organized the New Music Ensemble at Davis, California in 1963; it was made up of composers who performed free improvisations. Electronics were not initially employed, but have subsequently been incorporated into their performances.

The following year, Austin met Italian composer-pianist Franco Evangelisti in Rome. Evangelisti, who had previously realized tape compositions at Cologne (1956–7) and at the Polish Radio in Warsaw (1959), formed the Gruppo di Improvvisazione Nuova Consonanza as a result of his contact with Austin. This was the first European improvisation ensemble made up entirely of composers.

176

The Nuova Consonanza included Mario Bertocini, John Heineman, Roland Kayn, Ennio Morricone, Jerry Rosen, Frederic Rzewski, Ivan Vandor, and Evangelisti. The timbral possibilities of conventional instruments were extensively explored in order that they might give the impression of involving electronic sources and modifications. Some instrumental techniques that frequently appear are: prepared piano, piano interior, clarinet "squeaks" and "squawks," bowed cymbal, trumpet and trombone mutes, and Hammond organ mixtures that contain very high upper partials, e.g., 1/3. Due to the incorporation of the Hammond organ, which is electronic, oscillators generate pitches that can be filtered by changing their registration, while the use of the 2/3 mixture approximates ring-modulated sonorities. Additional timbral variety proceeds from diverse instrumental groupings and the use of voice. "Cantata" (1964), by the Nuova Consonanza, is derived from four filtered and reverberated voices; the appearance of phonemes, pops, coughs, groans, and breathing create homogeneous textures reminiscent of "Visage."

The Nuova Consonanza's more recent improvisations involve prerecorded tapes interspersed with silence; while the taped material does not dominate, it does assume the role of performer. Electronic devices are also employed to modulate the instruments and to generate sound. Extremely high oscillator pitches, contrasted against subaudio pulses, supply the basic timbral framework of "Credo" (1969). The subaudio pulses appear as square waves, so that the upper partials sound as "clicks" in the absence of a fundamental. The frequency continuum is completed by filtered noise. The prerecorded tape consists of multi-lingual spoken fragments, some of which contain the word "credo." In addition, musical excerpts appear on the tape in collage form. Periodic silences within the tape create a well balanced texture; "Credo" sounds like a notated composition rather than a free improvisation.

Shortly after the formation of the Nuova Consonanza, the British composer Cornelius Cardew formed the AMM ensemble in London (1965). Cardew states that AMM stands for "a very pure form of improvisation operating without any formal system or limitation." Like Evangelisti, Cardew had worked at the Cologne studio, where he was closely associated with Stockhausen. With the exception of Cardew, the members of the AMM quintet are jazz musicians, but stylistic jazz traits are not overtly apparent in their improvisations. Their instrumentation includes piano, cello, tenor saxophone, electric guitar, and percussion. Prerecorded electronic and concrète tapes are frequently used, and the taped sonorities blend well with the instruments because of the diverse instrumental timbres suggestive of electronic effects. Similar procedures were followed by the Nuova Consonanza. This gradual textural evolution characterizes both ensembles.

The AMM relies on sustained sounds as a sonorous frame of reference, like the orchestral compositions of Mahler. Feedback is also admitted for this purpose, and the instruments concentrate on rhythmic and timbral extensions rather than on melodic development. In this respect, the improvisations of the AMM resemble the Indian raga popularized in the West during this period by Ravi Shankar. The presence of Indian rhythmic traits in not surprising, for many jazz musicians of the late 1960s were quite involved with this music. Since most members of the AMM had jazz backgrounds, it follows that their improvisations would reflect Indian influences.

Live electronic improvisation ensembles continued to flourish in Europe at the end of the 1960s. A group of American composers residing in Rome formed the Musica Elettronica Viva (MEV) in 1966. Two members of the group, Frederic Rzewski and Ivan Vandor, had originally been associated with the Nuova Consonanza, and influences from that ensemble are apparent in the music of the MEV. Besides Rzewski, other American composers in the MEV included Alan Bryant, Alvin Curran, and Richard Teitelbaum.

In addition to conventional instruments, the MEV utilized tape recorders, a Moog synthesizer, brainwave amplifiers, photocell mixers, and contact microphones. Brainwave amplifiers, which are included in the realm of bio-music, derive control voltages from electrical impulses associated with neurological responses like opening and closing the eyes. Control voltages, in this instance, operate voltage-controlled amplifiers in a manner analogous to the synthesizer. According to Manford Eaton: "Bio-Music is the term used by ORCUS Research to describe a class of electronic systems that use biological potentials in feedback loops to induce powerful, predictable, repeatable, physiological/psychological states which can be elegantly controlled in real time."

Photocell mixers designed and constructed by Rzewski are similar to the one used by Roger Reynolds in "Ping." Light intensity determines amplitude, and the spatial movement of sound is easily accomplished by altering the direction of the light source, usually a small penlight. Rzewski's mixer accepted up to four input signals, each of which can be directed to any of four loudspeakers. The ease of operation enhances the usefulness of this device in live performance.

Both brainwave amplifiers and photocell mixers admit new resources in an improvisational situation. The former is directly related to the physiological responses of the performers to their environment, while the mixer introduces a nonmusical element, light, to control sonorous events within that environment. Performers no longer need to develop improvisations based solely on abstract musical concepts. These can now be transcended so that any sensory stimulus can effect a sonorous response, and thus a dialogue among musicians is extended to include all aspects of the performance. The MEV has developed this to the point of audience participation; total involvement is their ideal.

The use of electronics in "Spacecraft" helps to attain this goal. Textures evolve slowly while sustained sounds predominate, corresponding to the previously mentioned AMM improvisation. Continuous strands of subaudio square waves generated by a Moog synthesizer are also similar to those employed by the AMM. The appearance of elongated phonemes produced by filtered voices is an example of the Nuova Consonanza's influence on Rzewski.

Sustained tones, subaudio pulses, vocal sounds, modulated percussion, and recurring bell sonorities constitute a dense textural web that supplies a fundamental timbral structure. A gradual crescendo is accompanied by subaudio pulses of higher frequencies. Because of their rhythmic implications, subaudio pulses determine the tempo of "Spacecraft," which is a corollary of Stockhausen's use of pulse to generate timbre. Pulses subsequently modulate the instruments, but they disappear near the end of the improvisation. At that point, a timbral shift to instrumental sonorities is initiated. The articulation of this cycle reveals the basic idea of "Spacecraft," the transformation of musical space.

Performers and their music occupy space, but sounds are embodied in past experiences; they are reproductions of the known. Each performer plays within an individual sonorous microcosm defined by his own virtuosity and limitations. "Spacecraft" proceeds from a combination of autonomous, improvised elements that subsequently lose their individuality and form associations to create a space. The musicians gradually move away from their limited sphere of sounds, prompted by sonorous and visual stimulation, "and become one with the atmosphere in vibration." No distinction is made among sound sources, for they share a common purpose. The emphasis is on music, not on electronic devices.

In addition to collective improvisations such as "Spacecraft," the MEV performs improvisatory compositions by its individual members and by other composers as well. Allan Bryant, an American who moved to Rome after working at the Cologne studio from 1959 to 1964, was one of the founders of the MEV. His "Pitch Out" (1968), performed by that ensemble, demonstrates the production of quasi-electronic sounds from newly designed instruments. Strings are loosely stretched along strips of wood and amplified by magnetic guitar pickups. Each of four instruments is assigned a loudspeaker, one in every corner of the room. Diverse playing techniques such as pizzicato, rolling an iron pipe over the strings and pickup, sliding a metal bar along the strings, drawing a large file across the low strings, and the regulation of amplitude, contribute to a simulation of oscillators, subaudio pulses, filtering, modulation, and tape transposition.

Although electronics do appear in improvisations by the Nuova Consonanza, the AMM and the MEV, their music seldom evolves only from these procedures. Similar concepts emerge as fundamental principles for an ensemble formed by Stockhausen in 1967, in which their chief concern is improvisational techniques. Originally conceived as a vehicle for predominantly improvised compositions, this group reveals a considerable refinement of Stockhausen's original ideas on collective improvisation. "Prozession" (1967), the immediate successor of "Hymnen," is the first work to employ a fixed ensemble consisting of piano, elektronium, electric viola, tam-tam, and filters. Stockhausen abandons the kind of complex tape delay networks found in "Solo," and limits electronic techniques to amplification and filtering of the viola and tam-tam.

In order to appreciate the significance of "Prozession" in relation to the evolution of compositional procedures, it must be approached with regard to Stockhausen's earlier electronic works. His initial electronic pieces, "Studies I and II" (1953, 1954), "Gesang" (1956), and "Kontakte" (1960), show a strict control of all their elements. The tape medium was ideal for this purpose, but the incorporation of prerecorded voice in "Gesang," and of performers in the second version of "Kontakte," reveals a preference for live sound sources. This change of attitude is reflected in his next series of compositions, "Mikrophonie I" (1964), "Mixtur" (1964), "Mikrophonie II" (1965), and "Solo" (1966). Ensembles of various sizes are modified by ring modulation, filtering, or tape delay, but the performers are subject to relatively strict compositional controls, as in the previous works.

Stockhausen synthesizes his concepts of control and live sources in "Telemusik" (1966) and "Hymnen" (1967), and approaches the ideal of a universal or world music. With these tape compositions, the composer was able to construct a fixed portrayal of a universal concept. Since there is no provision in them for change, "Telemusik" and "Hymnen" will eventually assume their place among historical documents.

This dilemma was progressively resolved by Stockhausen in "Prozession," "Kurzwellen" (1968), and "Aus den Sieben Tagen" (1968). The aforementioned ensemble is employed in the first two works, but the compositional controls are gradually relaxed so that the responsibility shifts from the composer to the performers, as evidenced in the format of the score. Rather than allotting complete freedom to performers in "Prozession," Stockhausen provides a skeletal formal scheme through use of the signs " +," " −," and " =." These represent relative increase, decrease, and equality of such elements as pitch and amplitude with respect to the preceding sonorous events. The musicians are forced to respond among themselves, so that a situation conducive to dialogue is created.

Within this loose framework, Stockhausen exercises rather strict control over what is played, but leaves all other musical decisions to the performers. The thematic materials, derived from earlier works, are memorized by the musicians. The pianist plays fragments from "Klavierstücke I-XI" and "Kontakte," the elektronium part is derived from "Telemusik" and "Solo," an amplified viola performs from "Gesang," "Kontakte," and "Momente," and a tam-tam and filters are based on "Mikrophonie I." These compositions appeared from 1952 to 1966, and establish a thematic continuum or tradition for "Prozession." Severe demands are placed upon the musicians, for it is assumed that they are thoroughly conversant with Stockhausen's work. The object is not to reiterate musical excerpts, but to recompose Stockhausen's music in such a way that the will of the composer is practically absent. These compositions are vehicles for the improvisational process; they are an attempt to insure musical coherence. As a result, performers play melodic fragments and develop timbre.

"Kurzwellen" extends the concepts of collective improvisation through the further relaxation of predetermined elements. A descendent of "Hymnen," this work utilizes shortwave radios as a source of sonorous material. The familiar musical fragments of "Prozession" are replaced by the unknown; in this case, radio broadcasts. Although the format of the score is the same as that of "Prozession," "Kurzwellen" demands that musicians react to more diverse sounds. Modulated shortwave reception imitated by the instrumentalists maintains a homogeneous distribution of sources. Universality will remain a distinctive trait of "Kurzwellen" because shortwave radios are included in it; a dialogue among the performers proceeds from the imposed necessity to listen, contained within the notational method devised by Stockhausen.

All of these improvisational processes culminate in his next work, "Aus den Sieben Tagen," which contains fifteen ideas conceived during a week of fasting and meditation. For the first time, Stockhausen relinquishes fundamental compositional controls. In "Kurzwellen," as we have seen, shortwave broadcasts, usually distorted, characterize the sonorous nature of the improvisation, and Stockhausen determined the basic elements, or type of sounds that would define aural boundaries. No such limits are present in "Sieben Tagen"; only vague verbal instructions that denote abstract processes, as "think nothing," or "play a vibration," are offered. Instrumentation is not suggested, and electronics need not be included. The composer assumes the role of guru. This distillation of the compositional process to the primordial stage led Stockhausen to the brink of silence. Nothing remains to be said; all sounds have been included; everything is possible, and nothing can be denied.

Many of these concepts exist in one or another of Stockhausen's earlier works: "Plus Minus" (1963) and "Solo," for instance, do not specify the choice of instruments, but contain elaborate instructions for their realization. The quest for universality, a dominant characteristic of his later compositions, stems from studies in perception that Stockhausen carried out during the 1950s. Having realized the role of proportions as determinants of duration and frequency, Stockhausen applied proportional relations to structural plans. If all elements are treated in this manner, a universal process results, i.e., a:b:c: . . . x:y:z:a: . . . . This cycle is described by Stockhausen in the score of "Kurzwellen:" "EVERYTHING is the WHOLE and SIMULTANEOUS".

Significant among European based electronic ensembles is the importance they place on improvisational techniques. Electronics function in a subordinate capacity; they complement such underlying musical substances as melody, rhythm, and timbre. Electronic configurations are usually less complex than those found in studio-produced works because of the obvious necessity of facility in performance. Even if electronic devices are omitted, improvisations can still be executed successfully.

The opposite is true of the music of the Sonic Arts Union, organized in 1966 by the American composers Robert Ashley, Gordon Mumma, David Behrman, and Alvin Lucier. Most of their works are improvisatory, and some involve theatrics. Electronics are essential in many instances, and comparatively less attention is paid to improvisational procedures. Gradual timbral and rhythmic transformations dominate, so that the music tends to proceed slowly.

Robert Ashley and Gordon Mumma established the Cooperative Studio for Electronic Music in 1958 at Ann Arbor, Michigan, and within the next two years, both were actively engaged in the production of theatre pieces. Ashley's "The Wolfman" (1964) has already been mentioned in reference to experiments with the Bob James jazz trio, but this work can also be realized with amplified voice and tape. In the latter instance, the vocal part is textless, derived from vowel sounds transformed by a change of mouth position. Each vocal phrase begins and ends with sustained tones three seconds long, while the gradual timbral transition of the vowels separates the sustained tones. The central portion of each phrase lasts between seven and ten seconds, so that the total duration of the vocal phrases is predetermined, between thirteen and sixteen seconds.

Vocal feedback is also employed, for which Ashley establishes a timbral connection with the voice by requiring the performer to stand close to the microphone. In addition, the tongue must touch the roof of the mouth in producing all vocal sounds, to emphasize feedback possibilities. Further timbral links arise from the use of feedback as connecting material between successive vocal phrases. The resultant sonorities are noise-laden, while the restricted placement of the tongue reduces timbral variety. This static atmosphere is contrasted against a tape collage of predominantly dense textures.

Amplified voice is again employed in "Purposeful Lady Slow Afternoon," the first song of the theatrepiece "The Wolfman

Motorcity Revue." Ashley chose a text that describes a woman's first fellation experience, accompanied by taped patterns of bell sonorities outlining a second inversion major triad. The delicate web of bell sounds, reminiscent of "His Last Journey" by Josef Zawinul, reinforces the subtle nature of the text.

After his association with Ashley at the Cooperative Studio, Gordon Mumma performed with the Merce Cunningham Dance Company. His application of electronics involves the cybersonic console, a small device designed and built by Mumma and William Ribbens that is worn by the performer. The console contains electronic circuitry that responds to both live and resonated sounds which are either transformed, or generate electronically-produced sounds.

Cybersonic modifications were introduced in "Medium Size Mograph" (1963), and by 1965 Mumma utilized this instrument almost exclusively in his electronic compositions. "Mesa" (1966), for cybersonic bandoneon, is the fifth work of this type. The bandoneon, a member of the accordion family, contains buttons to produce single tones. In this instance, a monophonic texture is extended to include chordal formations from ring modulation, while filtering produces subtractive processes. Extensive timbral variety results; complex harmonic spectra are prevalent because of the nonharmonic partials generated by ring modulation.

Similar processes are used in "Hornpipe" (1967), in which the French horn is camouflaged by the substitution of double reeds for the conventional metal mouthpiece. The direction of the sound is changed by rearranging the position of the slides, so that electronic sonorities are simulated prior to their actual appearance. As in "Mesa," the cybersonic console functions as a source of timbral and textural complexity. The nature of this device permits timbral structures to be predetermined, for the soloist can learn what responses to expect from the console through practice. The same is true of "Mesa," but since both works involve only one performer, the results of such preliminary experimentation need not be duplicated in performance.

Influenced by the custom-designed equipment of Rzewski and Mumma, David Behrman constructed electronic sound generators, modulators, and a photocell distribution network for "Runthrough" (1967). No instructions are given the performers, but the composer clarifies his intentions when he states that ". . . any sound which results from any combination of switch and light positioning remains part of the 'piece'." Frequency and amplitude modulation of repetitive patterns produce corresponding pitch and rhythmic variations, timbre is controlled by filtering, and sound paths are determined by photocells. The indeterminate nature of "Runthrough" and of "Wave Train," for amplified piano, recalls works by John Cage. Both Behrman and Cage have been associated with the Merce Cunningham Dance Company, which may indicate a reason for the similarity between the two.

The amplification of the piano in "Wave Train" is obtained from magnetic guitar pickups placed on the strings; each pickup possesses the means for volume control. Feedback loops are generated, and timbre altered, by changing the pickups' position. Powerful amplifiers and high amplitude settings on the guitar pickups produce feedback without activating the strings, so that the regulation of amplitude results in alternation between complex sonorous masses and feedback oscillations of a single frequency. Optional equipment for "Wave Train" consists of a prerecorded tape and an equalizer. In addition, this piece can be realized by two to five performers. The forgoing description pertains to the two-performer version, whereas other versions expand the technical resources to include ring modulation of a guitar pickup by a subaudio sine-square oscillator.

The fascination for specialized electronic devices revealed in the works of Mumma and Behrman is characteristic of the Sonic Arts Union as a whole. A unique approach in this area is found in two improvisatory pieces by Alvin Lucier, "North American Time Capsule" (1967) and "Vespers" (1968). The former, for voices and Vocoder (voice coder), treats vocal elements as audio and modulation signals. The Vocoder, produced by Sylvania Electronic Systems, is employed commercially for speech transmission over telephone lines or radio channels. Its operation is analogous to the digital-analog conversion processes used in computer systems. Speech is converted to digital information, transmitted over appropriate channels, and subsequently restored to its original form. It is used in space communication.

Like Behrman's "Runthrough," no score for "Time Capsule" exists. Lucier instructed the performers to choose sounds descriptive of contemporary society, and suitable for inclusion in a hypothetical time capsule. Any sound that satisfies this criterion is acceptable. Filtering creates the impression of distant voices, or transmissions from interplanetary space, accompanied by modulated speech distorted beyond intelligibility. The textures are so complex that they make comprehension of the speech impossible.

Theatrical elements appear in "Vespers," performed in darkness and based upon the principle of echolocation. Echolocation is a process for locating distant or invisible objects by means of sound waves reflected back to the emitter by the objects. Blindfolded performers armed with sondols wander about the performance area in an attempt to avoid colliding with one another. This is facilitated by the sondols, electronic devices that emit clicks to survey the environment, like the sensory perception of dolphins and bats. The manually-variable click rate produces complex rhythmic structures and textural changes when more than one performer plays. In the existing recording, periods of silence are interspersed with clicks, followed by gradually accelerated pulse rates perceived as pitch rather than as rhythm, i.e., they are faster than 16 pulses per second (16 Hz). A transition from subaudio to audio frequencies constitutes the structure of "Vespers."

Aside from "Purposeful Lady," the improvisations of the Sonic Arts Union are dependent on electronic networks. Although their European counterparts do not emphasize electronics to such an extent, the ensembles discussed in this chapter do develop a creative application for electronic devices. Sonorous transformations are extended to include all the elements of music: pitch, amplitude, duration, timbre, texture, and so forth, to supply coherent structural relations.

Another contributing factor to their successful improvisations is that all the ensembles, with the exception of the Stockhausen and AMM groups, are comprised of composers. Since improvisation is a form of composition, the performers, in addition to making sounds, must relate to the sonorous environment. Composers are trained to think in terms of structural associations, so that this process is initiated instantaneously.

Discography

AMM	ASHLEY, ROBERT
Live Electronic Music	"Purposeful Lady Slow
Improvised, Main. **5002**	Afternoon," Main. **5010**

"The Wolfman," Source Record No. 1

BEHRMAN, DAVID
"Runthrough," Main. 5010

———

"Wave Train," Source Record No. 1

BRYANT, ALLAN
"Pitch Out," Source Record No. 2

LUCIER, ALVIN
"North American Time Capsule," Odys. 32160156

———

"Vespers," Main. 5010

MUSICA ELETTRONICA VIVA
"Spacecraft," Main. 5002

MUMMA, GORDON
"Hornpipe," Main. 5010

———

"Mesa," Odys. 32160158

NUOVA CONSONANZA
"Cantata," MLDS 20243 (RCA Italiana)

———

"Credo," DGG 137007

STOCKHAUSEN, KARLHEINZ
"Aus den Sieben Tagen," DGG 2530255 and DGG 2530256

———

"Kurzwellen," 2—DG— 2707045

———

"Prozession," Can. 31001

CHAPTER NINE

SYNTHESIZERS IN LIVE PERFORMANCE

COMMERCIALLY MARKETED BUCHLA AND MOOG SYNTHESIZERS did not appear until 1966; Moog had presented his famous paper, "Voltage-Controlled Electronic Music Modules," at the Sixteenth Annual Fall Convention of the Audio Engineering Society in October, 1964. In the two-year interim, Paul Ketoff designed and built a portable voltage-controlled synthesizer, the Synket, in Rome. Ketoff, a technical supervisor of NIS Films in Rome, developed the Synket for use in live performance. The synthesizer was never made readily available to the general public, but it was adopted by the American composer John Eaton in 1965 as a performance instrument.

The Synket is made up of three identical "sound-combiner" systems, each of which includes a square wave oscillator (5–20,000 Hz.), frequency dividers, a bandpass filter that also functions as a sine oscillator, a waveform controller, a frequency modulator, and an amplitude modulator. The wide frequency range of the square oscillator provides subaudio pulses, while frequency division by 2, 3, 4, 5, and 8 enriches the harmonic spectrum. Each combiner network possesses a keyboard, and all functions can be interconnected. Additional devices on the Synket are a white noise generator, three amplitude modulators, and an octave filter bank. Internal connections reduce the necessity of external patching, although it is available. In performance, however, the use of patch cords would probably be minimized.

John Eaton first employed the Synket with soprano and piano

in "Songs for R.P.B." (1965), written at the American Academy in Rome. His fascination for quarter-tones is immediately apparent, and is found in both the vocal and synthesizer parts. Incidentally, Eaton formed his Microtonal Music Ensemble at this time, but no commercial recordings were made from it. Piano interior sonorities are produced, and indicate Eaton's timbral mastery.

A concern for microtonal and timbral relations reappears in the "Concert Piece for Synket and Symphony Orchestra" (1967), in which the orchestra is divided into two groups tuned a quarter-tone apart. The instrumental writing sometimes suggests electronic sonorities, especially the chordal masses played by both groups; but timbral associations usually proceed from instrumental simulation by the Synket. Motivic recurrences among all the parts help to establish relations between the instruments and the synthesizer; microtonal writing is present in both. A striking feature of the "Concert Piece" involves the use of the synthesizer, for Eaton rarely relies upon keyboards as an extension of the piano or organ. The ability to approach the Synket as an autonomous device allows the composer to create an electronic part comparable to prerecorded tape, a significant achievement for 1967.

Eaton expanded his electronic resources in "Blind Man's Cry" (1968) to include an ensemble of synthesizers with voice. Traditional melodies are replaced by a recitative style of vocal writing. This archaic technique, applied to high, middle, and low registers, forms a structural basis for the work. Example 51 illustrates this progression.

An intense vocal style, blended with Synkets, produces an Expressionistic atmosphere permeated by both pitch and timbral correspondence between the voice and electronics. Synthesizers often share similar frequency ranges with the voice, so that aural identification of the sound sources is difficult, particularly in high registers. A further correlation between sonorous categories, like

EXAMPLE 51.   John Eaton, "Blind Man's Cry"

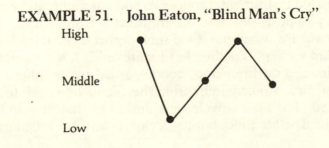

the voiced tremolo analogous to amplitude-modulated sine tones, confirms the homogeneity of "Blind Man's Cry," and makes it reminiscent of works by Davidovsky and Subotnick.

Eaton's preference for dramatic soprano can be seen again in "Mass" (1970), based on the Latin text, for voice, clarinet, Synket, and prerecorded tape. Eaton continues to display a mastery of timbre, evidenced in this case by his employment of clarinet multiphonics and flutter tonguing to simulate ring modulation and amplitude modulation respectively. As it did in "Concert Piece," the Synket synthesizes string, percussion, and vocal sounds. String and vocal timbres can be produced by sine tones or filtered square waves, whereas subaudio pulses and filtered noise, with their characteristic short attack and decay times, generate percussive sonorities. Finally, voiced vibrato and tremolo are representative of frequency and amplitude modulation.

Eaton treats the Latin text in a quasi-liturgical manner through the use of musical elements characteristic of Medieval and Renaissance practice. Parts of the Kyrie exhibit Gregorian melodic patterns. Modulated and filtered tape delay occurs in the Credo, in which a man recites selected textual excerpts in English, recalling antiphonal choral settings. The Agnus Dei contains microtonal relations within an imitative duet between voice and clarinet, superposed over an electronic drone.

Donald Erb employs a Moog synthesizer, Moog polyphonic, violin, piano, string bass, and percussion in "Reconnaissance" (1967), a five-movement work. Like Eaton, he maintains stable timbral relations among the instruments and synthesizers by treating the latter as part of the ensemble. Additional cohesion results from motivic interchanges among all the parts, which leads the composer to treat the synthesizer as a keyboard instrument, imitative of pianistic technique. Imaginative timbral associations between the synthesizer and conventional instruments are always present.

Simulated instrumental sonorities such as violin and percussion frequently appear; but smooth transitions from natural to electronic sound are also found. One such occurrence, at the beginning of the third section, is outlined in Example 52. A low pitch is struck sforzando (sfz) on the piano, accompanied by its inherent decay characteristics. Immediately after the piano tone, white noise is introduced. The noise envelope is similar to that of piano, i.e., it has no steady-state time, but its decay is considerably longer. This

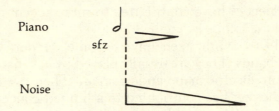

EXAMPLE 52. Donald Erb, "Reconnaissance"

technique enables Erb to transform instrumental sonorities to electronic ones without direct modification, concurrently establishing a homogeneous textural progression.

The vast number of rock and jazz ensembles that use the synthesizer cannot be discussed in entirety in this text, but the following selective survey should adequately cover this topic. The rock groups involved with electronics during the late 1960s like the Beatles, Hendrix, and the Velvet Underground, relied on recording studio techniques and feedback. Although commercial synthesizers were available, they were not regularly used by rock musicians until the next decade.

The first American rock band to extensively employ electronics, the United States of America (USA), appeared in 1967 and disbanded within one year. The leader of the group, Joseph Byrd, had organized the UCLA New Music Workshop in 1963; it included composers, engineers, sculptors, painters, filmmakers, photographers, and poets. In addition to solo tape pieces, Byrd had combined electronics with jazz and rock ensembles.

USA made use of electronically-generated sounds from the custom designed Byrd-Durrell synthesizer, combined with ring modulator and echo units controlled by foot pedals. California-based and contemporary with the Grateful Dead and the Mothers of Invention, USA, which consisted of electrified harpsichord, drums, bass, guitar, and violin, exceeded all other groups in instrumental amplification. Even voice was ring-modulated, a novelty for rock audiences, who had recently been exposed to tape transposition and voice reversal by the Beatles, the Stones and Hendrix. Without a doubt, his compositional training and awareness of the works of Stockhausen, Cage, *et al.*, enabled Byrd to conceive this ensemble.

Similar influences have contributed to more recent developments in the rock medium.

In the 1970s, synthesizers have become standard equipment in many rock bands. They are usually played by keyboard performers, in addition to electric piano and/or organ. Their oversimplified use of the synthesizer has contributed to a limited concept of the synthesizer as an extension of keyboard instruments. Aside from such clichés as oscillator glissandi and white noise (the latter suggestive of the ocean), synthesizers are commonly used to play melodic lines in either solo or ensemble contexts. Two oscillators are often tuned to the unison or octave to produce a full sound, while subsequent filtering, usually derived from descending control voltages analogous to glissandi patterns, simulates the "wah-wah" effects associated with the electric guitar, sonorities popularized by Jimi Hendrix and Eric Clapton during the late 1960s.

Much of this problem revolves around early synthesizer design, for mechanical keyboards were included by manufacturers to make their product more easily accessible to musicians unfamiliar with the principles of electronic music composition. Without understanding the basic concepts of control voltage, modulation, timbral transformation, and so on, performers will be unable to derive maximum flexibility from their equipment. Although live performance demands operational ease, and keyboard orientation is a solution to it, the possibility for instrument modification via synthesizer is a viable approach. Part IV includes suggestions for live performance synthesizer application; diverse methods of timbral, frequency, and amplitude control are outlined in it.

Stevie Wonder, blind singer-pianist-composer, derived instrumental timbres from a Moog synthesizer in "Living for the City" (1973). Electronic elements appear as melodic interludes and background accompaniment, enhanced by filter sweeps to provide timbral diversity. The formal organization recalls pieces by Pink Floyd that utilize concrète sources like speech, footsteps, and automobile engines, to evoke environmental impressions. Approximately two-thirds through "Living for the City," the text of which deals with racial prejudice toward blacks, a concrète sequence appears that depicts migration from Mississippi to New York. Sonorous events progress from a bus station to a speech, a police station, a false arrest and quick conviction, followed by the resumption and conclusion of the song.

Synthesized instrumental timbres characterize the style of George Duke, keyboard player for the Mothers of Invention. Since this group includes trumpet, trombone, and tenor saxophone, with an expanded rhythm section, the synthesizer helps to create full textures similar to those employed by Blood, Sweat and Tears and Chicago. Smooth timbre shifts accomplished by control voltage filter sweeps contribute to a well-balanced ensemble sound. These procedures are found in "Echidna's Arf" (1974), "Don't You Ever Wash That Thing" (1974), and "Penguin in Bondage" (1974); the latter also incorporates tape delay on the final word of some of its phrases. Filtered guitar, the wah wah, is often present; while the rarely-employed guitar fuzz appears in "Son of Orange County" (1974).

New rock during the late 1960s frequently entailed the use of flashing lights, slides, and films, as evidenced by such groups as the Velvet Underground. This trend has gradually progressed to include the performance of extramusical activities during concerts; usually they are visual representations of the lyrics or song title. "Be-Bop Tango" (1974), by the Mothers of Invention, involves the demonstration of a "perverted" tango, first by the musicians, then by audience volunteers, followed by complete audience participation. In this satirical context, the synthesizer appears in both ensemble and solo passages, while white noise and glissandi effects share a minor role.

Unlike Zappa's earlier pieces, in which electronic effects were achieved through recording studio tape manipulation, the addition of the synthesizer has effected a reorientation of timbral relations. Vocal transformations, originally a source of new sonorities, were replaced by synthesized equivalents of musical instruments. Since the album under discussion, *Roxy and Elsewhere*, consists of concert performances, tape modification would have been too cumbersome; hence, two distinct forms of electronic rock, recording studio and live performance, exist at present.

The Tubes' staging of the most elaborate rock spectacles of all incorporate costumes, props, and actions for individual songs, resulting in miniature theatrical productions. Despite their sensationalism, the Tubes have emerged as one of the best American electronic rock groups. They have assimilated elements from the

Mothers of Invention, the Velvet Underground, and electronic composers, so that the synthesizer, and tape transformations, provide varied timbral resources.

Taped voice echo appears in "Up From the Deep" (1975) and "White Punks On Dope" (1975). The former begins with speech, followed by wind effects via white noise, as background material for the remainder of the song. Oscillator glissandi alternated between two channels are superposed to create more diverse textures. Glissandi are also used in "White Punks," while tape delay is applied to the word "dope" near the end of the song. Further vocal treatment, found in "Malagueña Salerosa" (1975), consists of material spoken in English juxtaposed with the lyrics sung in Spanish. The conclusion of "What Do You Want From Life" (1975) gradually introduces high-pass filtering to speech, accompanied by continual movement between channels.

Filtered glissandi evoke eerie effects in "Space Baby" (1975), in which electronic clichés reinforce its satirical nature. "Mondo Bondage" (1975), however, contains the most successful application of electronics. The synthesizer sometimes doubles the lead guitar; glissandi are frequency-modulated; and a transposed tape fragment concludes the piece: the electronic sonorities are appropriately chosen to complement the instrumental timbres.

The long instrumental interludes that characterize songs by the Tubes stem from earlier groups like the Mothers of Invention and the Grateful Dead. The bilingual "Malagueña" is reminiscent of the Credo from Eaton's "Mass," and the combination of speech with song is also found in tunes by the Velvet Underground. Although the exaggerated use of glissandi becomes too predictable, it is compensated for by imaginative tape techniques, vocal transformations, and the melodic treatment of the synthesizer.

The music of Todd Rundgren is electronically more complex than that of the Tubes; it includes tape delay, mellotron, piano, and "keyboard computer". "Born to Synthesize" (1975), a blues-style vocal solo, receives textural contrast from tape delay and timbral variation through ring modulation of the voice. A complete range of electronic manipulations occurs in "A Treatise On Cosmic Fire" (1975), recorded and mixed in a studio. Additional timbral diversity is supplied by a mellotron, a keyboard instrument that plays prerecorded tapes of conventional instruments, voice, and sound effects. Since the instrumental sonorities are not synthesized, the mellotron is a suitable substitute for an orchestra. In this instance, a great variety of keyboard instruments make smooth timbral progression possible, although the excessive repetition of sonorous elements, frequently juxtaposed to form layers of sound, also contributes to textural associations.

The British electronic rock groups are generally superior to their American counterparts, for their electronic modifications often assume structural significance. The timbral subtlety of the mellotron, for instance, characterizes King Crimson's music. One of his early works, "Pictures of a City" (1970), combines guitar fuzz and reverberation with the mellotron, while additional sonorous relations proceed from the saxophone and flute. The song's strophic structure is reinforced by timbral repetitions, but a change of mood and texture halfway through the piece destroy its predictability—and that associated with rock music. After a classic return to the beginning, "Pictures" concludes in chaos, an unfortunate cliché derived from the earlier psychadelic bands. King Crimson's music typifies the use of the mellotron, which has become a popular instrument among groups desiring extensive timbral resources. The Moody Blues made similar use of the mellotron. Although it is not a synthesizer, both of these instruments provide means for controlling timbre, an essential aspect of electronic music.

One reason for the recent sophistication of electronic rock groups is the influence of other forms of music. A very imaginative ensemble, Yes, has been affected by the music of Stockhausen, Mimaroglu, Stravinsky, Jimi Hendrix, the Beatles, the Mahavishnu Orchestra, and jazz; yet, they have avoided the danger of eclecticism. Formed in 1968, Yes gradually approached the electronic medium via the addition of orchestra, mellotron and synthesizer. Their songs are long, contain extended instrumental interludes, and exhibit a wide range of timbres.

Electronics complement a simple three-part formal structure in "South Side of the Sky" (1971; *Fragile*). After beginning with filtered noise, the piece's melody is played in octaves by the guitar and the synthesizer. The gradual textural transformation procedes from the juxtaposition of old and new sonorities, i.e., filtered noise and acoustic piano, which evolves into a section with piano alone. The filtered noise motive recurs to initiate the recapitulation of the initial section, followed by a short coda derived from the filtered noise. Electronics are not used extensively, but they do add substance to the piece. The creative application of synthesizer revealed here is not found in other rock groups like the Tubes and Todd Rundgren until a few years later.

Motivic repetitions achieve greater importance in "Close to the Edge" (1972; *Close to the Edge*), which is segmented into four continuous movements. The opening sonorities of filtered noise, bird chirps (frequency modulated tones), bells, organ chords, and rapid sequencer patterns, appear intermittently, while chords are shared by the organ, acoustic piano, and mellotron. The incorporation of additional small synthesizers and mellotrons with conventional keyboard instruments, all played by one performer, enhances the sonorous possibilities in performance. The equipment can be preset to facilitate the timbral shifts, so that such an elaborate configuration actually renders great flexibility of structural relations dependent upon timbre. In this instance, the smooth progression among the electronic and acoustic keyboard instruments defines the formal divisions within the piece.

Excerpts from "The Six Wives of Henry VIII" (1973; *Yes Songs*), keyboard solo by composer Rick Wakeman, are less successful than Yes's earlier works. Purposeless stylistic shifts encompassing diverse keyboard mannerisms of Bach, Debussy, silent movie accompaniment, jazz, and rock, followed by the Alleluia Chorus from Handel's "Messiah," contribute to the formation of a collage. War clichés of bombs and air raid sirens produced from filtered noise and oscillator glissandi do little to affect timbral cohesion, one of Yes's most refined aspects.

"The Remembering" (1973; *Tales from Topographic Oceans*), one of the final songs recorded by Yes before Wakeman's departure, exhibits frequent mood changes accompanied by corresponding textural transformations. The mellotron supplies sustained string sonorities, while synthesizers simulate organ chords. Wakeman produces the effect of tape reversal by setting the envelope attack times to maximum duration, so that the total envelope time exceeds the duration of the individual pitches. When this is applied to a synthesizer keyboard, the depression of a key may generate pitch and activate an envelope generator, in which case the resultant envelopes end prematurely as melodic progressions occur more quickly. Example 53 illustrates the following envelope characteristics: (a) quick attack and long decay, typical of many instrumental timbres; (b) reversal of (a); (c) long attack and quick decay as employed by Wakeman; and (d) truncated version of (c). The similarity

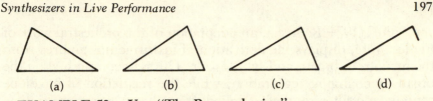

(a)   (b)   (c)   (d)

EXAMPLE 53.   Yes, "The Remembering"

between (b) and (d) is sufficient to produce the impression of tape reversal.

Patrick Moraz, formerly of Refugee, replaced Rick Wakeman in 1974. Like his predecessor, Moraz performs surrounded by a variety of synthesizers and keyboard instruments, each of which possesses a unique sonorous quality. His refreshing approach to the synthesizer is revealed in his statement that "the ultimate goal is to make a Moog or an Arp or a string synthesizer not sound like a Moog or an Arp or a string synthesizer," a sentiment shared by many composers and performers.

Even though Wakeman had left Yes, the group retained the technique of timbral structure to enforce sectional division. In "The Sound Chaser" (1974; *Relayer*), Moraz displays jazz influences that recall Miles Davis and Chick Corea; sonorous associations among guitar, synthesizer, and mellotron, contrasted against electric piano, permeate the piece. The electronic effects are subtly integrated within the work's textural context. "The Gates of Delirium" (1974; *Relayer*), in which fast sequencer patterns occur periodically in the background, makes use of more elaborate electronics. The synthesizer and the mellotron, treated as complements of each other, are used for solos, accompaniment, countermelodies, and guitar doubling, while filtered guitar enhances its relation to the electronic instruments. Moraz appropriately combines ring modulation and noise to create dense textures, followed by pedal tones, much reverberation, and the use of an echoplex near the conclusion.

Although Wakeman is a capable performer, his use of electronics is not as imaginative as that of Moraz, who relies less upon clichés. His restricted use of white noise, for instance, along with the introduction of ring modulation, reveal Moraz to be a sensitive performer. Both musicians base their work upon structural considerations, a major factor in determining Yes's musical effectiveness.

Before Moraz joined Yes, he led the trio Refugee, where he played piano, organ, mellotron, and synthesizer. "The Grand Canyon Suite" (1974; *Refugee*), an adaptation of the orchestral work of Ferde Grofé, displays the derivation of instrumental timbres from the mellotron, organ, and synthesizer. This is accomplished on the organ by changing registration, while the regulation of envelope contour and filter response applied to oscillators produces similar results on the synthesizer. In contrast to this piece, "Credo" (1974; *Refugee*) is a virtuosic keyboard work in the tradition of Keith Emerson, in which rapid alternations among piano, organ, and synthesizer provide timbral and structural associations. Another instance of Moraz's refined musical judgment is revealed in his application of glissandi. Like the orchestral music of Xenakis, Moraz develops the concept of glissando rather than relying on a momentary effect. Slow glissandi that encompass a few bars are contrasted against quick glissandi and similar filter patterns, so that a homogeneous network of melodic and timbral relations arises.

I (1976), the first album produced by Moraz since his tenure with Yes, is a composition of approximately forty-five minutes' duration. Although subdivided into fourteen sections, the music is continuous, and the progression between the successive parts is smooth. Moraz states that "*I* stands for initiation, identity, idealism, integration, illumination, immortality, infinity . . . ," but this profound generalization is too serious for the musical content of "*I*."

As one would expect of Moraz, "*I*" exhibits an imaginative application of electronic processes to produce the timbral interest from which the structural relations proceed. Those timbres most noteworthy are: water drops recorded with a time delay via an echoplex; stereo separation of French and English texts; and stereo separation of Arp and Moog synthesizers, while ring-modulated harpsichord appears on both tracks. Timbral resources are extended by the employment of acoustic and electric guitar and bass, cello, drums, timpani, and a percussion ensemble from Rio de Janeiro. In addition, Moraz plays piano, organ, mellotron, electric piano, harpsichord, gongs, cymbals, and a variety of synthesizers, including string and drum synthesizers. Sections are delineated by timbral changes similar to those found in the works of Yes.

The problem with "*I*" rests in its eclectic nature; its stylistic elements are derived from Baroque and Romantic keyboard literature, rock, jazz, and a Brazilian Macumba chant. Even though the combination of such diverse idioms stems from a desire to achieve "integration," their presence often assumes the nature of a cliché; the value of the intermodulation proposed by Stockhausen becomes evident.

While Rick Wakeman was with Yes, he also produced an album, *The Six Wives of Henry VIII* (1972), in which his lack of imagination is apparent. His realization of six long compositions that focus on various keyboard instruments requires a special effort to avoid unnecessary repetitions and clichés. A baroque keyboard style and harmonic vocabulary, in addition to filter sweeps, are used in "Catherine of Aragon" and "Catherine Howard," the latter also characterized by frequent shifts from the keyboard style of Bach to rock, honky tonk, and Mozart. Timbral changes are derived from filtering and alternation among the instruments; ring modulation is never incorporated, but the sounds of the sea, via filtered noise, are present in "Catherine Parr". In addition, two mellotrons generate string, woodwind, brass, vocal, and vibraphone sonorities. As in his Yes arrangements, timbral changes articulate a shift of mood, and Wakeman has mastered that technique. However, since this is not accompanied by substantive development, a superficial virtuosity permeates the work.

The only group to employ electronics as effectively as Yes is Emerson, Lake and Palmer. Keith Emerson's keyboard artistry is unequaled in electronic rock, while his approach to the synthesizer demonstrates a refined sensitivity toward timbral relations. Classical influences are obvious, but rather than extract stylistic mannerisms as Wakeman does, Emerson chooses compositions upon which he structures improvisations. An example is his arrangement of Mussorgsky's "Pictures At An Exhibition" (1971). Emerson keeps some sections, like "Promenade," intact, but most of them serve as frameworks for variation and development. Varied synthesizer applications include amplitude, frequency, and ring modulation; slow filtering rates; white noise; and oscillators tuned in seconds and fifths. The character of "Pictures" is retained, while Emerson's musical effects are used by the rest of the group to improvise.

Similar treatment is given to "Toccata" (1973), adapted from the fourth movement of Alberto Ginastera's first piano concerto. Synthesizers often simulate orchestral sonorities, since a mellotron is not employed. Choral effects, produced by oscillators of identical waveforms tuned in unison, are varied by changing waveforms, or played in unison with the guitar. All forms of modulation, together with filtering and the use of the sequencer and echoplex, constitute timbral associations that adhere to the formal structure established by Ginastera.

Keith Emerson, one of the few rock keyboard performers to use ring modulation, bases his choice of timbre on structural relations. His music is always intersting because he avoids triteness and unnecessary literal repetition. The constant search for new sonorities that characterizes contemporary composition is not an end in itself, but rather results from compositional necessity.

The Matching Moles, contemporaries of Emerson, Lake and Palmer, do not attempt to overwhelm the listener with electronic effects, but employ them within a definite timbral structure. "Gloria Gloom" (1972) is among their most successful pieces because of the synthesizer artistry of Brian Eno. It combines simple melodic patterns on the synthesizer with sustained tones, glissandi, filtering, ring modulation, reverberation, and tape delay. The entire song is soft, and its rich textures blend to create an Impressionistic atmosphere. This is especially evident at the beginning, where conversational speech is accompanied by a synthesizer and a rock band. The voices gradually fade into the background and the song begins, with the synthesizer, voices, and instruments playing and singing the melody. A more extensive use of modulation, in conjunction with tape delay, appears in "Smoke Signal" (1972), whereas "Flora Fidgit" (1972) relies on filtering for sonorous transformation. In the latter, the synthesizer and instruments also play the melody in unison.

Eno's contribution on "Gloria Gloom" is obvious when the song is compared to the others on this album, for he performs only on this one. His absence on the remainder of the album is marked by a less imaginative utilization of electronics: the synthesizer is generally treated as a melodically-oriented keyboard instrument. The Soft Machine is a further example of this kind of use of the synthesizer. Whereas their initial compositions involved tape manipulations (see Chapter 5), *Soft Machine VII* (1973) replaces these with a synthesizer played in the aforementioned manner, e.g., "Nettle Bed" (1973). In addition to doubling melodic materials with the synthesizer and instruments, the Soft Machine frequently applies glissando patterns to voltage-controlled filters. The inferior musical quality of their more recent albums may be attributable to both the use of the synthesizer and a personnel change in the group.

Tape effects reminiscent of those employed by Pink Floyd and the Mothers of Invention, combined with synthesizer and mellotron, reappear with the Who. Their *Quadrophenia* (1973) album is dominated by white noise and taped fragments that function as interludes between successive pieces. The former appears throughout "I am the Sea," accompanied by a tape echo of a voice, while a news broadcast occurs at the conclusion of "Cut My Hair." Although "The Punk Meets the Godfather" incorporates filtered voice, electronics and tape techniques are treated purely as effects, a by-product of the late 1960s.

Roxy Music began as a promising group. They explored timbral resources derived from the synthesizer, the oboe, guitar fuzz, and ring-modulated saxophone. Taped sequences also appear, as in "Re-make/Re-model" (1972), in which sounds from a cocktail party introduce the song. Extreme high and low frequency ranges, combined with modulation in the background, again show Eno, their keyboard player, to be an imaginative musician. Further timbral variety is included in "Ladytron" (1972), achieved by adding reverberation to the oboe, while amplitude modulation and the filtering of instruments is restricted to the end of the piece; ring-modulated and reverberated saxophone in "Chance Meeting" (1972) account for its increased textural complexity. Despite the inclusion of such stereotyped elements as filtered noise and taped fragments, Roxy Music originally displayed a creative application of electronics in their songs.

Unlike the results of Wakeman's replacement by Moraz in Yes, Eno's departure from Roxy Music caused their electronic music to suffer. Their recent music displays nostalgia for the 1950s, and their lyrics focus on sex and drugs, abandoned by most rock groups by the late 1960s. "Love is the Drug" (1975), for example, begins with sounds of footsteps and a departing automobile. Electronic effects such as white noise and modulation are often restricted to the introductory material. Their absence during the main part of "Sentimental Fool" (1975) weakens any structural relations that might have developed. The synthesizer is generally a source of melodic material and simple accompaniment, and contains much less modulation and sonorous associations among other instruments.

Another Green World (1975), an album produced by Eno following his association with Roxy Music, exhibits a refined application of electronics similar to the first Roxy Music album. A prerecorded tape composed of concrète and electronic elements appears in "Over Fire Island," while the simple use of oscillators tuned in unison is expanded to encompass intervals of thirds, fifths, and sixths to produce chords. Eno's inventiveness is further demonstrated on "In Dark Trees," in which delayed guitar chords are superposed over a rhythmic accompaniment derived from electronic percussion instruments. The guitar chords are then interspersed with the melodic lines, so that simple musical ideas yield a refreshing timbral and rhythmic structure.

Voltage-controlled oscillator glissandi representative of air raid sirens; machine gun fire simulated by filtered noise with short attack and decay characteristics; and fragmented conversations, provide a stereotyped programmatic introduction to "War Child" (1974), by Jethro Tull. Like recent pieces by Roxy Music, the effects cease upon commencement of the song, but they intermittently reappear in the background. The recapitulation of the introductory sonorities establishes a superficial formal plan, but since the electronics are not integrated with the other musical elements, their effect is weakened.

In "The Third Hoorah" (1974), a more meaningful use of synthesizer is made with the synthesizing of realistic harpsichord sonorities. Derived from two oscillators tuned in unison, a harpsichord timbre is produced from the addition of a percussive envelope, while its authenticity is enhanced by the employment of diverse oscillator waveforms that are then filtered. Although the synthesizer is capable of more varied applications, and could have been replaced effectively by mellotron, its use in this piece exemplifies a more creative approach than that of "War Child."

Songs by the various rock groups are either short, between three and five minutes, or rather long, more than ten minutes. Surprisingly, groups tend to restrict themselves to one of these categories. As may be expected, the shorter songs generally do not possess elaborate electronic modifications, but utilize the synthesizer chiefly as a melodic instrument. "Just the Same" (1975), by the Gentle Giant, displays these qualities. The synthesizer often plays in unison with the piano or guitar; timbral variety is accomplished by filtering. Sustained chords modified by filter sweeps provide a simple accompaniment to the song. Because of the time limitation, electronic complexity is not possible, but as a result, a series of formulae to guarantee a modern, "electronic" sound have rapidly evolved. These stereotyped sonorities, however, must be extended if interesting timbres are to prevail. Since there are presently a few musicians who understand this, hopefully others will follow their example.

One of the most popular Italian rock bands is Premiata, Forneria, Marconi (PFM). Their keyboard instruments, typically found in most electronic groups, include a synthesizer, acoustic and electric piano, organ, and mellotron, but their application of electronics is generally limited to melody. Most of the PFM songs are related stylistically to those of Emerson, Lake and Palmer, like "Celebration" (1974) and "Mr. Nine Till Five" (1974). The former entails using a filtered synthesizer for prime melodic material, in addition to unison passages between synthesizer and guitar; the mellotron appears in the conventional context of sustained string tones. The mellotron is replaced by the organ in the second piece, while acoustic piano provides an accompaniment for a melodically oriented use of the synthesizer. Like the British groups, PFM's timbral changes often reflect the sectionalization of a song, and they derive these contrasts from a variety of keyboard instruments. While excessive stereotyped electronic effects are avoided, synthesizer and guitar filtering are the only modifications employed. Their timbral shifts are therefore too predictable; for a limited number of sonorities, each assigned to a particular mood, continually recur. The synthesizer plays the melodic lines, the electric piano and organ supply the chordal accompaniment, and the mellotron and organ provide the sustained sonorities.

The mellotron is used extensively by I Pooh, sometimes accompanied by the synthesizer playing melodic lines in the background. Piano, harpsichord, and filtered guitar increase the timbral possibilities, but electronics are assigned a minor rule. A similar use of electronics appears in the songs of Claudio Baglioni, where a limited number of effects such as white noise and a Moog bass ornament the instrumental accompaniment.

The influence of Emerson, Lake and Palmer reappears in the music of G. P. Reverberi, who arranges works of Chopin, Schumann, and Liszt for orchestra, piano, organ, synthesizer, textless soprano, and rhythm section. The fourth prélude of Chopin, for instance, includes ornamental melodic figurations on the synthesizer, in addition to unison passages for synthesizer and orchestra. An excerpt from "Carnaval", Schumann's solo piano composition, includes overdubbed synthesizer, piano, and organ, and recalls Keith Emerson's adaptation of works by Mussorgsky and Ginastera.

Compared to their British counterparts, the Italian electronic rock groups are conservative in their application of electronics. Although the British influence exists, it involves stylistic similarities rather than an extensive use of electronics.

Edgar Froese, the principal exponent of German electronic rock, does not employ guitar, bass, and drums as other groups do. Extremely long pieces, realized on tape in a studio, are derived from synthesizers and tape manipulations. Three characteristics of his work, slow pulse, gradual timbral transformation, and superposed layers of sound, are apparent in "ngc 891" (1974). The stratification of sonorous elements produces a transformation from monophonic to polyphonic textures, ornamented by tape echo and filter sweeps. Froese's compositions bear little resemblance to rock music, including that by Yes and Emerson, Lake and Palmer. Except for the inclusion of an extended bass sequencer pattern, "ngc 891" could be considered a "classical" electronic composition.

Tangerine Dream, a trio formed by Froese, consists of synthesizers, mellotron, organ, electric piano, guitar and gong. The characteristics of "ngc 891" mentioned above recur in "Rubycon" (1975), so that static elements are varied by timbral and textural transformations. The presence of additional keyboard instruments increases the sonorous resources, which are complemented by filtering and by a concentration on high, middle, and low frequencies to elicit structural divisions. Since the emphasis is upon "consonant" harmonics, ring modulation is excluded; glissandi and white noise appear as embellishments of the dense textural web.

German electronic rock is unique in its exclusion of percussion and its rare use of the guitar, both of which are considered essential by other rock groups. Rock's rhythmic characteristics have already begun to disappear with its recent fusion with jazz, manifested in the keyboard styles of George Duke, Keith Emerson, Patrick Moraz, and Rick Wakeman. The use of electronics, particularly ring modulation, feedback, and tape manipulation, has extended its sonorous elements into the realm of classical electronic music. Finally, the classical and jazz backgrounds of many musicians has facilitated stylistic borrowing that has ultimately led to new methods of structural organization. The definition of fusion music, which originally included only jazz and rock, must now be broadened to encompass electronic music. Similarly, electronic composers including Pierre Henry, Ilhan Mimaroglu, and Kenneth Gaburo have incorporated elements from jazz and rock in their music, and when Stockhausen speaks of a universal music, he is referring to the highest level of fusion. At this point categorization is no longer useful, for sound has transcended its usual connotations.

This phenomenon is not restricted to electronics; it appears in ensembles involved in improvisation as well. In many respects, improvisation is a strict discipline, for performers must exercise compositional choices that do not reflect personal musical habits, and must avoid clichés. Musicians are forced to shed stylistic crutches to seek meaningful sonorous relations at any given moment. No formulae exist; everything depends on the sensitivity of the performer. This situation has united and equalized musicians on a level where stylistic mannerisms no longer have meaning; each sound contributes to the formation of the whole.

The introduction of the synthesizer in jazz groups achieved popularity in the early 1970s, a few years after its use by rock bands. Contrary to rock, the utilization of electronic keyboard instruments in jazz poses particular problems. More emphasis is generally placed on the keyboard in jazz, especially for solos; the counterparts to this in rock are Emerson, Lake and Palmer; Yes; and Tangerine Dream. Furthermore, rock groups always include at least two chordal instruments, keyboard and guitar, so that the guitar can supply harmonies when the synthesizer is played. This is because until recently, all synthesizers possessed monophonic keyboards. If two or three oscillators were connected to the keyboard, the depression of a single key generated two or three pitches whose intervallic relation remained constant, regardless of which key was depressed. Example 54 illustrates this situation.

If three oscillators are tuned to a C major triad (Example 53a), the depression of the middle C key will produce the chord, so that one key controls all three oscillators. Although only one control voltage is present, each of the oscillators is tuned initially to a different pitch. Therefore, when the control voltage changes, that is, when another key is pressed, the voltage will transpose the three pitches uniformly, so the intervallic distance between the three

(a)

(b)

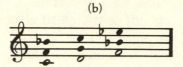

(c)

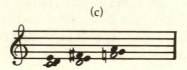

White notes denote keys to be depressed.

EXAMPLE 54. Monophonic synthesizer keyboards

frequencies remains constant. Examples 54b and c portray other tunings. As can be imagined, few pieces can be harmonized by a single vertical harmony, whether triadic, quartal, or a cluster. In most instances, there is not enough time to change oscillator tunings during the performance of a song, so that these polyphonic possibilities enjoy only limited application. Keith Emerson, for example, utilizes quartal tunings in "Aquatarkus." Since jazz groups do not always include guitar, the keyboard player must supply the chords, but this is not always possible because of the limitations of most synthesizers.

There are three possible solutions to this dilemma: first, tune three oscillators to a given harmony as shown in the preceding example; second, avoid polyphonic applications entirely; and third, treat the synthesizer as a monophonic instrument, but simultaneously play chords on the piano or organ with the other hand. Emerson, Moraz, Wakeman, *et al.* generally follow the latter procedure, which is one of the reasons they surround themselves with keyboard instruments, although timbral variety and performance facility are other benefits of this configuration.

Paul Bley, one of the first jazz musicians to use the synthesizer within a trio, is among the best of the synthesizer performers, yet he is surprisingly underated. *The Paul Bley Synthesizer Show* (1970–71), perhaps the best electronic jazz album to date, includes the ARP synthesizer with the electric piano and rhythm section. Bley treats the synthesizer according to the context of the music, so that the range of modifications spans the spectrum from simple to complex. "Mr. Joy," for instance, involves only slight frequency modulation on high sustained tones. The melodic material is played on the ARP synthesizer, while the electric piano supplies the chordal accompaniment. In this example, the synthesizer assumes the timbre of an accordion; the simplicity of the electronic application emphasizes the song's musical substance, rather than electronic effects.

A more elaborate use of the synthesizer is made in "The Archangel," but subtlety still prevails, and the electronic transformations still proceed from the song's musical context. A chordal effect obtained by tuning two oscillators in unison is again combined with the electric piano; glissandi are used as melodic development rather than as superficial effects. Bley then employs high frequency glissandi and amplitude modulation as accompaniment for a subsequent bass solo, so that his electronic modifications achieve real structural significance.

Bley's most complex treatment of electronics occurs in "Nothing Ever Was, Anyway." Sonorities articulate the structure of this piece to such an extent that the listener forgets the source of the sounds. A rare example of ring-modulated keyboard solo, along with sequencer patterns that are extensions of previous melodic and rhythmic elements, demonstrate creative, musical applications of modulations and sequential material.

During the next few years, jazz musicians, particularly exponents of the jazz-rock fusion music, increasingly adopted the use of synthesizers. The Mahavishnu Orchestra, with Jan Hammer playing keyboards and synthesizer, is among the earliest bands of this type. Timbral homogeneity among the electronic keyboards, guitar, and violin characterizes their music, and it is often difficult to aurally separate the individual instruments. Layers of sound composed of repetitive melodic and rhythmic elements are superposed to establish a rock feeling. In addition, guitar fuzz and filter sweeps on synthesizer constitute other elements of "Birds of Fire" (1973; *Birds of Fire*). Similar procedures, along with much unison synthesizer, violin, and guitar playing, characterize "Miles Beyond" (1973; *Birds of Fire*).

An increasingly subtle application of electronics occurs in "One Word" and "Sanctuary," both from the *Birds of Fire* album. In the former, an accompanying pedal point derived from two oscillators tuned in octaves, is subjected to filter sweeps; while "Sanctuary" applies slow filter changes, along with amplitude and frequency modulation, to sustained octaves. Filtered noise also appears, but Jan Hammer successfully conceals the familiar nature of white noise and filter sweeps so that they assume structural importance.

An extremely short piece from this album, "Sapphire Bullets of Pure Love," portrays what the essence of electronic jazz could be. Only twenty-one seconds long, "Sapphire" includes noise, modulation, glissandi, and instrumental effects. Its rhythmically volatile character recalls similarly brief compositions of the early serialist Anton Webern, like his "6 Bagatellen" Op. 9 (1913), for string quartet.

In contrast to such brevity, "Trilogy" (1973; *Between Nothingness and Eternity*) lasts approximately twelve minutes. Surprisingly, the music's increased duration does not entail a corresponding increase in electronic complexity; instead, the reverse takes place. Three continuous sections share timbral associations, the first of which includes noise, guitar fuzz, and filter sweeps. The second movement contains many filter sweeps, whereas the final part is dominated by guitar fuzz. The initial section, therefore, is a timbral exposition from which the remainder of the piece is derived.

Although Jan Hammer does not exploit the synthesizer to the extent that Paul Bley does, his refined treatment of comparatively common electronic sonorities is effective and structurally coherent. Hammer's goal is to relate electronics to the other instruments, and this is remarkably achieved. Like Paul Bley, The Mahavishnu Orchestra is fascinated not with the electronic effects themselves, but with their contribution to musical substance.

In his electronic solo album, *The First Seven Days* (1975), Hammer derives instrumental sonorities from synthesizers accompanied by piano, mellotron and string synthesizer. Filtered sequential patterns and electronically-generated guitar and percussive timbres frequently appear. In order to obtain further timbral complexity, Hammer applies the familiar method of tuning two oscillators of diverse waveforms to the unison or octave; sometimes one of the oscillators is filtered to yield an even greater subtlety of color. The Biblical reference involves the sectionalization of this lengthy composition, while the internal division of these seven sections is based upon timbral, thematic, and rhythmic aspects. Aside from some segments employing Latin percussion patterns on the album, Hammer uses the aforementioned electronic and acoustic instruments to realize this recording.

Less interesting albums of Hammer's are *Like Children* (1974), made in conjunction with jazz violinist Jerry Goodman; and an album by drummer Elvin Jones, *On the Mountain* (1975), in which Hammer plays keyboards within a conventional jazz trio format. The first was recorded on separate tracks and then mixed; it includes string quartet sonorities along with standard jazz–rock elements, while plucked string patterns are generated by a sequencer. *On the Mountain* is more successful with respect to improvisation than to electronic transformation. Hammer uses conventional keyboard instruments in combination with the synthesizer, but the resulting electronic sounds are predictable and stereotyped. Neither of these albums is as effective electronically as *The First Seven Days*.

Like Moraz's *I* and Wakeman's *The Six Wives of Henry VIII*, *The First Seven Days* is an indication of a new direction being followed by jazz and rock musicians. The urge to extend the song form to encompass long temporal durations had already been manifested in the music of Zappa, the Grateful Dead, and Yes, and the 1970s have seen the proliferation of this type of music. The desire to create large compositional structures, is due at least in part to these performers' musical training. It can be considered another step toward the fulfillment of Stockhausen's ideal of a universal music. All musical styles are gradually being amalgamated into a single framework, so that the categorization of music as classical, jazz, rock, and folk, has begun to lose its significance.

Although the Mahavishnu Orchestra generally avoids performing such long pieces, John McLaughlin, their guitarist and leader, employs a variety of electronic devices, including a polyphonic frequency-to-voltage converter, a frequency shifter, a sequencer, and a polyphonic mini-Moog synthesizer for guitar and modified guitar. As its name implies, the frequency-to-voltage converter produces electronic analogues to the guitar's pitches; these voltages can then control other sound generators and modifiers as oscillators and filters. The frequent appearance of modulated sonorities on some of the album *Inner Worlds* (1976) is an outgrowth of Mahavishnu's earlier piece "Sapphire Bullets of Pure Love." Both "Miles Out" (1976) and "Inner Worlds" superpose harmonically complex, modulated textures with recurrent rhythmic patterns, so that the pulse of the music is not destroyed; hence, these pieces retain a fundamental association with the jazz idiom. Oscillator glissandi sometimes serve as modulating signals for frequency shifting in "Miles Out," while "Inner Words" mixes noise with modulated guitar. The other works on this album incorporate less modulation.

In some instances, fusion groups include musicians who have performed both in jazz and rock ensembles. Such is the case with George Duke, formerly of the Mothers of Invention. His performance with percussionist Billy Cobham reveals a sensitivity comparable to that of Bley and Hammer. Duke's early style reflects a cautious application of electronic modifications in which the electric piano is given a more prominent role than the synthesizer. Introductory sections generally composed of diverse electronic sonorities are followed by electric piano, filtered, and modulated guitar, which seem anticlimatic after the initial sounds. The introductions are nonetheless well worth listening to. "Stratus" (1973; *Spectrum*), for instance, begins with amplitude-modulated noise and melodic elements, followed by the entrance of a filtered sequencer. This sonorous progression could easily have been reduced to a cliché, but percussionist Billy Cobham develops the rhythmic ideas present in the sequencer pattern to result in a dialogue between synthesizer and drums. The structural unity generated by this process is sufficient to have constituted an entire improvisation, so it is all the more unfortunate that it was restricted to introductory material.

"Snoopy's Search" (1973; *Spectrum*) contains greater timbral coherence, for the introduction is followed by filtered guitar and filtered and ring-modulated synthesizer. Rapid sequencer patterns subjected to gradual pitch transposition, in addition to glissandi and filtered noise with a percussive envelope, combine to form the opening sonorities. The subsequent appearance of ring-modulated tones enhances the timbral associations with the introduction. Later works establish more sophisticated relations.

"Heather" (1974; *Crosswinds*), whose opening is made up of filtered sustained tones on the synthesizer, accompanied by electric piano, concludes with similar sonorities. A reliance on particular timbres as motivic elements is also found, and extended, in "Spanish Moss" (1974; *Crosswinds*), which is divided into four continuous movements. Filtered noise, and ring modulated tones analogous to wind and gong sounds, appear at the outset. Treated as timbral motives, these sonorities recur as interludes between successive sections, each of which is defined by individual kinds of sounds. In the second part, "Savannah the Serene," filtered electric piano is prominant. It is followed by "Storm," a filtered drum solo accompanied by white and filtered noise. The final section, "Flash Flood," incorporates filtered trumpet, filtered guitar, and echoplex, so that the control of timbre operates on two levels: in addition to connecting the separate sections, the diverse timbres also delineate the different movements. Particularly apparent in the *Crosswinds* album, electronic applications provide structural cohesion without dominating the music's texture. George Duke continues to use the synthesizer sparingly but judiciously, with the electric piano providing contrasting sonorities.

In contrast to Billy Cobham's ensemble, Weather Report utilizes a synthesizer for melodic purposes and special effects. "Nubian Sundance" (1974) displays electronically-generated bass patterns and filtered melodic lines, while preference is given to unison passages between the synthesizer and the saxophone. Keyboard performer Joe Zawinul employs oscillator glissandi as effects, concluding with a brief segment of modulated sonorities. As with the Mahavishnu Orchestra and Billy Cobham, timbral association among synthesizer and instruments is the prime concern, although Jan Hammer and George Duke incorporate the synthesizer to a greater extent than Zawinul does.

Homogeneous textures also characterize the music of guitarist Larry Coryell and the Eleventh House, but the electronic transformations are more apparent than they are in Weather Report. Electric piano is used as a source of melodic and harmonic materials, while filtered trumpet frequently reinforces the timbral associations between electronic and acoustic instruments. "Birdfingers" (1974) is a typical example. The increased timbral complexity of "Yin" (1974) proceeds from filtered trumpet and guitar in conjunction with filtered and frequency-modulated glissandi from the synthesizer. The piece is further unified by the glissandi that grow out of the melodic development. Electronic modifications and thematic interchanges between the instruments prevail to the extent that it is difficult to distinguish the individual instruments. The sonorities are absorbed into a massive texture in which musical elements receive the foremost attention.

Many of the jazz musicians discussed so far have been influenced by personal contact with Miles Davis, who was one of the first to use electric piano in his group. Chick Corea, the founder of Return to Forever, is one of these. Corea employs electronic keyboard instruments for two diverse reasons, timbral variety, and the ability to be heard above strong drummers, which is a purely practical consideration. *Hymn of the Seventh Galaxy* (1973), although it does not contain any synthesizers, displays the variety of timbres available from the organ, the harpsichord, and the electric and acoustic piano.

Corea's style revolves around his use of the electric and acoustic piano, so it is not surprising to find that he also treats the synthesizer melodically. The periodic appearance of filtered noise and slight modulations in the background are used only as effects; the more interesting sonorities stem from the filtered and fuzz guitar. Timbral relations between keyboards and guitar do not display the refinement encountered in other jazz ensembles.

Corea tends to use a wide variety of keyboard instruments and synthesizers on his later albums. *Romantic Warrior* (1976), for instance, includes acoustic and electric piano, organ, clavinet, ARP Odyssey synthesizer, and four different models of Moog synthesizers, an impressive collection of equipment worthy of Patrick Moraz, Keith Emerson, or Rick Wakeman. From a stylistic point of view, the new Polymoog is the most important of these instruments, for it enables the performer to play chords in a manner analogous to traditional keyboard instruments, so that there is no longer a need to rely on the piano or organ for the production of chords, which increases the possibility of maintaining structural relations based on timbre.

Although polyphonic synthesizers can be considered a valuable asset for keyboard-oriented performers, David Friend of ARP Instruments cautions inexperienced musicians concerning the substitution of a melodic structure for one based upon harmonic principles: "When you start playing in a fully polyphonic manner you get back to harmony and structure as being the musical elements that you're dealing with, rather than melody." There is no reason for a keyboard player to feel restricted when using a monophonic synthesizer, but he must be able to work within a melodic framework. Once this has been mastered, polyphonic applications will evolve out of musical necessity.

Such is the case with Chick Corea, for his "Medieval Overture" (*Romantic Warrior*) displays a high level of timbral organization which, when combined with thematic recurrences, results in a standard ABA song form. Like his earlier pieces with Return To Forever, there are rapid stylistic changes, while monophonic synthesizers frequently play melodic lines in unison with the electric guitar.

Another veteran of the Miles Davis group, Herbie Hancock, accurately describes the dilemma of most pianists who adopt the use of synthesizers: "I don't want to make the synthesizer sound like a keyboard instrument, but I'm still new to it, so I have a hard time avoiding it." This revealing statement made by an excellent pianist and musician leads to the fundamental limitation of keyboard-oriented synthesizers. It is ironic that since manufacturers purposely designed synthesizers with a keyboard to facilitate adoption by musicians, performers must struggle to avoid keyboard mannerisms. Although the control voltage options of synthesizer keyboards supply a variety of functions other than pitch generation, some of which will be discussed in Part IV, it is the keyboard itself that seems to overpower most performers, who think in terms of it. Part of the problem certainly rests with performers who must learn to overcome technical difficulties and treat the synthesizer as an instrument. On the other hand, electrical engineering is so advanced that improved synthesizers ought to be forthcoming.

The reservations expressed by Hancock in the foregoing statement are manifested in his application of electronics. "Butterfly" (1974) makes a minimal use of the synthesizer; the piece's textures are dominated by electric piano. The mellotron is also employed as a source of sustained string sonorities, and it often emphasizes the high pitches in instrumental solos. A wide range of timbres result from the presence of four woodwind instruments which, when combined with electric piano, mellotron, synthesizer, bass, and percussion, afford a smooth sonorous progression. As Hancock attains more experience with electronic devices, his music should reflect greater a structural unity derived from synthesizers, for he is among the finest contemporary jazz pianists.

Discography

BAGLIONI, CLAUDIO
Sabato Pomeriggio,   RCA
TPL 1—1161

BLEY, PAUL
*The Paul Bley Synthesizer
Show,* Mile. MSP 9033

COBHAM, BILLY
Crosswinds, At. SD 7300

Spectrum, At. SD 7268

COREA, CHICK
*Hymn of the Seventh
Galaxy,* Poly. PD 5536

Romantic Warrior, Cd.
PC—34076

*Where Have I Known You
Before,* Poly. PD 6509

CORYELL, LARRY
The Eleventh House, Van.
VSD—79342

EATON, JOHN
"Blind Man's Cry," CRI
S—296

"Concert Piece," Turn.
TV—S 34428

"Mass," CRI S—296

"Piece for Solo Synket No.
3," Dec. 710154

"Songs for R.P.B.," Dec.
710154

EMERSON, LAKE AND PALMER
Brain Salad Surgery,
Mant. MC 66669

Pictures At An Exhibition,
Cot. ELP 66666

ENO, BRIAN
Another Green World,
Island ILPS 9351

ERB, DONALD
"Reconnaissance," None.
H 71223

FROESE, EDGAR
Aqua, Virg. VR 13—111

GENTLE GIANT
Free Hand, Cap.
ST—11428

HAMMER, JAN
Like Children, Nemp.
NE 430

The First Seven Days,
Nemp. NE 432

HANCOCK, HERBIE
Thrust, Col. PC 32965

JONES, ELVIN
On The Mountain, PM
PMR—005

KING CRIMSON
In the Wake of Poseidon,
At. SD 8266

MAHAVISHNU ORCHESTRA
*Between Nothingness and
Eternity,* Col.
KC 32766

Birds of Fire, Col. KC
31996

Inner Worlds, Col.
PC 33958

MATCHING MOLES
Little Red Record, Col.
KC 32148

MOODY BLUES
Seventh Sojourn, Thresh.
THS 7

MORAZ, PATRICK
I, At. SD 18175

———

Refugee, Char.
CAS 1087

POOH
*Un Po' Del Nostro Tempo
Migliore*, CBS 69118

**PREMIATA, FORNERIA,
MARCONI**
Live in U.S.A., Numero
Uno, DZSLN 55676

REVERBERI
Reverberi, Pausa
PA—USA 7003

ROXY MUSIC
Roxy Music, Rep. MS
2114

———

Siren, Atco SD
36—127 0698

RUNDGREN, TODD
Initiation, Bears. 6957

SOFT MACHINE
Soft Machine VII, Col.
KC 32716

TANGERINE DREAM
Rubycon, Vir. VR
13—116

TUBES
The Tubes, A and M
SP—4534

TULL, JETHRO
War Child, Chrys. CHR
1067

UNITED STATES OF AMERICA
*The United States of
America*, Col.
CS—9614

WAKEMAN, RICK
*The Six Wives of Henry
VIII*, A and M SP—4361

WEATHER REPORT
Mysterious Traveller, Col.
KC 32494

WHO
Quadrophenia, MCA
MCA—2 10004

YES
Chase to the Edge, At.
SD 7244

———

Fragile, At. SD 7211

———

Relayer, At. SD 18122

———

*Tales from Topographic
Oceans*, At. SD
2—908

———

The Yes Album, At. SD
8283

———

Yes Songs, At. SD
3—100

ZAPPA, FRANK
Roxy & Elsewhere, Disc.
2DS—2202

Part Four

Compositional Techniques

Man has qualities which can never be replaced by a robot . . . they [robots] are there so that he shall have more time for the truly human tasks—those of creation.

Karlheinz Stockhausen, 1958

THE CONCLUSION OF THIS TEXT is directed toward composers and performers. Compositional techniques and methods of formal organization will be covered in detail. In order to avoid needless repetition of previously-published material on synthesizers, such discussions will be eliminated whenever possible. Readers who need more specific information concerning the operation of particular electronic devices are referred to the previously cited book by Hubert Howe, or to instruction manuals published by the synthesizer manufacturers themselves.

Once the sonorous elements of a composition have been chosen, the feasibility of using them in specific transformation processes must be determined. All sounds, for example, do not produce acceptable results when they are ring-modulated or filtered. Frequency, harmonic content, and amplitude are determining factors in making a reasonable decision concerning their subsequent modifications.

By the 1950s, two fundamental concepts concerning the derivation of new sounds from preexisting ones had been formulated. In Paris, Pierre Schaeffer employed the technique of subtractive synthesis, while his German contemporary Karlheinz Stockhausen initiated the use of an additive process. Both methods are most successful when applied to particular categories of sound. Because of its degenerative nature, subtractive synthesis is best employed when the sonorous elements possess a rich harmonic content. The amplitude of the original sounds must also be sufficiently high to avoid the introduction of unwanted noise and hiss during the recording process.

Subtractive results are obtained by filtering. A filter is an electronic device that segments a sound into component groups based on frequency content. An octave filter divides the frequency spectrum into octaves starting at, e.g., 100, 200, 400, 800, 1600, 3200, 6400, and 12,800 Hz. A sound processed by this type of filter is therefore available as eight different timbres, depending on which frequency range is selected. Low-pitched sounds with complex harmonic structures produce the greatest variety of timbres, although higher sounds can also be treated in this manner. A sound whose fundamental frequency is 1000 Hz, for example, would only yield four individual timbres if it were modified by the aforementioned octave-filter; 1600, 3200, 6400 and 12,800 Hz. As long as the harmonic content is of adequate complexity, any sound will produce useful results when filtered.

A less common device, the third-octave filter, divides the frequency spectrum in a manner similar to that of the octave filter. Each octave is divided into three equal parts, e.g., 100, 133, 166, 200, 266, 372, 400, 533 . . . 12,800 Hz. A third-octave filter affords increased selectivity and generates a greater number of timbral variations than its counterpart, the octave filter.

Additional kinds of filters include high-pass, low-pass, bandpass, and band-reject (notch); their names describe their functions. A high-pass filter allows all frequencies above a predetermined pitch or cutoff frequency to sound, or pass, so that the pitches below the cutoff frequency are attenuated. Conversely, the lowpass filter suppresses pitches above the cutoff frequency while resonating those below it. As its name implies, a band-pass filter resonates a selected band of frequencies, attenuating pitches above and below the range of the band, or bandwidth. The bandwidth is adjustable; its range encompasses components equidistant from a variable center frequency. Similarly, the band-reject or notch filter, functions as the complement of the band-pass filter. An adjustable frequency band determined from the center frequency is attenuated, while frequencies exceeding the bandwidth are still pre-

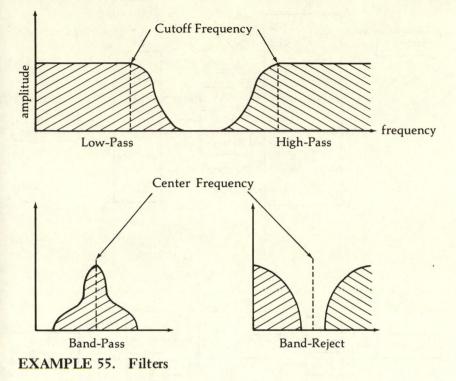

EXAMPLE 55.   Filters

sent. Example 55 portrays the effect of these filters on the frequency continuum.

A composer often wishes to utilize related sounds in a piece in order to establish timbral relations. Filtering can be applied to this situation. The timbral variants that result are analogous to changes of orchestration in instrumental music, so that a single sound can assume a variety of colors. Furthermore, the process of filtering permits the composer to work within a timbre continuum, proceeding from the original sound to gradually removed correlates. Such procedures avoid the necessity of literal repetition, although rhythmic characteristics, when present, remain intact.

Additional subtleties are obtained by processing a single sound through an octave filter bank or a series of filters. Example 56 illustrates both possibilities, in which the modified outputs are subjected to further transformations. Treated in this manner, a sole sound source may generate enough material for an entire composition.

In Example 56a, the multiple outputs from an octave filter are

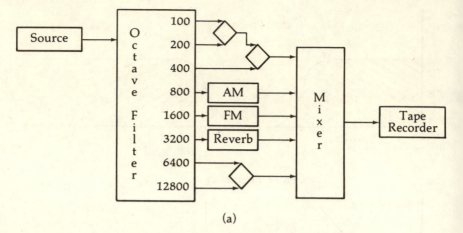

(a)

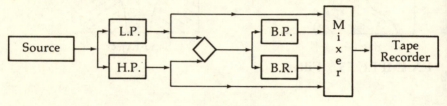

(b)

EXAMPLE 56. Filtering techniques

subjected to ring modulation, double ring modulation, amplitude modulation, and reverberation. The resultant transformations are then mixed and recorded. Example 56b separates the frequency components of the sound source into two ranges by simultaneous low- and high-pass filtering, and the outputs are both mixed and ring-modulated. The separation of the ring-modulated output into complementary segments by employing band-pass and band-reject filters is followed by the mixing and recording of all four signals.

Sounds possessing a low fundamental and a substantial number of upper partials are best suited for subtractive procedures. Simple tape manipulations, however, can be utilized to provide these characteristics for sounds lacking these characteristics. This is shown in Example 57. By slowing down a recording of a sound source, the fundamental frequency and accompanying harmonic spectrum are lowered. The transposed version can then be mixed

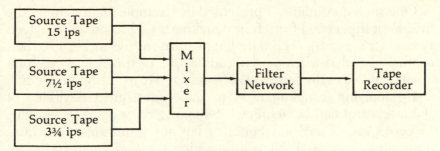

EXAMPLE 57.   Tape transposition and mixing

with the original sound to yield a more appropriate input signal to a filter. The manual control of the respective amplitudes insures attainment of the desired results. Incidentally, preamplification before and after the filtering process helps to eliminate extraneous noise resulting from equipment and second generation recordings. A preamplifier is an amplifier that raises the output of a low level signal.

As noted earlier, additive synthesis is a second method of deriving new timbres. Three developmental stages account for a gradual extension and sophistication of Stockhausen's ideas regarding this technique. The first approach, in "Studie II," consists of splicing together recordings of sine frequencies .05 seconds long. The tedious nature of this procedure should not be a deterrent to those interested in acquiring basic electronic skills, for the construction of timbres is contingent upon understanding the principles of aural perception. In this instance, timbre is treated as a function of pitch, so that high frequencies produce bright timbres and low pitches yield dark colors. A frequency continuum emphasizing a multitude of timbral shades can be defined by selecting its appropriate components, while the proximity among individual pitches determines the actual degree of timbral change.

"Kontakte" demonstrates a second method of additive synthesis by incorporating the tape transposition of subaudio impulses. Timbre is the result of both pitch and duration because a variable speed tape recorder is used to accomplish the tape transpositions. Perception of duration is of prime importance, and Stockhausen has referred to this in the article ". . . How Time Passes . . ." (1956), in which he concludes that timbre is the result of individual durations perceived as proportions. This implies a duration continuum from which timbral transitions can be derived.

One such continuum is presented in Example 58, including the division of the second from four equal parts (.25 seconds) to sixteen parts (.063 seconds). The tape lengths are for use at 7½ ips; their length is doubled when working at 15 ips. In this text these fractional divisions of the second will be referred to as "sampling rates."

By applying sampling rates to sine tones, great flexibility of timbre control can be achieved. Sampling rates below 8 result in the perception of individual pitches, but not of timbre. As the sampling rate is increased, pitch recognition is transformed to timbre perception. This occurs in the region of 12 to 14 samples per second, depending on the frequency and amplitude of the sine tones. The speed of the timbral transitions can therefore be regulated by working within the duration continuum.

These procedures need not be restricted to electronic sounds, but can be employed for the modification of concrète materials as well. More harmonically complex sources produce correspondingly complex timbres. Rhythmic relations can also be established by devising repetitive patterns of sampling rates such as 16, 12, 13, 14, 15, 16, 12. As with pitch, familiar timbres lose their identity as faster sampling rates are chosen.

The constituent components of a sound must be chosen with a specific resultant timbre in mind, even though it will usually be impossible to predict precisely the quality of the final sound. For example, if a bright timbre is desired, the sonorous sources could include flute, clarinet, trumpet, siren, and train whistle, all sounding in a high register. The speed of the timbral transformations is governed by sampling rates, and establishes the degree to which the original elements are recognizable. Emphasis on a particular color like the trumpet can be maintained by ascribing a longer sampling duration to specific sources. A possible sequence of events follows, in which the numbers in parentheses refer to sampling rates: siren (16), clarinet (12), flute (14), trumpet (7), trainwhistle (14). This pattern can then be made into a tape loop and subjected to envelope control by regulating the amplitude of the tape loop.

Stockhausen eventually extended the application of additive synthesis to include intermodulation, which was discussed in the second chapter in reference to "Telemusik." Amplitude and frequency modulation, in addition to double ring modulation, are the most obvious ways of producing intermodulation. In this instance, the additive process is more selective, for the resultant frequencies can be calculated in advance if both input frequencies are known.

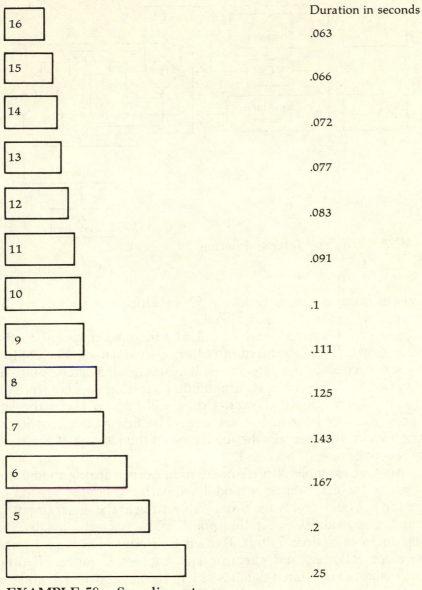

Duration in seconds

16 — .063

15 — .066

14 — .072

13 — .077

12 — .083

11 — .091

10 — .1

9 — .111

8 — .125

7 — .143

6 — .167

5 — .2

.25

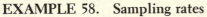

EXAMPLE 58.   Sampling rates

The application of intermodulatory processes in determining overall timbre structures is a viable compositional technique. Timbre can be treated as a function of pitch, duration, and amplitude, thereby establishing many degrees of sonorous associations within a composition. An instance employing minimal sound

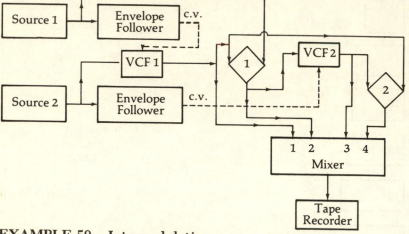

EXAMPLE 59. Intermodulation

sources is contained in Example 59, in which two sounds are filtered, ring-modulated, and mixed.

Source 2 is filtered, and its output simultaneously sent to the mixer (input 1) and the input of both ring modulators. The control voltage needed to activate the voltage-controlled filter (VCF) is obtained from Source 1, its amplitude converted to a control voltage by the envelope follower. (More will be said about the envelope follower later in this section.) The first instance of intermodulation, then, entails the regulation of the filtering of Source 2 by the amplitude of Source 1.

Another example of intermodulation occurs at ring modulator 1, where the first Source is modulated with the filtered version of Source 2. The output is again split, appearing at the mixer (input 2) and the second VCF. At this point VCF_2 is controlled by the amplitude of Source 2, transformed to a control voltage by the envelope follower, and effecting still another instance of intermodulation. The filtered signal is sent to the mixer (input 3) and the second ring modulator, subsequently modulating both filtered sounds. These appear at the mixer (input 4), and provide a final example of intermodulation.

The variety of timbres obtainable from such a restricted number of sound sources guarantees the presence of close timbral relations within a work. Furthermore, such processes allow the composer maximum flexibility in his choice of sonorous elements without compromising the resultant sound. Simple melodies, as well as complex electronic sounds, are suitable to intermodulatory techniques.

With the advent of voltage-controlled devices, some of the time spent in splicing has been eliminated. The sequencer, for example, can produce effects similar to those of manually-derived sampling rates. If only one sound source is employed, the sequencer can generate a multitude of voltages within a fraction of a second, resulting in alternate recurrences of sound and silence. This technique is illustrated in Example 60.

Voltages from the sequencer are alternately set between positive and zero values to control the operation of the voltage-controlled amplifier (VCA). Sampling rates much faster than those derived from splicing are produced, although the exact rate is difficult to determine because of the absence of precise speed calibrations on the sequencer. An additional limitation of this procedure is the necessity of employing a single sound source. In order to maintain an alternation between two or more sources, the number of sequencers must be increased and, most important, their operation must be synchronized. The latter consideration is essentially impossible to satisfy without the aid of sophisticated digital equipment.

There is, however, a solution to this problem. A computer can be programmed to accept a number of sound sources that can be converted to a digital, or binary, format by means of an analog-to-digital converter. Individual sources, stored in labeled memory blocks, can then be recalled at specific times for any duration. Input data would consist of the following: call number to identify the appropriate sound, entry time, duration, and amplitude. Absolute flexibility and precision are provided by these procedures, whereupon the computer output is processed by a digital-to-analog converter to derive an analog signal. A block diagram of this procedure is illustrated in Example 61.

EXAMPLE 60. Sequencer

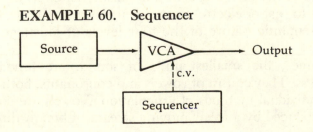

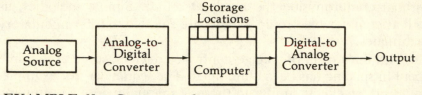

EXAMPLE 61. Computer editing

Criteria for the classification of compositions in the main body of this text were based upon the nature of sources employed: either voice, instruments, or concrète and electronic sounds. Each of these elements suggests a particular manner of composing internal structural relations, just as the piano and other instruments imply certain stylistic characteristics. Chopin Etudes, for instance, demonstrate an idiomatic style of piano writing; hence their transcription for another instrument or ensemble would not produce the sonorous qualities originally intended by the composer. Just as composers of vocal and instrumental music conceive a piece in terms of the instruments employed, so must electronic composers realize appropriate applications of the sonorous elements to be incorporated in a composition.

The voice is perhaps one of the most fertile sonorous sources, for its applications range from intelligible speech, or semantics, to purely timbral effects. In order that a composer be able to work successfully within this medium, a clear understanding of all aspects of language is essential. This may also be a plausible explanation for the comparatively few examples of tape compositions derived solely from voice.

The function of language is to carry meaning, based upon syntactic rules that establish semantic expectations for a listener. Rules of syntax must be followed for meaningful speech to result. Furthermore, language proceeds from the systematic combination of basic elements or phonemes that lead to the formation of syllables, words, and sentences. To develop linguistic materials in a manner analogous to that of electro-mechanical transformations, the physical and semantic nature of the four levels of language must be studied.

Phonemes, the smallest units of sound, are fundamentally meaningless. They consist of vowels and consonants, both of which involve individual methods of articulation. Vowels are continuous sounds produced by a freely moving stream of breath through the mouth, whereas consonants involve stopping the breath stream. The four categories of consonants are stopped, fricative, affricate, and nasal. Stopped consonants shut off the air flow completely, while fricative consonants result from narrowing the air passage so that they come through noisily. Affricate sounds are the combination of stopped and fricative, and nasal consonants are produced by diverting the air through the nose. Example 62 includes the four categories of consonants along with additional subdivisions. The terminology is derived from the manner of their articulation.

This information is especially useful in constructing timbral relations on the linguistic level, for it enables the composer to isolate suitable words from a text, followed by their rearrangement according to sonorous characteristics. Berio's "Thema" is an example of this procedure. Based on a text by James Joyce, "Thema" entails a gradual progression or disintegration to the fricative-alveolar "s." Conversely, a composer can utilize this information to construct a text in which predetermined timbral associations are realized. In dealing with phonemes, the fundamental structural level of language, only timbral considerations are possible. In this instance, meaning, if present at all, is a function of timbre.

Meaning is also absent from the second, or syllabic, structural level of language. Syllables differ from phonemes by the presence of a vowel in conjunction with one or more consonants. There is, however, one important exception, monosyllabic words like boy, dog, bird. Because they exhibit fundamental traits of the syllabic

EXAMPLE 62. Classification of consonants

Stopped

1. Bilabial (pale, bad)

2. Alveolar (tool, did)

3. Velar (can, good)

Fricative

1. Labiodental (far, verse)

2. Dental (thin, that)

3. Alveolar (sent, zoo)

4. Palatal (ash, rouge)

Nasal

1. Labial (ram)

2. Alveolar (ran)

3. Velar (rang)

Affricate

1. Palatal (chip, jump)

and word (third) levels of linguistic structure, the overlap introduces the element of ambiguity within the realm of meaning.

Words, the principal disseminators of meaning, may be broken into constituent parts, so that new meanings evolve. For example, the word "wonderful" could be divided into three syllables, wonder-ful. If the temporal separation is of sufficient length, three monosyllabic words appear: won (sounds like the number "one"), der (the German article "the"), and ful (sounds like "full" or "fool"). The word's semantic structure is destroyed, and then replaced by new word-meanings. This procedure was incorportaed by Stockhausen in "Gesang der Jünglinge."

The fourth structural level of language includes sentences, in which syntax is a function of meaning. Sentences, like words, can be dissolved into separate phrases, words, or syllables. Both semantics and syntax can be altered to produce various degrees of intelligibility. The complete range of compositional procedures associated with language is illustrated in Example 63, a language continuum.

Should a composer decide to deal with language, the preceding example would indicate some possibilities of formal organization on the linguistic level. Syntax is a prime factor where meaningful speech is concerned, whereas the absence or transformation of syntax is characteristic of meaningless speech. At the timbral end of the continuum, syntax is replaced by pure sound.

Additional elements pertaining to language include intonation and accent. These can be utilized within any of the aforementioned contexts, for they contribute significantly to the establishment of a sonorous resemblance to linguistic patterns. Meaningless speech, for instance, can be made to appear meaningful, as exemplified by Berio's "Visage."

Electro-mechanical transformations involving additive or sub-

EXAMPLE 63.   Language continuum

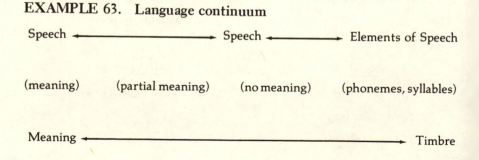

tractive methods increase the number of possible speech variants. Filtering systems similar to those depicted in Example 56 are a source of timbral components, whereas the intermodulatory procedures shown in Example 59 generate more complex timbres, usually accompanied by a decrease in comprehensibility when meaning is initially present. The timbral complexity of the ensuing modifications remains the choice of the composer, so it is helpful to remember that reverberation and filtering produce less drastic effects than ring modulation, whereas mixing and overdubbing tend to yield collage-related effects obscuring most of the word content. The formal organization of speech-derived materials must take into account both textual intelligibility and the timbral resources of the voice. The twofold nature of this procedure constructs a multitude of relations between semantics and timbre.

Instrumental sources, when treated in an additive manner, tend to yield complex and varied timbral structures. Their harmonic content is increased by intermodulation, whereas splicing techniques in the form of sampling rates produce a degree of harmonic complexity proportional to the sampling rate. Slower rates are more readily perceived as autonomous events, while an increased speed of execution increases the likelihood of composite sounds being formed.

Since envelope characteristics and harmonic content define the sonorous quality of musical instruments, familiar timbres may be effectively transformed by altering temporal and frequency relations. Experiments by Schaeffer and Poullin confirm the feasibility of envelope alteration by tape editing in which attack, steady state, and decay times are shortened or removed entirely. A piano, for example, can be recorded playing isolated pitches. Its envelope, shown in Example 64, consists of an attack followed by a continuous decay. The piano does not possess any steady state characteristics.

EXAMPLE 64.   Piano envelope

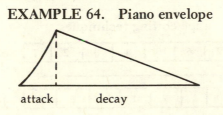

attack   decay

A wide range of related timbres can be derived from this source. By separating the attack and decay portions, two sounds result: tape reversal produces organlike sounds, and tape transposition at faster rates approaches the sound of a harpsichord, whereas slower playback speeds sound like a gong striking. Additional sounds can be extracted by subjecting the transposed fragments to tape reversal as well. The internal reordering of attack and decay segments produces subtle timbral differentiations. This is achieved by dividing a recorded sound into any number of parts, and splicing and rearranging the physical location of the individual components, as indicated in Example 65.

The forgoing technique can be applied to more than a single sound, thereby yielding a greater variety of timbral changes. It must be remembered that the duration of individual segments, or their sampling rate, governs the possibility of aural identification of the sources. Rhythmic patterns can also be produced by employing different sampling durations; this results in timbral rhythms. Finally, the effect of low-frequency amplitude modulation can be realized by separating successive segments with blank tape (silence).

An advantage afforded by the use of tape is that the choice of sonorous elements is extended to include concrète sources other than voice and instruments. Both additive and subtractive processes can be employed; their choice depends on the timbral nature of the initial sound. One way of handling such material is to prepare an environmental-type piece in which electronic modifications are minimized to insure the aural recognition of familiar sounds like footsteps, barking, and automobile engines. Elementary tape manipulations, filtering, reverberation, and mixing can be applied without necessarily interfering with this plan, since their main function would be to supply timbral nuances.

Electronic sounds are produced by oscillators and noise generators. Oscillators produce definite pitches and a variety of

EXAMPLE 65. Tape editing techniques

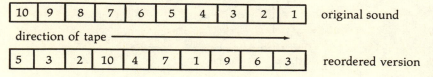

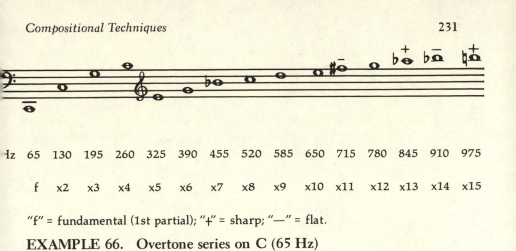

Hz 65 130 195 260 325 390 455 520 585 650 715 780 845 910 975

f   x2   x3   x4   x5   x6   x7   x8   x9   x10   x11   x12   x13   x14   x15

"f" = fundamental (1st partial); "+" = sharp; "—" = flat.

EXAMPLE 66. Overtone series on C (65 Hz)

waveforms, while the individual waveforms derive their sonorous characteristics from the nature of the accompanying harmonic spectra, the overtone series. The patterned distribution of frequencies, in addition to corresponding amplitude relations, constitute the nature of these spectra. Example 66 contains the first sixteen partials of an overtone series on the pitch C (65 Hz).

Upper partials exist as simple arithmetic ratios to the fundamental, e.g., 2 : 1, 3 : 1, and so on; the series can be extended indefinitely. Before specific waveforms are considered, a means of accurately measuring amplitude should be understood. The timbral characteristics of complex sounds are dependent upon both frequency proportions and amplitude relations.

Our perception of loudness is relative, not absolute. For example, a sound described as soft may denote something different to a musician and to a worker continually exposed to factory noises. Because of these inherent differences in amplitude perception, scientists have formulated a system of measurement based on logarithms, in which the basic unit of measurement is the decibel (dB). To double the loudness of a sound is to increase it by 3 dB. If the threshold of hearing is considered as 0 dB and painfully loud noise as 120 dB, a soft sound would be approximately 45 dB. Measurement by decibels does not eliminate the relativity of amplitude perception, but it does enable one to work more accurately after a point of reference has been decided upon, and it is an invaluable tool for the electronic composer. Example 67 gives degrees of loudness with their corresponding decibel ratings, which have been rounded to the nearest tenth.

Number of times as loud	dB
initial sound	0
2	3
3	4.8
4 (2^2)	6 (3+3)
5	7
6	7.8
7	8.5
8 (2^3)	9 (6+3)
9	9.5
10	10
11	10.4
12	10.8
13	11.1
14	11.5
15	11.8
16 (2^4)	12 (9+3)
17	12.3
18	12.6
19	12.8
20	13
30	14.8
32 (2^5)	15 (12+3)
40	16
50	17
60	17.8
64 (2^6)	18 (15+3)
70	18.5

EXAMPLE 67.   Decibel ratings

Sine, square, triangle, sawtooth, and ramp waves are normally generated by modern oscillators. The sine tone is the only one of these to possess a fundamental without its accompanying partials. Whereas the frequency ratios among the remaining waveforms are constant, their amplitude relations vary. A graphic representation of a 65 Hz square wave, 60 dB, is shown in Example 68.

A square wave consists of a fundamental (f) and of odd-numbered partials (f × 3, f × 5 . . .) whose amplitude relations are inversely proportional to their numerical order within the

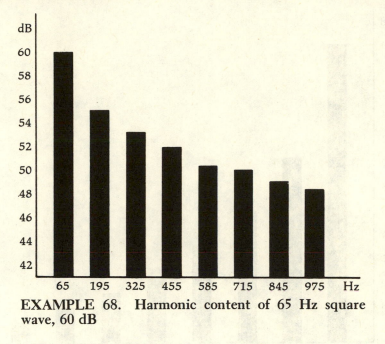

EXAMPLE 68. **Harmonic content of 65 Hz square wave, 60 dB**

series (1/3, 1/5 . . .). In Example 68, the third partial has a frequency of 195 Hz (65 × 3) and an amplitude of 55.2 dB (60 − 4.8). An increase of 4.8 dB represents a sound three times louder; conversely, one-third as loud is achieved by subtracting 4.8 dB.

The harmonic content of a triangle wave can be deduced in similar fashion, as shown in Example 69. Possessing identical frequencies to the square wave, the triangle wave contains amplitudes that are both inversely proportional and the squared ratios of their numerical order within the series ($1/3^2$ or 1/9, $1/5^2$ or 1/25 . . .). The third partial of a 65 Hz triangle wave is 195 Hz (65 × 3), whereas its amplitude is one-ninth as loud as the fundamental, i.e., 50.5 dB (60 − 9.5).

Square and triangle waves partake of selected portions of the overtone series, but the ramp or sawtooth wave is a manifestation of the complete series. The amplitude of the partials exists in a relation that is reciprocal to their numerical position within the series (1/2, 1/3, 1/4 . . .), a situation identical to that of the square wave. Both the rich harmonic content of the ramp wave, and its resemblance to the square wave, are illustrated in Example 70.

A knowledge of the overtone series and of the harmonic content of specific waveforms can be applied to the execution of additive

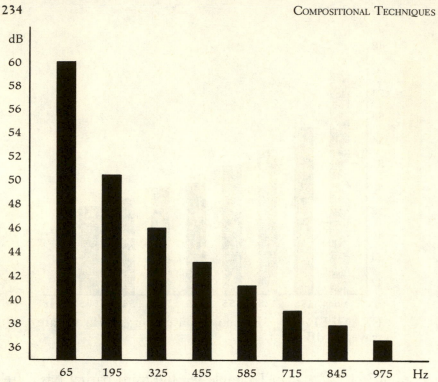

EXAMPLE 69. Harmonic content of 65 Hz triangle wave, 60 dB

and subtractive processes. Establishing the square wave as a point of reference, additive synthesis can be accomplished by choosing a fundamental pitch and its appropriate partial frequencies. These would be generated by a sine oscillator, as shown in Example 71, in which timbral transformation of the square wave results from the deviation of the amplitude relations from their normal setting. In this instance the amplitude succession is reversed, creating an undertone series, or subharmonic spectrum, in which the fifteenth partial (975 Hz) appears as the fundamental due to its increased amplitude.

The extension of this technique yields an infinite array of timbres. The original complex waveforms can be synthesized from frequency and amplitude successions that are not derivatives of the overtone series. An illustration of this procedure is contained in Example 72, in which the intervallic distance between successive pitches is diminished by semi-tones, and the amplitudes are reduced by half, −3 dB. Octave doublings are avoided so that specific pitches are not emphasized.

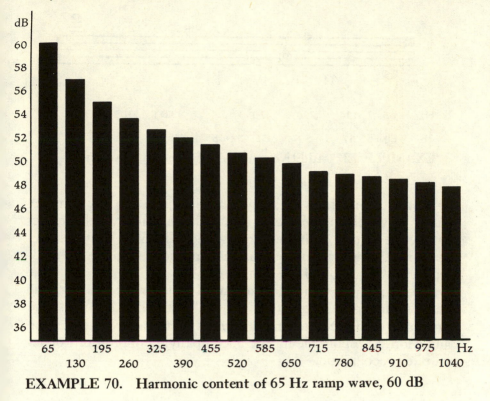

EXAMPLE 70. Harmonic content of 65 Hz ramp wave, 60 dB

EXAMPLE 71. Additive synthesis of a square wave

| Square Wave | Altered Square Wave | |
Amplitude	Frequency	Amplitude
60 dB	65 Hz	48.2 dB
55.2	195	48.9
53	325	49.6
51.5	455	50.5
50.5	585	51.5
49.6	715	53
48.9	845	55.2
48.2	975	60

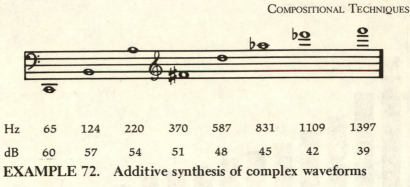

Hz	65	124	220	370	587	831	1109	1397
dB	60	57	54	51	48	45	42	39

EXAMPLE 72. **Additive synthesis of complex waveforms**

Subtractive methods by filtering can be applied to any complex timbres in which the degree of harmonic complexity helps to determine the texture of the resultant sound. The filter networks presented in Example 56 are typical configurations that can be modified at the discretion of the composer.

Electronic noise generators are most suitable for filtering, and filtered noise is often referred to as "pink" noise. Bands of noise are frequently employed to simulate wind, jets, and the like; the band-width is responsible for the accompanying impressions of actual pitch recognition.

The formal organization of sonorous materials within the tape medium can be based on melodic, rhythmic, and timbral relations, among others. Regardless of the type or number of structural levels, smooth transitions and transformed repetitions of elements are readily available from electro-mechanical devices. Internal coherence is maintained by modifying all sounds in a similar fashion, by filter, reverberation, and so forth.

The structural possibilities are increased, however, when a performer plays in conjunction with tape, while the sonorous relations between a performer and tape are dependent upon the ability of the composer to establish them. If substantial thematic cohesion is desired, both parts will most likely share melodic or rhythmic motives. On the other hand, should a composer wish to establish timbral connections between a performer and tape, a knowledge of the acoustical properties of the voice or of various instruments is essential in order to transfer them to prerecorded sounds. Envelope and harmonic content are the two basic elements to control.

The attack, steady state, and decay times of vocal or instrumental sources can be approximately determined by careful listening, or the sounds can be routed to an oscilloscope, where their envelope contour is projected on a screen. Many percussion instruments, for instance, possess sharp attack rates and fast decay times, without steady state characteristics, like wood sounds. Similarly, piano and plucked string sounds do not exhibit steady state segments, but are differentiated from percussive sources by more gradual attack and decay rates. Detailed information concerning the envelope properties of orchestral instruments and the voice is contained in the scientific journals listed in the bibliography.

The harmonic content of instrumental sources is usually derived from filtered square, triangle, or ramp waves. The sine wave cannot be filtered, but it closely resembles the sound of a flute. When the amplitude of a sine tone is increased to border on distortion, it assumes vocal characteristics. The appropriate envelope contour applied to a sine tone approximates the sound of an electric piano. Middle to low range square frequencies approach a clarinet timbre, whereas high pitched sine tones appear as violin harmonics. Cymbal and gong sounds are effectively produced by the ring modulation of sine tones with square, triangle, or ramp frequencies.

Finally, prerecorded and transformed versions of instrumental or vocal sources can be incorporated with electronic and concrète elements, and the resultant tape displays close timbral associations with the accompanying instruments. Example 73 presents a few ideas for the formal organization of pieces that combine performers with tape. A common procedure (Example 73a) divides a composi-

EXAMPLE 73. Formal plans for performer and tape

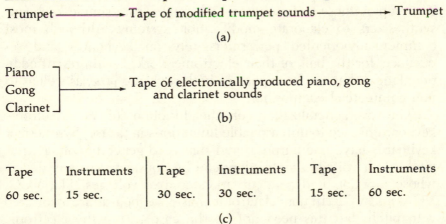

Trumpet ⟶ Tape of modified trumpet sounds ⟶ Trumpet

(a)

Piano
Gong ⟶ Tape of electronically produced piano, gong
Clarinet   and clarinet sounds

(b)

Tape	Instruments	Tape	Instruments	Tape	Instruments
60 sec.	15 sec.	30 sec.	30 sec.	15 sec.	60 sec.

(c)

tion, or one of its parts, into three related sections. A timbral progression of trumpet sounds is produced by a performer, transformed by tape and electronic techniques, and followed by the recapitulation of the natural trumpet.

Example 73b illustrates a more sophisticated design than the previous example. Instrumental sounds are here contrasted against electronically produced analogues. Although this method could result in confusion between the natural and synthesized instrumental timbres, the electronically-derived instruments can be assigned elements like melody, rhythm, and register, that are physically impossible to execute on unmodified instruments. The tape thus fulfills a compositional need, rather than providing mere imitative effects.

The formal divisions of Example 73c incorporate simple and inverse durational proportions to articulate delineations between tape and instruments. In this instance, more effective results would be obtained if the taped material were of a contrasting nature, not instrumental, so that the aural recognition of individual sonorous categories would be facilitated. The durations of the taped sections decrease by a rate of 2:1, e.g., 60, 30, and 15 seconds; whereas the intervening instrumental segments increase inversely (1:2), 15, 30, and 60 seconds. Structures based on multitude proportions provide logical formal relations, and their appearance can be heard.

The addition of voltage controlled devices to the electronic medium during the mid-1960s was influential in the evolution of live electronics in performance. All forms of contemporary music can employ these techniques, which range from simple keyboard synthesizers to elaborate modification systems. Although most commercially-oriented performers rely on keyboards and sequencers for the bulk of their electronic work, I will present additional ideas that can be applied to both rock and jazz, as well as to non-commercial composition.

The overgeneralization of the function of an electronic keyboard has led to unreasonable limitations in its use. Synthesizer keyboards have one purpose, and that is to generate voltage, not pitch. As a voltage source, they can be connected to any device whose function is dependent upon control voltages, like VCO, VCA, and VCF. In non–electronic music, keyboards are associated with pitch, but this need not be the case within the electronic medium. Both synthesizer performers and electronic composers must divorce themselves from this antiquated concept.

Since their association with oscillators is obvious, other uses of the keyboard will be explained. Rhythmic patterns executed on a keyboard can activate a voltage-controlled amplifier to which one or more instruments have been connected. Each time a key is depressed, a voltage is sent to the VCA, turning it on, and allowing the input signals to be heard. When the key is released, the amplifier is shut off and no other sounds come from the loudspeakers. In order to differentiate the amplified sounds from their natural states, a reverberation unit can be placed between the output of the VCA and the preamplifier. If, for example, a trumpet, saxophone, and trombone are treated in this manner, the natural sounds will always be present, while reverberated rhythmic extractions will periodically be transmitted over the loudspeakers. A diagram of this configuration is shown in Example 74.

By substituting a voltage-controlled filter for the VCA in the previous example, timbral rhythms are produced. Since each key generates a different voltage, its filter characteristics vary accordingly. Omission of the VCA causes the modified sounds to be continuous, but their timbre changes as various keys are depressed. Although such effects are rarely employed by commercial groups, if used discriminately, they will not interfere with the predominant elements of melody, harmony, and rhythm. Conversely, structural cohesion could be increased by articulating the rhythmic patterns and motives occurring in various parts of the composition. Keyboards are flexible devices capable of controlling pitch, duration, and timbre.

EXAMPLE 74. Keyboard as rhythmic source

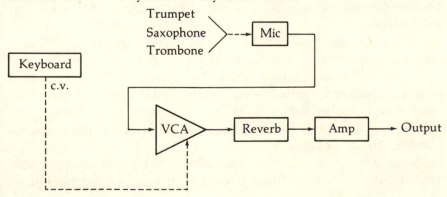

The sequencer is another versatile voltage source that is usually restricted for use with voltage-controlled oscillators. There is no reason for such a limited application, although extremely complex sounds are obtainable when a VCO is activated by a sequencer. The repetitive nature of this instrument affords a means of constructing interesting masses of sound when it is connected to a VCO. If the sequencer is set faster than approximately twelve events per second, the individual pitches will lose their autonomy, and timbre will be perceived in an effect similar to that achieved by Stockhausen in "Studie II." Subtle timbral changes are easily derived by adjusting the control voltages.

Complex envelope contours are available by controlling a VCA with a sequencer, although a volt-meter must be used to accurately measure output voltages. Examples 75a and b illustrate some typical patterns produced by a twelve-stage sequencer where the voltage range is 0 to +5 volts. The voltage of each stage is preset, and a smooth transition between successive stages can be made through the appropriate setting of a "glide" control, available on most commercial sequencers. The interconnection of equipment is shown in Example 75c.

This application is feasible when conventional instruments are the sound sources, for their characteristic timbres can be transformed. If applied to sustained pitches, the effect is one of continuous repeats superposed over a long tone. When a melodic line is treated in this manner, unpredictable accents, crescendi, and diminuendi contort the melody.

Timbral rhythms analogous to those produced by keyboard control of a VCF are also possible with a sequencer. Modified instrumental sounds, particularly when played in conjunction with unaltered instruments, can be effectively distinguished by such further transformations as reverberation, tape delay, and ring modulation.

The envelope generator, a control voltage source, provides a less elaborate means of producing envelope contours than does the sequencer. Connected to a VCA, the envelope generator offers separate controls for attack, steady state, and decay rates, but these are not comparable to the multistage sequencer. Nevertheless, the envelope generator is a useful device, and its capabilities are sufficient for most applications.

Voltage inverters, although not sources of control voltages, provide the flexibility of changing the direction of a voltage. This is

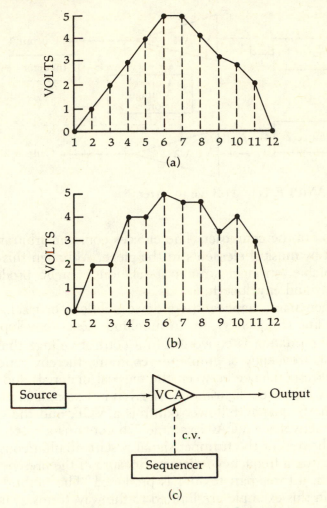

(a)

(b)

(c)

EXAMPLE 75.   Sequencer as envelope source

advantageous when a single voltage source operates two pieces of
equipment. As shown in Example 76, two sound sources are sent to
individual VCA's. The control voltage is unaltered at VCA_1, but is
inverted at the second VCA, yielding a ping-pong effect. Any voltage source can be used in this instance, and the amplifiers can be
replaced by filters—or by oscillators, if the analog sound sources are
omitted.

The voltage sources discussed so far have existed outside any
musical context, and the resultant voltages have been preset at the

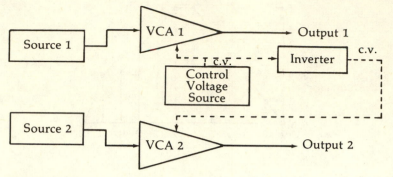

EXAMPLE 76.   Voltage inverter

discretion of the composer. The choices could be arbitrary, or influenced by musical elements in the piece. Although this practice is acceptable, stronger structural relations can be produced by frequency and envelope followers.

As their name implies, these devices follow, or track, either a melodic line (frequency), or an amplitude level (envelope). This analog information is converted to a control voltage that closely represents frequency or amplitude contours, thereby generating a direct correspondence between the musical materials and the voltage. Two simple configurations are given in Example 77a and b, in which the frequency follower controls a VCF, and the envelope follower activates a VCA. Example 77b contains a more sophisticated scheme, for the trumpet signal is sent simultaneously to an envelope and a frequency follower. Because of the presence of two oscillators, a three-part texture is produced. The timbral characteristics in this example are limited to the waveforms available on each oscillator.

Numerous structural relations are obtainable from these devices, and it would be futile to attempt to exhaust the possibilities. A final, quite elaborate, scheme, is offered as an incentive to those interested in exploring structural relations on an advanced level. Incidentally, these procedures need not be restricted to live performance, but can also serve as material for prerecorded tape.

Example 78 achieves a high degree of structural unity by utilizing envelope and frequency followers, while the voice is distinguished from the instruments by the addition of reverberation. Furthermore, the voice is the only source that undergoes multiple modifications and generates control voltages. Complex connections

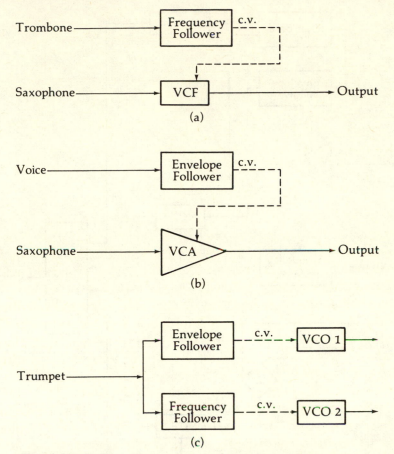

EXAMPLE 77. Frequency and envelope followers

among the instruments are avoided by systematic groupings: voice, flute, and saxophone; trumpet, electric bass, and keyboard; and cymbal. The saxophone is the only instrument that is not modified, but its melodic phrases are converted to control voltages. Other voltages are supplied by the sequencer, voice, and keyboard, while the latter instrument produces only voltages, not pitches. The modification devices are typical, consisting of a filter bank, reverberation unit, and two ring modulators, voltage-controlled amplifiers, and filters. Only four additional sounds are produced; their amplitude is regulated at the mixer. Depending on the nature of the playback system, the output from the mixer can be monaural, stereo, or quadraphonic.

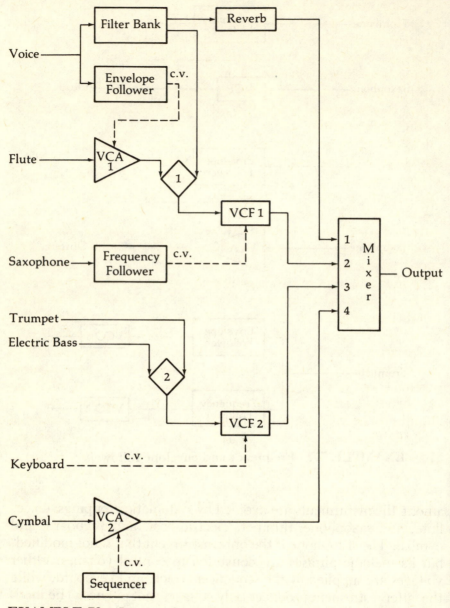

EXAMPLE 78.   Live performance scheme

Computer-generated sounds deserve special discussion because of the manner in which they are produced. The precision afforded by computers is one of their primary advantages over other types of electronic equipment; each sound is accurately described by a series of numbers. Since a variety of sound synthesis programs are currently available, only a general explanation of possibilities will be given. Readers interested in specific details are once more referred to the bibliography.

Most computer programs require a series of preliminary instructions indicating sources, modifications, waveforms, and envelope contours. The first two categories are combined to form "instruments," whereas the latter are function-generating subroutines, or GEN functions. Oscillators are essential to most instruments, and typical modification devices, including filters, ring modulators, and envelope generators, can be included to construct more complex sources.

Among the descriptive information required to form an oscillator are instrument numbers (1, 2, 3 . . .), the GEN function number for the waveform, the point of entry and duration in seconds, the frequency in Hertz, and the amplitude in decibels. The ordering of these elements may vary among different programs, but it is defined and constant within an individual one. Their inherent accuracy and flexibility permit more sophisticated formal relations on all structural levels. Frequency can be calculated to one-hundredth of a Hertz, while amplitude and temporal elements, as well as modification devices, can be controlled with similar precision.

The derivation of GEN functions resembles the methods employed with the sequencer, although the twelve sequencer stages are replaced by five hundred twelve storage locations within the computer. Waveforms and envelopes unavailable from synthesizers can be gotten from computers, in which harmonic content, amplitude, and envelope characteristics are susceptible to limited variation. Since sound synthesis programs are usually patterned on studio and synthesizer techniques, computers frequently duplicate these functions. In this respect, there is not much that needs to be learned, but all the operative sonorous elements must be predetermined unless provisions are made for random operations.

Because of the complex pitch and amplitude relations of most instrumental envelopes, the derivation of instrumental timbres is particularly suited to computer synthesis. Each overtone can pos-

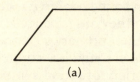

(a)

Entry Time	Instrument Number	Duration	Amplitude	Frequency
0.0	1	5	40	440
0.05	1	4.95	43	462
0.1	1	4.9	44.8	484
0.15	1	4.85	46	506
0.2	1	4.8	47	528
0.25	1	4.75	47.8	550
0.3	1	4.7	48.5	572
0.35	1	4.65	49	594
0.4	1	4.6	49.5	616
0.45	1	4.55	50	638
0.5	1	4.5	50.4	660
0.55	1	4.45	50.8	682
0.6	1	4.4	51.1	704
0.65	1	4.35	51.5	726
0.7	1	4.3	51.8	748
0.75	1	4.25	52	770
0.8	1	4.2	52.3	792
0.85	1	4.15	52.6	814
0.9	1	4.1	52.8	836
0.95	1	4.05	53	858
1.0	1	4.0	53	880

(b)

EXAMPLE 79.   Computer generated sounds

sess individual attack, sustain and decay characteristics, while pitch
fluctuations and noise transients peculiar to attack segments are
easily attainable. Noise transients are extraneous sounds that sometimes accompany the initiation of a pitch produced by string and
wind instruments; "scratching" is common to bowed string instruments, and "hissing" to wind instruments. The timbral extension of
instrumental families, including brass, woodwind, string, and per-

cussion, is an example of the resources available from computer applications.

Example 79 is a description of a simple computer sound generating process. Since computer methodology permits the sonorous representation of graphically conceived ideas, the figure in Example 79a may be considered a sound analogue. A sine oscillator, instrument 1, is the sole, unmodified sound source. The numerical information is in typical input data format (Example 79b), indicating the entry time in seconds, the instrument number, the duration in seconds, the amplitude in decibels, and the frequency in Hertz.

The total duration of the sonorous event is five seconds, and the number twenty has been chosen as a basis from which pitch, amplitude and temporal relations are derived. The time of the initial slope segment is one second, or twenty per cent of the total. The subdivision of this part into twenty smaller units provides entry times for the twenty pitches 1/20 or .05 seconds apart. Since all the pitches stop simultaneously, their individual durations are obtained by subtracting their time from five seconds. An increasing amplitude scale from one to twenty times as loud is formed on the value of 40 dB (decibel ratings are contained in Example 67). Finally, the octave 440 to 880 Hz is segmented into twenty equal parts, whereby the perception of discrete pitches is no longer possible.

Although the work required to formulate and realize such a short section may be formidable, there are modifications possible by changing some of the input data. Subsequent transformations of pitch, amplitude, or duration include the establishment of additional instruments, including filtering and ring modulation; the formulation of different frequency and amplitude scales; and temporal alterations of the original sound events. The precision by which these variations are accomplished strengthens the internal structural relations from which a large scale formal plan may evolve.

Until recently, computer facilities have been restricted to a small number of institutions. The expensive operating time and conversion equipment have also been obstacles for composing computer music, but the increased appearance of mini-computers during the last few years is beginning to place computers within the price range of synthesizers. These computers are available in kit form, and cost as little as three hundred dollars. More flexible systems with larger core memories, along with terminals, converters, display units, etc., can be purchased for approximately one thousand dollars, a price competitive with most synthesizers. Although it is too early to ascertain the importance that small computer systems will have on electronic music, one variable application is within the realm of hybrid systems. Control voltages to govern synthesizers can be obtained, thereby transferring the characteristic attributes of speed and precision from synthesizers to analog devices.

Although such a brief exposition of compositional techniques is not all-inclusive, it categorizes basic procedures so that students can begin to experiment in this medium with a minimum of difficulty. It is essential to listen carefully to records and to analyze scores. A mastery of synthesizer or computer technique will enable a composer to formulate an individual language, for technique serves no other purpose. A statement by the Italian pianist Pietro Scarpini seems an appropriate conclusion here: "If one knows exactly what one wishes to do musically—I mean with complete exactitude, down to the smallest final detail—the technique will be there."

SELECTED BIBLIOGRAPHY

I. General Readings

APPLETON, JON. "Additive vs. Subtractive Synthesis." *Electronic Music Review* 5 (January, 1968), 37–38.

———. "Reevaluating the Principle of Expectation in Electronic Music." *Perspectives of New Music* 8 (Fall-Winter, 1969): 106.

APPLETON, JON, AND PERERA, RONALD, EDS. 1975. *The Development and Practice of Electronic Music.* Englewood Cliffs, N.J.: Prentice-Hall.

ASHLEY, ROBERT, AUSTIN, LARRY, AND STOCKHAUSEN, KARLHEINZ. "Conversation." *Source* 1 (1967): 104–107.

AUSTIN, LARRY, *et al.* "Groups." *Source* 3 (1968): 14–27.

BABBITT, MILTON. "An Introduction to the RCA Synthesizer." *Journal of Music Theory* 8 (1964): 251–265.

———. "Edgard Varèse: A Few Observations of His Music." *Perspectives of New Music* 4 (Spring-Summer 1966): 14–22.

———. "Twelve-Tone Rhythmic Structures and the Electronic Medium." *Perspectives of New Music* 1 (Fall-Winter, 1962): 49–79.

BANCS, LESTER. "How to Succeed in Torture Without Really Trying." *Creem* 7 (1976): 30.

BASART, ANN PHILLIPS. 1963. *Serial Music: A Classified Bibliography of Writing on Twelve-Tone and Electronic Music.* Berkeley: University of California Press.

BAUMGARTH, CHRISTA. "I Futuristi in Germania." *Il Verri* 33/34 (1970): 71–76.

BERIO, LUCIANO. "Poesie e musica—un'esperienza." *Incontri Musicali* 3 (1959): 98–111.

BIVONA, JOE. "Patrick Moraz: Keyboardist for 'Yes.'" *Contemporary Keyboard* 1 (1975): 8.

BOLINGER, DWIGHT. 1968. *Aspects of Language*. New York: Harcourt, Brace and World.

BYRD, JOSEPH. "New Sounds for Christmas: A Carol for Synthesizer." *Contemporary Keyboard* 1 (1975): 22–25.

CAGE, JOHN. 1961. *Silence*. Middletown, Conn.: Wesleyan University Press.

CAGE, JOHN, AND HILLER, LEJAREN. "HPSCHD." *Source* 4 (1968): 10–19.

CARDEW, CORNELIUS. "Note sulla musica AMM con riferimenti indiretti a una etica di improvvisazione." *Il Verri* 30 (1969): 116–126.

CEELY, ROBERT. "Electronic Music Three Ways." *Electronic Music Review* 1 (January, 1967): 18–21.

CHADABE, JOEL. "New Approaches to Analog-Studio Design." *Perspectives of New Music* 6 (Fall-Winter, 1967): 107.

CHAPIN, LOUIS. "The Future Started Here." *BMI: The World of Music* (Summer, 1970): 23–30.

CHAVEZ, CARLOS. 1937. *Toward a New Music*. New York: W. W. Norton.

CHILDS, BARNEY, AND SCHWARTZ, ELLIOTT, EDS. 1967. *Contemporary Composers on Contemporary Music*. New York: Holt, Rinehart and Winston.

CLOUGH, ROSA TRILLO. 1961. *Futurism*. New York: Philosophical Library.

COPE, DAVID. 1971. *New Directions in Music*. Dubuque: Wm. C. Brown.

COREA, CHICK. "The Electronic/Acoustic Controversy." *Contemporary Keyboard* 1 (1975): 42.

COTT, JOHNATHAN. 1973. *Stockhausen: Conversation with the Composer*. New York: Simon and Schuster.

COUTTS-SMITH, KENNETH. 1970. *Dada*. New York: E. P. Dutton.

COWELL, HENRY. 1930. *New Musical Resources*. New York: Something Else Press.

CROSS, LOWELL. 1966. *A Bibliography of Electronic Music*. Toronto: University of Toronto Press.

――――. "Electronic Music, 1948–1953." *Perspectives of New Music* 7 (Fall-Winter, 1968): 32–65.

CUMMINGS, BARTON. "New Techniques for Tuba." *The Composer* 6 (1975): 28–32.

DAVIES, HUGH, ED. 1967. *International Electronic Music Catalogue*. Cambridge, Mass.: M.I.T. Press.

DOCKSTADER, TOD. "Inside Out: Electronic Rock." *Electronic Music Review* 5 (1968): 15–20.

DRAKE, RUSSELL, HERTER, RONALD, AND MODUGNO, ANNE. 1975. *How to Make Electronic Music*. Pleasantville, N.Y.: EAV Vineyard Edition.

EATON, MANFRED. "Bio-Music." *Source* 9 (1971): 28–36.

———. 1969. *Electronic Music: A Handbook of Sound Synthesis and Control*. Kansas City: Orcus Publications.

EDWARDS, JOHN HAMILTON, AND VASSE, WILLIAM. 1971. *Annotated Index to the Cantos of Ezra Pound*. Berkeley: University of California Press.

EIMERT, HERBERT. "What Is Electronic Music?" *Die Reihe* 1 (1955): 1–10.

ERNST, DAVID. 1972. *Musique Concrète*. Boston: Crescendo.

FENNELLY, BRIAN. "A Descriptive Language for the Analysis of Electronic Music." *Perspectives of New Music* 6 (Fall-Winter, 1967): 79.

FERRIS, JOAN. "The Evolution of Rameau's Harmonic Theories." *Journal of Music Theory* 3 (1959): 231–256.

GOEYVAERTS, KAREL. "The Sound Material of Electronic Music." *Die Reihe* 1 (1959): 35–37.

GROPIUS, WALTER, ED. 1961. *The Theatre of the Bauhaus*. Middletown, Conn.: Wesleyan University Press.

HARVEY, JONATHAN. 1975. *The Music of Stockhausen*. Berkeley: University of California Press.

HEILINHEIMO, SEPPO. 1972. *The Electronic Music of Karlheinz Stockhausen*. Translated by Brad Absetz. Helsinki: Acta Musicologica Fennica.

HILLER, LEJAREN. "Electronic Music at the University of Illinois." *Journal of Music Theory* 7 (1963): 99.

HOLLANDER, JOHN. "Notes on the Text of 'Philomel.' " *Perspectives of New Music* 6 (Fall-Winter, 1967): 134–141.

HOWE, HUBERT. 1975. *Electronic Music Synthesis*. New York: W. W. Norton.

———. "Compositional Limitations of Electronic Music Synthesizers." *Perspectives of New Music* 10 (Spring-Summer, 1972): 120–129.

JUDD, FREDERICK. 1961. *Electronic Music and Musique Concrète*. London: Neville Spearman.

KAGEL, MAURICIO. "Tone Clusters, Attacks, Transitions." *Die Reihe* 5 (1959): 40–55.

———. "Translation-Rotation." *Die Reihe* 7 (1960): 32–60.

KAUFMANN, HENRY. "More on the Tuning of the Archicembalo." *Journal of the American Musicological Society* 23 (1970): 84–94.

KETOFF, PAUL. "The Synket." *Electronic Music Review* 4 (October 1967), 39–41.

KIRBY, MICHAEL. 1971. *Futurist Performance*. New York: E. P. Dutton.

KOENIG, GOTTFRIED MICHAEL. "Studium im Studio." *Die Reihe* 5 (1959), 52–54.

KOESTLER, ARTHUR. 1959. *The Watershed.* New York: Doubleday Anchor.

LUCIER, ALVIN. "The Making of North American Time Capsule." *Electronic Music Review* 5 (January, 1968), 30–36.

LUENING, OTTO. "An Unfinished History of Electronic Music." *Music Educators Journal* 55 (1968): 35.

————. "Some Random Remarks about Electronic Music." *Journal of Music Theory* 8 (1964): 89–98.

LYONS, LEN. "Herbie Hancock: Keyboard Wizard." *Contemporary Keyboard* 1 (1975): 18.

MACONIE, ROBIN. "Stockhausen's 'Mikrophonie I.' " *Perspectives of New Music* 10 (Spring-Summer, 1972): 92–101.

MARKS, STEVEN. "Eddie Harris: Plugged In Pioneer Turns Up His Lungs." *Down Beat* 43 (1976): 16.

MAUD, RALPH. 1963. *Entrances to Dylan Thomas' Poetry.* Pittsburgh: University of Pittsburgh Press.

MILANO, DOMINIC. "Bob Moog." *Contemporary Keyboard* 1 (1975): 14.

MOOG, ROBERT. "Voltage-controlled Electronic Music Modules." *Journal of the Audio Engineering Society* 13 (1965): 200–206.

MOTHERWELL, ROBERT, ED. 1951. *The Dada Painters and Poets.* New York: Wittenborn, Schultz, Inc.

MUMMA, GORDON. "An Electronic Music Studio for the Independent Composer." *Journal of the Audio Engineering Society* 12 (1964): 240.

NOLAN, HERB. "Urszula Dudziak: Vocalese Vistas Unlimited." *Down Beat* 43 (1976): 14.

OLIVEROS, PAULINE. "Tape Delay Techniques for Electronic Music Composition." *The Composer* 1 (1969): 135–142.

POUSSEUR, HENRI. "Calculation and Imagination in Electronic Music." *Electronic Music Review* 5 (January, 1968): 21–29.

RHEA, THOMAS. 1974. *Minimoog Sound Charts.* Lincoln, Ill.: Norlin Music.

ROXON, LILLIAN. 1971. *Rock Encyclopedia.* New York: Grosset and Dunlap.

RUSSCOL, HERBERT. 1972. *The Liberation of Sound.* Englewood Cliffs, N.J.: Prentice-Hall.

RUSSOLO, LUIGI. 1967. *The Art of Noise.* Translated by Robert Filliou. New York: Something Else Press.

RZEWSKI, FREDERIC. "A Photoresistor Mixer for Live Performance." *Electronic Music Review* 4 (October, 1967): 33–34.

————. "Plan for Spacecraft." *Source* 3 (1968): 66–68.

RZEWSKI, FREDERIC, AND ESPOSITO, SALVATORE. "Zuppa' e altri processi." *Il Verri* 30 (1969): 102–115.

SALZMAN, ERIC. 1967. *Twentieth Century Music: An Introduction.* Englewood Cliffs, N.J.: Prentice-Hall.

SCHAEFFER, PIERRE. "Introduction a la musique concrète." *Polyphonie* 6 (1950): 30–52.

———. "L'objet musical." *La Revue musicale* 222 (1952): 65–76.

———. 1967. *Musique Concrète.* Paris: Presses Universitaires de France.

———. "Note on Time Relationships." *Gravesaner Blätter* 5 (1960): 50–77.

———. 1966. *Traité des objets musicaux.* Paris: Editions du Seuil.

SCHERCHEN, HERMAN. 1950. *The Nature of Music.* Translated by W. Mann. Chicago: H. Regnery.

SCHILLINGER, JOSEPH. "Electricity, A Musical Liberator." *Modern Music* 8 (1931): 26–31.

SCHWARTZ, ELLIOTT. 1973. *Electronic Music: A Listener's Guide.* New York: Praeger.

SHAW, ARNOLD. 1969. *The Rock Revolution.* London: Crowell-Collier Press.

STANFORD, DEREK. 1954. *Dylan Thomas.* New York: The Citadel Press.

STRANGE, ALLAN. 1972. *Electronic Music.* Dubuque: Wm. C. Brown.

STOCKHAUSEN, KARLHEINZ. "Actualia." *Die Reihe* 1 (1955): 45–51.

———. "Electronic and Instrumental Music." *Die Reihe* 5 (1959): 59–67.

———. ". . . How Time Passes . . ." *Die Reihe* 3 (1957): 10–40.

———. "Music and Speech." *Die Reihe* 6 (1960): 40–64.

———. "Registrazione d'una Conferenza." *Il Verri* 30 (1969): 78–85.

———. "The Concept of Unity in Electronic Music." *Perspectives of New Music* 1 (Fall-Winter, 1962): 39–48.

STOKOWSKI, LEOPOLD. "New Horizons in Music." *Journal of the Acoustical Society of America* 4 (1932): 11.

STUCKENSCHMIDT, H. H. "The Third Stage." *Die Reihe* 1 (1955): 11–13.

———. 1969. *Twentieth Century Music.* New York: McGraw Hill.

TRYTHALL, GILBERT. 1973. *Principles and Practice of Electronic Music.* New York: Grosset and Dunlap.

USSACHEVSKY, VLADIMIR. "Notes on 'A Piece for Tape Recorder.'" *The Musical Quarterly* 46 (1960): 202.

———. "The Process of Experimental Music." *Journal of the Audio Engineering Society* 6 (1958): 202.

———. "The Making of Four Miniatures." *Music Educators Journal* 55 (1968): 76.

VARÈSE, EDGARD. "The Liberation of Sound." *Perspectives of New Music* 5 (Fall-Winter, 1966): 11–19.

VERKEN, MONIQUE. "An Interview with Frederick Rzewski." *The Drama Review* 14 (1969): 93–97.

WHITNEY, JOHN. "Moving Pictures and Electronic Music." *Die Reihe* 7 (1960): 61–71.

WINGLER, HANS. 1969. *The Bauhaus.* Translated by Wolfgang Jabs and Basil Gilbert. Cambridge, Mass.: M.I.T. Press.

WORNER, KARL. 1973. *Stockhausen: Life and Work.* Berkeley: University of California Press.

YATES, PETER. 1967. *Twentieth Century Music.* New York: Pantheon Books.

II. Computers

BEAUCHAMP, JAMES, AND VON FORESTER, HEINZ, EDS. 1969. *Music by Computers.* New York: John Wiley and Sons.

CLOUGH, JOHN. "TEMPO: A Composer's Programming Language." *Perspectives of New Music* 9 (Fall-Winter, 1970): 113–125.

DIVILBLISS, J. L. "The Real-Time Generation of Music with a Digital Computer." *Journal of Music Theory* 8 (1964): 99.

GABURA, JAMES. "Computer Control of Sound Apparatus for Electronic Music." *Journal of the Audio Engineering Society* 16 (1968): 49–51.

GHENT, EMMANUEL. "Programmed Signals to Performers: A New Compositional Resource." *Perspectives of New Music* 6 (Fall-Winter, 1967): 96–106.

HELMERS, CARL. "Add a Kluge Harp to Your Computer." *BYTE* 2 (1975): 14–18.

HILLER, LEJAREN, AND ISAACSON, LEONARD. 1959. *Experimental Music.* New York: McGraw-Hill.

HILLER, LEJAREN, AND BAKER, ROBERT. "Computer Cantata: A Study in Compositional Method." *Perspectives of New Music* 3 (Fall-Winter, 1964): 62–90.

HOWE, HUBERT. 1975. *Electronic Music Synthesis.* New York: W. W. Norton.

KOBRIN, EDWARD. "I Ching." *Source* 8 (1970): 1–7.

LINCOLN, HARRY, ED. 1970. *The Computer and Music.* Ithaca: Cornell University Press.

MACINNIS, DONALD. "Sound Synthesis by Computer: MUSICOL, a program written entirely in extended ALGOL." *Perspectives of New Music* 7 (Fall-Winter, 1968): 66.

MATHEWS, M. V. 1969. *The Technology of Computer Music*. Cambridge, Mass.: M.I.T. Press.

MATHEWS, M. V., AND ROSLER, L. "Graphical Language for the Scores of Computer-Generated Sounds." *Perspectives of New Music* 6 (Spring-Summer, 1968): 92–118.

RANDALL, J. K. "Three Lectures to Scientists." *Perspectives of New Music* 5 (Spring-Summer, 1967): 124–140.

TENNEY, JAMES. "Sound Generation by Means of a Digital Computer." *Journal of Music Theory* 7 (1963): 24.

XENAKIS, IANNIS. 1971. *Formalized Music*. Bloomington: Indiana University Press.

ZINGHEIM, T. J. "Introduction to Computer Music Techniques." *Electronotes* 42 (1974): 1–5.

III. Acoustics

BACKUS, JOHN. 1969. *The Acoustical Foundations of Music*. New York: W. W. Norton.

DOUGLAS, ALAN. 1957. *The Electrical Production of Music*. New York: The Philosophical Library.

FLETCHER, HARVEY, *et al*. "Quality of Organ Tones." *Journal of the Acoustical Society of America* 35 (1963): 314–325.

FLETCHER, HARVEY, BLACKHAM, E. DONNELL, AND STRATTON, RICHARD. "Quality of Piano Tones." *Journal of the Acoustical Society of America* 34 (1962): 749–761.

FLETCHER, HARVEY, AND SANDERS, LARRY. "Quality of Violin Vibrato Tones." *Journal of the Acoustical Society of America* 41 (1967): 1534–1544.

HELMHOLTZ, HERMAN. 1954. *On the Sensations of Tone*. Translated by A. J. Ellis. New York: Dover.

HOLLIEN, HARRY, AND WENDAHL, RONALD. "Perceptual Study of Vocal Fry." *Journal of the Acoustical Society of America* 43 (1968): 506–509.

LUCE, DAVID, AND CLARK, MELVILLE. "Durations of Attack Transients of Nonpercussive Orchestral Instruments." *Journal of the Audio Engineering Society* 13 (1965): 194–199.

OLSON, HARRY F. 1967. *Music, Physics and Engineering*. Second edition. New York: Dover.

PLOMP, R. "Beats of Mistuned Consonances." *Journal of the Acoustical Society of America* 42 (1967): 462–473.

———. "Detectability Threshold for Combination Tones." *Journal of the Acoustical Society of America* 37 (1965): 1110–1123.

Rainbolt, Harry, and Schubert, Earl. "Use of Noise Bands to Establish Noise Pitch." *Journal of the Acoustical Society of America* 43 (1968): 316–323.

Scharf, Bertram. "Loudness Summation and Spectrum Shape." *Journal of the Acoustical Society of America* 34 (1962): 228–233.

Schultz, Theodore, and Watters, B. G. "Perception of Music Heard via Interfering Paths." *Journal of the Acoustical Society of America* 36 (1964): 897–902.

Slawson, A. W. "Vowel Quality and Musical Timbre as Functions of Spectrum Envelope and Fundamental Frequency." *Journal of the Acoustical Society of America* 43 (1968): 87–101.

Small, Arnold, and Daniloff, Raymond. "Pitch of Noise Bands." *Journal of the Acoustical Society of America* 41 (1967): 506–512.

Strong, William, and Clark, Melville. "Perturbations of Synthetic Orchestral Wind-Instrument Tones." *Journal of the Acoustical Society of America* 41 (1967): 277–285.

Taylor, C. A. 1965. *The Physics of Musical Sounds.* New York: American Elsevier.

Winckel, Fritz. 1967. *Music, Sound and Sensation.* Translated by Thomas Binkley. New York: Dover.

Wood, Alexander. 1962. *The Physics of Music.* London: University Paperbacks.

Young, Robert. "Inharmonicity of Plain Wire Piano Strings." *Journal of the Acoustical Society of America* 24 (1952): 267–273.

IV. SCORES

Arel, Bulent. "Electronic Music No. 1," American Composers Alliance.
———. "Music for a Sacred Service: Prelude and Postlude," American Composers Alliance.
———. "Stereo Electronic Music No. 1," American Composers Alliance.

Ashley, Robert. "The Wolfman," *Source* 4 (1968): 5–6.

Austin, Larry. "Accidents," *Source* 4 (1968): 20–22.

Babbitt, Milton. "Philomel," Associated Music Publishers.
———. "Vision and Prayer," Associated Music Publishers.

BADINGS, HENK. "Armageddon," Peters P66212.

———. "Capriccio," Donemus.

BEHRMAN, DAVID. "Wave Train," *Source* 3 (1968): 28–32.

BROWN, EARLE. "Times Five," Universal Editions UE 15385.

BRYANT, ALLAN. "Pitch Out," *Source* 3 (1968): 3–13.

CAGE, JOHN. "Aria," Peters P6701.

———. "Cartridge Music," Peters P6703.

———. "Fontana Mix," Peters P6712.

———. "HPSCHD," Peters P6804.

———. "Imaginary Landscape No. 1," Peters P6709.

———. "Imaginary Landscape No. 2," Peters P6721.

———. "Imaginary Landscape No. 3," Peters P6717.

———. "Imaginary Landscape No. 4," Peters P6718.

———. "Imaginary Landscape No. 5," Peters P6719.

———. "Solo for Voice 2," Peters P6751.

———. "Variations II," Peters P6768.

———. "Variations IV," Peters P6798.

———. "Williams Mix," Peters P6774.

CHIHARA, PAUL. "Logs," Peters P66364.

DAVIDOVSKY, MARIO. "Synchronism No. 1," McGinnis and Marx.

———. "Synchronism No. 2," McGinnis and Marx.

———. "Synchronism No. 3," McGinnis and Marx.

DRUCKMAN, JACOB. "Animus I," Mercury Music.

EATON, JOHN. "Songs for R.P.B.," Shawnee Press.

ERB, DONALD. "Reconnaissance," Theodore Presser.

ERNST, DAVID. "Exit," Shawnee Press.

ERICKSON, ROBERT. "Ricercar a 3," University of California Press.

HILLER, LEJAREN. "An Avalanche," Theodore Presser.

———. "Machine Music," Theodore Presser.

HILLER, LEJAREN, AND BAKER, ROBERT. "Computer Cantata," Theodore Presser.

ICHIYANAGI, TOSHI. "Extended Voices," Peters P66145.

KAGEL, MAURICIO. "Transicion II," Universal Edition UE 13809.

KOLB, BARBARA. "Solitare," Peters P66508.

LIGETI, GYORGY. "Artikulation," B. Schott (1970) 6378.

LORA-TOTINO, ARRIGO. "English Phonemes 1970," *Source* 9 (1971): 11–16.

LUCIER, ALVIN. "I Am Sitting In A Room," *Source* 7 (1970): 60.

———. "Vespers," *Source* 7 (1970): 60.

LUENING, OTTO. "Fantasy in Space," American Composers Alliance.

258 SELECTED BIBLIOGRAPHY

———. "Gargoyles," Peters P66002.

———. "Invention in 12 Notes," American Composers Alliance.

———. "Low Speed," American Composers Alliance.

———. "Synthesis," Peters P66003.

———. "Theatre Piece No. 2," American Composers Alliance.

Luening, Otto, and Ussachevsky, Vladimir. "Concerted Piece," Peters P66010.

———. "Incantation," American Composers Alliance.

———. "Poem in Cycles and Bells," Peters P66005.

———. "Rhapsodic Variations," Peters P66006.

———. "Suite from King Lear," American Composers Alliance.

Mache, François-Bernard. "Volumes," Editions Françaises de Musique.

Pousseur, Henri. "Rimes, pour differentes sources sonores," Edizioni Suvini Zerboni 5520.

Powell, Mel. "Events," Schirmer.

———. "Second Electronic Setting," Schirmer.

Reynolds, Roger. "Ping," *Source* 6 (1969): 70–88.

———. "Traces," Peters P66247.

Stockhausen, Karlheinz. "Hymnen," Universal Editions UE 15142.

———. "Kontakte," Universal Editions UE 13678.

———. "Mixtur," Universal Editions UE 14261.

———. "Prozession," Universal Editions UE 14812.

———. "Solo," Universal Editions UE 14261.

———. "Studie II," Universal Editions UE 12466.

———. "Telemusik," Universal Editions UE 14807.

Subotnick, Morton. "Lamination I, for Orch. and Electronic Sounds," MCA Music No. 15428-044.

Ussachevsky, Vladimir. "Creation: Prologue," American Composers Alliance.

———. "Linear Contrasts," American Composers Alliance.

———. "Metamorphoses," American Composers Alliance.

———. "Piece for Tape Recorder," American Composers Alliance.

———. "Sonic Contours," American Composers Alliance.

Varèse, Edgard. "Déserts," Colombo—NY 1794.

Wittenberg, Charles. "Electronic Study No. 2," American Composers Alliance.

Wourinen, Charles. "Time's Encomium," Peters P66455.

LIST OF RECORD LABELS AND ABBREVIATIONS

AR	Acoustic Research
Adv.	Advance
At.	Atlantic
BAM	Bôite à Musique
Can.	Candide
Cap.	Capitol
Char.	Charisma
Col.	Columbia
CRI	Composers Recordings, Inc.
Cot.	Cotillion
Dec.	Decca
DGG or DG	Deutsche Grammophon Gesellschaft
DUC	Ducretet-Thomson
ESP	ESP-Disk
Ev.	Everest
Finn.	Finnador
Fly. Dut.	Flying Dutchman
Folk.	Folkways
Harv.	Harvest
Hel.	Hellidor
Lime.	Limelight
Lon.	London
Lou.	Louisville
Lyr.	Lyrichord
Main.	Mainstream
Mant.	Manticore
Mile.	Milestone
Nemp.	Nemperor

None.	Nonesuch
Odys.	Odyssey
Point	Point Park College
Poly.	Polydor
Turn.	Turnabout
Van.	Vanguard
West.	Westminster

Index

INDEX

263

X

Z

Y